Creative Realism

A NEW METHOD OF WINNING

Rolf Alexander, M.D.
author of "The Doctor Alone Can't Cure You"

Pageant Press, New York

PUBLISHED BY PAGEANT PRESS, INC.
130 WEST 42ND STREET, NEW YORK 36, N. Y.

First Edition

LIBRARY OF CONGRESS CATALOG CARD NUMBER: 54-12353

MANUFACTURED IN THE UNITED STATES OF AMERICA

Foreword

"Parapsychology" means the study of those mental principles at present outside the conceptual schemes of science. The term embraces such things as hypnotism, telepathy, precognition, clairvoyance, psychokinesis, and related phenomena. These phenomena have been attested to by people of all nations and from earliest times. Records of them are spread through the historical documents collected in the Old Testament, and the New Testament is replete with stories of happenings which have no scientific explanations. The same holds true of the sacred literature of Buddhism, Jainism, Hinduism, Taoism, Shintoism, Zoroastrianism, Mohammedanism, and, in fact, of the sacred literature of all mankind, down through the ages.

With the founding of the Society for Psychical Research in London in 1882 there commenced a systematic and objective study of these phenomena and a great amount of authentic data was gathered and classified. Finally, in the 1930's Dr. J. B. Rhine of Duke University developed a method by which extrasensory powers could be adequately tested and evaluated. A tremendous increase in research activity followed this development, and since the founding of the *Journal of Parapsychology* in 1937, the psychology departments of over twenty universities have published reports of their researches in it. Among the competent investigators of the subject today, there is little doubt that man is possessed of powers and potentialities far beyond his present understanding and his ability to utilize them. Parapsychologists believe now that it is just a question of the amount of evidence required to overcome the huge a priori incredibility of the phenomena.

The essence of parapsychology, of course, is the possibility that in some unknown manner the human mind, in response to the will, can act at a distance from the brain of the operator. The experimental evidence is strongly in favor of the probability that all of our minds, all of the time, so act—and without our knowledge. If such be the case, the tremendous possibilities open to the person who can bring these now chaotic and unpredictable powers under conscious control and direct them creatively is obvious.

Over some forty years of painstaking research and the study of numerous primitive systems of magic and modern systems of psychology . . . all at first hand . . . the philosophy of Creative Realism as outlined in this book was evolved. It is a system of self-training which will yield results in accordance with the amount of persistent effort made to master it. It has completely revolutionized the lives of many of the author's private students, and every student has received benefits from the training, far in excess of what might have been logically expected. With this book, the course of training is offered to the general public for the first time.

The photographs following page 235 are of a demonstration given by this writer before reliable and qualified witnesses at Mexico City in January, 1952, and reported in the *Fairmont Daily Sentinel* (Minnesota) by W. Dale McLaughlin, in the issue of February 12, 1952. In the demonstration, a target cloud, heavy with rain, was selected from among many by McLaughlin, and with no aid other than the power mentioned above, the cloud was halted in its course, while others continued on; then, as the photographs show, it was disintegrated—without precipitation—in twelve minutes. There can, of course, be no collusion between a raincloud at 4000 feet and a man on the ground. This demonstration, which has been repeated hundreds of times, is evidence that parapsychological power exists, and that it can be controlled and directed by a trained operator.

ROLF ALEXANDER

Contents

Introduction

Despite the fact that today we have grown accustomed to thinking of scientific research as a team project, in which a problem under investigation is broken down and parcelled out among a number of specialists whose findings are later integrated, it should be remembered that every great discovery in science and philosophy has been primarily the work of a single brain. This has been true from the ancient days of Leucippus and Democritus, to the modern days of Einstein, Planck, Rutherford and Heisenberg. Basic and revolutionary discoveries have usually resulted from some pioneering individual's dissatisfaction over the difficulties of fitting certain by-passed stubborn facts into an established theory of science.

It was the difficulty of reconciling certain demonstrable facts of a parapsychological nature with the Western conceptions of science and psychology, which led Dr. Rolf Alexander into a lifelong program of private research, and experimentation, over forty years ago. After wide travels and the painstaking investigation of many little-known systems grew the new and revolutionary philosophy named Creative Realism, which this book outlines. Into its conceptual scheme may be easily fitted all of the old facts of both religion and science. I have followed Dr. Alexander's work closely for some years, and it is my considered opinion, based upon considerable experimentation with his method of hard-headed Western self-training that out of his "Creative Realism" will arise a host of new facts, which will contribute more to human advancement and enlightenment in the next few decades than the Eastern cultures have contributed in the past 3,000 years.

Dr. Alexander's repeated and spectacular demonstrations of psycho-kinetic power proves that the human will has powers and potentialities hitherto undreamed of by science, and correlates with the work of such men as W. Grey Walter of the Burden Neurological Institute of England, Leonard J. Ravitz of Yale, J. B. Rhine of Duke University, Wilder Penfield of the Montreal Neurological Clinic, and others.

It is in the process of being demonstrated by many independent investigators in the new science of electroencephalography, that the electrical rhythms of the individual's brain may be correlated with the state of his health. Alexander believes also that the habitual E.E.G. patterns of each of our brains are not only responsible for the effectiveness of our thinking, and the state of our health, but that they do work in our surroundings in correlating the flexible events of our daily lives with our innermost hopes, fears, ideals, and expectations. He has demonstrated that the *human will* may revise these basic electrical patterns which may determine our thinking, our health, and our success, and by doing so may be literally "born again" into a new world of happiness, health, and limitless possibilities.

EDWARD T. WHITNEY, M.D.

Boston, Massachusetts, 1954

Creative Realism

A NEW METHOD OF WINNING

CHAPTER I

Nature, Mind, and Science

Having insight into all the world, into all the world as it really is, he is yet detached from all the world, and without compare in all the world.

HSIN-HSIN-MING
The Believing Mind

YOUR WORLD

Your mind. Your world is your mind. Without a mind to behold it, the world would not exist for you. The coloring of the autumn woodlands, the witchery of moonlight over a woodland lake, the blazing desert sunset, the face of a loved one, in fact, every experience of your life is a construction of your mind, an interpretation of stimuli arriving from without. Heat and cold, light and darkness, form, velocity, color, sound, taste, feeling and emotion cause responses in the human mind. Yet the response of each mind to these stimuli is as individualistic as are a man's fingerprints.

THE MIND

Nonphysical, immeasurable. The human mind is not examinable as a physical system. It is not possible to measure it quantitatively as a form of energy, and all attempts to find a scale of equivalence between conscious experience and energy have been fruitless. *So mind is the only human reality.* The physical universe of matter-energy, space-time, mass-momentum, and so on, is a construction of the human mind, and a

3

temporary not a permanent edifice, for it is changing rapidly almost from day to day as new and sometimes revolutionary concepts are introduced by minds trained to think in the manner we term "scientific."

SCIENCE

Limitations. Despite the spectacular accomplishments of science during the past century, scientific investigation must by its very nature be limited to that which may be measured; in short, to physical systems. Its methods are only applicable to that which may be counted as to numbers; measured as to size or dimension; weighed as to mass; and timed as to duration. As the mind which computes these measurements cannot measure itself, for it is apparently nonphysical and therefore immeasurable, it has only one means by which to gauge reality . . . and that means is *conscious experience.*

CONSCIOUS EXPERIENCE

Psychic response. Our experience in consciousness—for instance, when we behold the beautiful in sound, form, or concept—is immeasurable. Our feeling of secret delight at the laughter of a child, our experience of indignation over an injustice, perhaps inflicted upon others in a distant part of the world—these are immeasurable. An experience in consciousness may be triggered by sense impressions, but it is in the nature of a total response of the psyche or soul to a situation, and is something quite different and infinitely more significant than a mere intellectual response.

The pointing finger. Direct conscious experience then is something quite different from a mere exercise of the intellect. Unless the intellect, like a pointing finger, shows the way to something bigger and more real beyond itself, man would be inferior in stature to the very machines he has created.

NATURE AND SCIENCE

Johnny-come-lately. Long before nature had designed a human brain capable of elaborating a science, she had already worked out most of the problems lately solved in our laboratories. Flight, radar, sonar, television, the harnessing of atomic energy from the sun, these and all other "miracles of modern science" had been set into operation millions of years before man, the "Johnny-come-lately" of nature, appeared on the scene.

Prima-facie evidence. The very existence of living nature seems prima-facie evidence of the existence of an all-embracing, directive mind, even from an intellectual viewpoint and without direct conscious experience of the reality. As human beings we cannot conceive a thing's transcending its own possibilities, and our experiences in our attempts at creative thinking by which we have produced our daubs and our gadgets should have taught us respect for the mind which "peopled the earth and the air" of our planet with its myriads of exquisitely balanced and beautiful creations.

Innate knowledge. The creations of nature as a rule are much more perfect than human creations. The technology which built a human brain was obviously of a superior order to that developed by the brain; the hand of even the most primitive savage is an engineering marvel contrasted with the crude instruments and weapons the hand fashions.

Unlearned knowledge. The knowledge of nature is innate, and it is not necessary for each generation of organisms to relearn it but only to wait for its spontaneous awakening. The bird flies though it has never studied the science of aerodynamics; in fact, the bumble bee flies directly in the face of that science by doing the aerodynamically impossible. The honey bee builds its six-sided geometrically perfect cells, yet it has never studied mathematics; the tree performs miracles of chemistry, yet it has never learned chemistry in a college.

Inorganic nature. Yet so far as this planet is concerned anyway, the inanimate objects of nature also co-operate in the incredible processes of evolution. The sun lifts the waters of the ocean as vapor, which form clouds to be carried over the earth and precipitated as rain to supply the life-giving moisture to land organisms and plant life. The atmosphere itself contains the exactly right proportion of each of the essential gases needed by breathing organisms; the atmosphere is so arranged that the exactly right amounts of the right kinds of radiation are allowed through, while forms of radiation which would prove inimical to life forms are filtered out. It would therefore seem evident that as a bird prepares its nest for its expected young, this planet was prepared over long aeons by our creative source for the coming of life.

Gems of truth. Primitive man seemed to have accepted the foregoing concept as simply and naturally as a bird accepts its knowledge of how to build a nest, or a bee its understanding of how to build a honeycomb. Coming fresh from the "wheel of the potter" and without the hard glaze of modern culture to divert his natural instincts, he was much closer to basic realities than is modern man. Thus the primitive faiths of man might be expected to contain many gems of actual truth scattered through the dross of fantasy and superstition.

Animism. Although there were, of course, wide variations in these primitive religions, they seem to have all followed an animistic pattern. In general, they held that all nature is the embodiment of a great spirit, which had, for its own purposes, fractionated itself into numerous different forms and aspects. These fractions formed the souls which animated all living things and even formed the cohesive element which bound nonliving matter into its various forms and properties.

THE MAGIC ARTS

Origins. We can trace the development and refinement of this primitive concept to the time of ancient Egypt, about six thousand years ago, where the art of magic was practiced by the priesthood, who were among the highest and most brilliant men in the land—and among whom Moses was raised as a prince, incidentally. We can trace the spread of this early science to India and its development there as Yoga, into Tibet where it formed the basis of the various lamaistic systems of spiritual discipline, into China where it developed as Taoism, and so on. Evidence of this art is also abundant in the Western world of long ago. According to Tacitus, Hippocrates used the "magnetic pass" or "laying on of hands" in the cure of disease, and Aesculapius was supposed to be able to relieve pain in inflamed parts by breathing upon them, and, by stroking with his hands, he could throw patients into refreshing sleep.

"Miracles." The miracles of the Old and New Testaments were probably produced by people familiar with the principles of this ancient science, and the medieval alchemists to some extent tried to create an analogical science by using physical elements as symbols of spiritual principles. In the seventeenth century, several writers, including Paracelsus,

Glocenius, Kirchner, Santanelli, Maxwell, and others, wrote books setting forth the theory that living bodies contained a magnetic fluid which was transmissible from one to another by the exercise of the will and imagination; then, of course, in the eighteenth century came the advent of Anton Mesmer, whose theory of hypnosis as a curative power swept through Europe like a conflagration.

THE MATERIALISTS

Anton Mesmer. Anton Mesmer was investigated in 1784 by a commission of physical scientists, which included Benjamin Franklin and Lavoisier, and they concluded that there was no evidence of the animal magnetic fluid; this report finished Mesmer, and the rapid development of nineteenth-century materialism under the impetus of the Darwin theory of evolution scorned the idea of an invisible power which produced visible phenomena.

Born too soon. Had Mesmer been born a century later and had he grown up in this age of field physics and atomic energy research, when even a microbe is conceived as giving off waves of energy, things might have been different, though not necessarily so. Many physical scientists still shy away from the obvious conclusions to be drawn from their own researches.

THE CLASSICAL FIELD

Tension. We now regard physical objects as being composed of atoms held together by electric fields. A classical field is a kind of tension which can exist in empty space in the absence of matter. It reveals itself by producing forces which act upon any material object within its scope. The electric and magnetic fields which act upon electrically charged and magnetized objects respectively are the standard example of the classical field.

The quantum theory. Quantum physics today gives us the picture of from ten to twenty qualitatively different quantum fields interpenetrating each other. Each fills the whole of space and has its own particular properties. *There is nothing else but these fields* . . . the whole of the material universe is built of them.

Interaction. Between various pairs of the fields there are various kinds of interaction. Each field brings forth its own type of elementary particle, and these particles are always identical, but the number of particles manifested by each field is not fixed, and particles are continually being brought forth, annihilated, or transmuted into one another. In this quantum concept, the electromagnetic field appears on an exactly equal footing with all other fields. The particle it brings forth is the light quantum or photon.

DEATH OF THE MACHINE

Quantum mechanics. So the mechanical universe of the nineteenth-century materialists with its inexorable sequence of cause and effect—the universe which found no room for the flow of a "magnetic fluid" between people—has been dissolved by the quantum mechanics which produced the Atomic Age and converted into a conceptual scheme which envisions the whole universe as a series of interpenetrating and inter-acting fields, each bringing forth its own kind of energy quanta or particles like bubbles which form and dissolve and sometimes amalga-mate with bubbles produced by other fields to form atoms of matter.

Principle of uncertainty. And what governs the creation of atoms? Chance. In a famous statement of physical law made in 1927, the German physicist, Werner Heisenberg, demonstated that a particle cannot have simultaneously a well-defined position and sharply defined velocity. All objects of atomic size fluctuate continually and cannot maintain a precisely defined position for a finite length of time; there-fore, the more closely we try to observe them, the less we know about their subsequent state. We can only treat them statistically in great numbers, as we might, after long and careful observation, be able to predict the numbers and sizes of bubbles formed in a certain area of the Atlantic Ocean. The individual bubble would be unpredictable and meaningless, and a chance happening of wind or eddy might even com-pletely upset our statistical prediction.

PROBABILITY

Principle. If we spin a coin in the air half a dozen times, the number of heads and tails which turned up would be quite unpredictable; but if we spun the coin ten thousand times, we should discover that we had turned up approximately five thousand heads and five thousand tails. This illustrates the principle by which mathematical probabilities are computed. Commencing with a fifty-fifty probability of either a head or a tail turning up with a single toss, the probability of an equal number of heads' and tails' turning up would decrease sharply as we continued to throw; then beyond a certain number of tosses, the heads and tails would commence to average out, until with a large enough number of throws we should approach near certainty of an equal number of heads and tails.

Creation. Now the mathematical probability of that "fortuitous concatenation of circumstances" happening by which living nature might have accidentally created itself upon this planet is so remote that it approaches zero. It is not the product of chance happenings. The human mind itself acts as a principle of "antichance." Our whole system of industrialized civilization is evidence of how it has outwitted the natural laws of chance in a million different ways. To account for living nature on this planet, like our primitive ancestors we are going to have to look behind the measurable manifestations for an immeasurable creative essence, a conscious field encircling the planet and interpenetrating all other fields to bring into the right combinations the energy quanta of other fields to produce the favorable conditions we find. It goes without saying that this great overmind would have to be superior in quality to those of its creations. It must not be lost sight of that quantum physics is merely a creation of the human mind, the same as was Newtonian physics, or, as a matter of fact, as was the religion of ancient Egypt. Each could produce what seemed like verification of its theories.

Fruitful equations. The equations of quantum mechanics though have proved immensely fruitful, and a majority of physicists believes that the concept is so useful and illuminating that it will survive for a long time to come. As Professor Erwin Schrodinger ironically pointed out in his lecture on "Our Conception of Matter" given at Geneva in 1952: "Their study promises, indirectly, a hastened realization of the plan for the annihilation of mankind which is so close to all our hearts."

Direct experience. Quantum mechanics can also help us understand the inner meanings of life by reconciling our intellectual knowledge with our direct conscious experiences. If it succeeds in this, it can easily prove a tool for the salvation of mankind, which is even closer to our hearts than its annihilation. Direct "mental experience" is a state in which *the vivid awareness of living through an event is coupled with a direct "intuitive" understanding of the inner meaning of the event.* Many of our acquired intellectual beliefs and dogmas are direct barriers to direct mental experience; yet unless intellection leads us to this threshold, it is as empty of content and inner significance as a computing machine.

THE CIRCLE

Familiar shores. In the 380 years from Copernicus to Heisenberg, science has erected many intellectual structures, only to tear them down and replace them with others, until gradually, almost imperceptibly, it has found its way back to strangely familiar shores. The intellect is nearing the limits of its possibilities, but the mind of man remains as a great unexplored hinterland. The system of training called Creative Realism here given may help to clear the pathway to this objective.

CHAPTER 2

Patterns and Fields

The miracle of the human mind is not only that it can observe, remember, and understand, but that it can also learn to observe itself in performing these acts.

Rolf Alexander

TWIN PILLARS

Mental experience. In the previous chapter, "mental experience" was defined as: *A state of awareness of living through an event, while at the same time responding to the meaning of the event by a mental state.* This must be an individual experience, and it cannot be verified by any technique of measurement. It can only be verified by each individual's repeating the experience for himself.

Intuition. A dictionary definition of "intuition" is: *Immediate perception by the mind without reasoning,* and the process of intuition also defies measurement. Mental experience and intuition are the twin pillars upon which the structure of human thought rests, for, as Einstein has pointed out, space and time are a form of intuition which do not exist apart from the human mind. As space-time forms the basis of all measurement, science itself rests upon this intuition.

QUALITIES

Conventional symbols. Every object is simply the sum of its qualities as these are discerned by the human mind. The human mind discerns the qualities in that particular way, because that is the manner in which

11

the human senses respond to them. Thus, all qualities are mere conventional symbols shaped by the human senses, and mathematics is a form of mental discipline which enables the intellect to think about these intuited qualities in terms of magnitudes and quantities.

THE SINGLE TRACK

Scientific method. The tremendous advantage of the scientific method is that it produces practical results in the physical aspects of life. Its disadvantage is that it is not applicable to the most important aspects of life, for these lie beyond measurement. As a world-famous physiologist* states, somewhat regretfully, "We must confess at this stage that no study of brain activity has thrown any light on the peculiar forms of behavior known variously as second sight, clairvoyance, telepathy, extrasensory perception, and psychokinesis" . . . and further: "It seems to be one of the cardinal claims of workers in this field that a signal may be received before it is transmitted. If we accept these observations for what they are said to be, we cannot fit them into the physical laws of the universe as we define them today."

PATTERN-MAKING

Three-dimensional patterns. The human mind is a maker of patterns . . . of three-dimensional patterns in a multi-dimensional world. Our intellects cannot grasp facts unless these be organized into a pattern. In this work three-dimensional patterns are used to form a highway leading to the realm of heightened powers of intuition and mental experience, which, taken together, form the only valid values to be derived from the business of living. Each step in this pattern which follows should first be read thoughtfully, then visualized as vividly as possible, for thus may be organized the master-pattern in the subconscious stratum of the mind which will draw all lesser patterns into its orbit, in this way resolving their conflicts—the conflicts which bar the way to mental experience and true intuition.

The ocean. To form the basic picture of our pattern, let us think of the atmosphere which surrounds our planet as an ocean. The surface

* W. Grey Walter, *The Living Brain* (W. W. Norton and Company: 1953).

of the earth forms the bottom of this ocean and its surface is the iono-sphere some two hundred odd miles above.

Ice. In the Polar seas of our real ocean, ice crystals form under certain conditions, and these amalgamate into solid masses ranging in size from tiny pin-point granules to mighty icebergs, large as good-sized islands. All of these ice-organizations are formed of the basic substance of the ocean . . . or water . . . and it is not necessary to understand exactly "why" some molecules of water become congealed into ice while other adjacent molecules remain as water. We accept ice as a fact. In short, we accept it intuitively and without having to reason about it.

EVOLUTION OF CONSCIOUSNESS

Ocean of mind. Now let us return in imagination to the ocean of atmosphere which surrounds our planet. We shall imagine that in addition to the measurable gases, there is an *immeasurable* element called "mind" in its composition. We shall think of this mind as being a great reservoir of *direct or unlearned knowledge,* something like an infinite expansion of the knowledge by which a bee builds its cell, or a bird builds its nest, or a single fertilized cell builds a human body.

Unconscious knowledge. Let us suppose that this ocean of mind, like the mind of a sleeping man which carries on the complex functions of the body without knowing that it is carrying these on, is unconscious. And let us suppose that the whole purpose of its operations on this planet is the same as the purpose which drives the fertilized human egg into building a body—*the evolution of consciousness.* The human foetus builds special types of cells, then organizes these into a special structure called a "brain" in order to manifest consciousness. There are some ten thousand millions of these cells in a single human brain. Well, let us imagine that nature has brought forth man—*Homo sapiens*—as the instrument of her consciousness, and that mankind as a whole is the "brain of nature."

CREATION

In the beginning. Now the ice crystals and larger organizations of these formed in a real ocean float to the surface, but let us imagine that in our "ocean of atmosphere" the reverse is true; that, in other words, the "granules" formed as virus, then organized into protoplasmic one-celled creatures, gravitated to the "bottom of the ocean"—the earth's surface.

Body of nature. When the fertilized human ovum starts on its long climb toward consciousness, it sets about organizing a body which will support a brain, the organ of consciousness. If biology is correct, nature set about her march toward consciousness in a similar manner. First came the production of the elementary building blocks of living forms, or protoplasm, organized into tiny one-celled, self-dividing creatures, such as the protozoa and algae; then came the organization of many-celled creatures of various kinds.

The climb. Soon came the organization of still more complex living forms, such as the club mosses, corals, jellyfish, mollusks, worms, and the like, and, after these again still more complex living forms, such as fish, frogs, reptiles, insects, and so on. Finally there came forth the salamanders, hoofed animals, birds, apes, and man.

LORD OF THE EARTH

Difference. Now the main difference between a man and an ape is difference in mental equipment. Man and ape have existed side by side and have shared the same environment for more than a million years, and so this difference cannot be accounted for in terms of "evolutionary opportunity."

Resemblances. Both man and ape have similar skeletons, musculature, internal organs, and basic nervous systems. . . . But the ape has no stratum of mind which can detach itself from the flickering automatic reflex patterns of the brain. The ape lives in his feelings, is his feelings, and possesses nothing which can separate itself from his feelings. These not only control him . . . *they are him.*

Brain of nature. If our surmise be correct—that the great purpose behind nature's long evolutionary climb is the evolution of consciousness—then there can be no doubt that the most conscious of all the species—mankind—forms in effect the brain of nature. Apart from the fact that humanity is not enclosed in a protective skull, the organizations of civilized humanity are not dissimilar to the organizations of a single human brain.

The cell. Man then is unique among all living things. Because of the special quality of his mind, and the unusual structure of his brain, he is Homo sapiens, the animal which thinks. Alone among all the animals, man is not forced to respond at once and automatically to a given situation. He can *imagine* himself making a number of responses, and judge which response is the better one, without having to commit himself to action. He is a "specialized brain cell" through which the mind of nature must express its consciousness.

Individuality. Each of the ten thousand million cells which make up an individual human brain is itself an individual with a life of its own; it is separated from all adjacent cells, although its activities contribute to the total activity of the brain. We can imagine that each individual cell of our brains has a little "private mind" to attend to its own internal economy; then a stratum of mind which mediates between the internal economy of the cell and the life outside the cell. Finally, we can imagine that each cell has a stratum of mind which can contribute to, and partake of, the collective mind of the whole brain.

FIELDS

Definitions. The dictionary defines a field as: "The space within which a certain force is operant." A magnetic field is easily rendered visible by shaking iron filings on a piece of stiff paper held above a magnet. A gravitational field is just as much of a physical reality as a magnetic field or an electrical field. Now the peculiar thing about the gravitational field is that *it is created by a body in the space which surrounds it.* In other words, no body, no gravitational field. And yet, as every body in space is simply a denser concentration of the electrons, protons, and neutrons everywhere present in space, it can be said that a body in space is produced by the "generalized" field (space), and that it then sets up a "specialized" or gravitational field.

Patterned space. Now let us imagine that a body in space, after setting up a specialized gravitational field, could disintegrate and disappear while leaving the field it created intact. Impossible? Not at all. Such a field need not be thought of as "motion" but rather as a capability for action . . . an inherent power to *initiate action* when brought together with the right circumstances. To all intents and purposes it would be a unit patterned of space.

Souls. The foregoing speculation is intended to point out the fact that if we accept the idea that the development of consciousness is the great purpose behind evolution, then the scrapping of each individual human mind at death of the physical body would be a most wasteful, tedious, and unnecessary process. So we can think of living organisms as "bodies in space" created by a "generalized field" we have called the "mind of nature." And we can think of each of these living organisms as setting up their own "specialized" individual field, which persists after the death and disintegration of its physical body. Perhaps such "specialized fields" return again and again to build new physical bodies, and so elaborating the structure of their particular fields a little more. In the case of human beings it is conceivable that each "tour of duty in the flesh" makes possible the gain of a little more consciousness.

The continuum of life. It is interesting to note in passing that more than half of the peoples of the world have always accepted the doctrine of reincarnation as self-evident. This should not be confused with the "transmigration of souls" concept in which the souls of people are reborn into the bodies of animals and vice-versa. The doctrine of reincarnation simply holds that life is a continuum—not a straight line from conception to death, but a great circle from conception to death and back again after a time to conception. Those who hold this view think it to be self-evident that of the species in nature each could only offer the hospitality of its own protoplasm to the souls of its own kind.

INFINITE MIND

The creator. Having read this far, the startled reader is no doubt asking: "Has this theory not merely pushed the problem back a little further? How did the 'world organism' or the 'mind of nature' originate?" The answer is that Creative Realism considers the physical universe as being separate from the phenomenon of mind; that the physical universe bears the same relationship to the mind of nature that a log of wood might to a colony of termites.

Suitable medium. The king and queen termites on their nuptial flight find a suitable log of wood or structure in which to start a colony. They do not, of course, create the log of wood or the structure. It is simply a suitable medium for their purpose—the founding of a colony. The queen lays up to 20,000 eggs a day, and the progeny becomes rapidly specialized as soldiers, workers, nurses, food specialists, and so on, the entire colony functioning as a superorganism.

Mind a special field. Regarding the "ocean of mind" (which, it was suggested, surrounds this planet) as a special field or as an area of "patterned space," a "world soul," in effect capable of organizing matter according to its innate patterns, is as a magnetic field capable of organizing iron-filings brought within its influence. And considering the fact that the evolution of consciousness seems to be its dominant purpose, might not this "world soul" itself be the product of a similar evolutionary process carried out elsewhere in this vast restless sea we call the universe? Like the queen termite, might it not have left the fully evolved colony in which it developed to found and develop a colony of its own? Might not we human beings on this little planet be destined to evolve similarly, and after aeons of development here eventually be destined to set forth, each to populate a new planet?

Speculation. The foregoing, of course, is the purest speculation—a rationalization without a shred of supporting evidence—but as the human subconscious demands a patterned structure as a highway to the land of direct mental experience, the picture will be found consistent with later mental experience.

SPACE-TIME

Electromagnetic field. To clarify the idea of mind as a *field:* In the nineteenth century Oersted and Faraday demonstrated that an electrical current is always surrounded by a magnetic field. It was demonstrated also that under certain conditions, magnetism can induce electrical currents; that electricity and magnetism are different states of the same thing. From this developed the concept of the electromagnetic field through which radio waves, light waves, and all other electromagnetic disturbances are propagated through space. Without a disturbance of the electromagnetic equilibrium of the field, however, the field would exist beyond space-time.

Reality. We should be unable to see the full moon, say, without the electromagnetic field which carries its reflected light waves to us. Which then is the more "real": the invisible, electromagnetic field or the moon made visible by it? To measure distance between two points, we must have the *space* separating them. To measure the ticking of a clock, we must have the soundless *pauses* separating the ticks. Thus, we only become aware of space and time *because there exists that which is not space and not time.*

Mental field. Like the electromagnetic field, the mind is only observable *by what happens in it.* To paraphrase Sir Charles Sherrington, we only become aware of the enchanted loom by the millions of flashing shuttles weaving a dissolving pattern. The dissolving patterns are subject to measurement—they belong to space-time—but the field which *directs the pattern and may alter it at will* does not belong to space-time and is therefore not subject to measurement.

SUMMARY

THE OVERSOUL

By the foregoing rationalization then we have offered a concept of an ocean of mind like a great "oversoul" enveloping this planet as a *special field.* Just as a magnetic field or a gravitational field has a specific structure, we have suggested that this special field or oversoul has a special structure—and a vastly more complex one than anything known to physics.

ANALOGY

Just as a human body is a *functional unity* formed of billions of diversified individual cells, it is suggested that the oversoul is a functional whole, formed of countless billions of individual, lesser fields or souls.

PURPOSE

According to the "Accretion Theory," a sun or a planet is a creation of the spatial field, built up little by little from elements (electrons, etc.) existent everywhere in space. Once formed though, the sun or planet modifies the field which originally created it. We suggest that the special field or oversoul enters into a relationship with matter for a similar purpose: to bring about a structural modification (or elaboration) which will result in consciousness.

MAN

Let us imagine that an individual human soul enters into a relationship with matter at the fertilization of the ovum. That it builds a body and a brain, and that by its actions through the medium of this brain, it is able to further elaborate the structure of its permanent field or soul. In short, that *what we learn by direct experience* becomes a permanent part of our imperishable selves.

LEARNING

All learning leads eventually to direct mental experience, to *a more vivid state of awareness of living through events called "consciousness."* And learning commences with failure. It is only when we have an urge to do a thing and fail in the attempt to do it a number of times before we are successful that it can be said we have learned something. In doing the thing thereafter, we are mentally detached from the doing . . . and we pass from the stage of being involved in, and therefore a part of the act, to being detached from it, and so able to live through it in its completeness as an act of consciousness. While learning to drive an auto we cannot enjoy the scenery we are passing through. . . . We are part of the act of manipulating the car. When we have mastered the art of driving, we can detach ourselves from it and so enjoy the mental experience of the changing scenery.

CONSCIOUS EXPERIENCE

After practicing the exercises which follow in this book, we shall discover that the more vividly conscious we become, the less involved our minds are with our bodies. Like good drivers we are then able to enjoy the changing scenery of life that we are passing through.

CHAPTER 3

Mental Types

Aesthetics is not mere feeling, but feelings induced by insight into the perfect pattern of means and ends.

WILLIAM J. SANDERS

BRAIN RESEARCH

The electrical brain. We do not all use the same technique of thinking. Brain research during the past ten or twelve years, aided by new electrical apparatuses and techniques, have given us a picture of this organ as a vast galaxy of some ten thousand million tiny electrical dipolar batteries, which charge and fire in thousands of interlacing rhythms. When a million or so of these cells repeatedly charge and fire together, their discharge becomes measurable by an electroencephalographic recording.

Individuality. These major measurable rhythms have been found to possess significance. For instance, the earliest observed rhythm called the "Alpha rhythm" has been clearly associated with the process of mental imagery. The rhythm is in the nature of a "radar" scanning for a significant target: the moment a "target" is found, the Alpha rhythm disappears. When the eyes are shut and the mind is at rest, this scanning rhythm is strongest; when the eyes are open, or when a mental effort involving mental imagery is made, the Alpha rhythm vanishes. The accumulation of thousands of encephalographic recordings, however, has demonstrated that each person's *method* of thinking is as individualistic as are his fingerprints. Nevertheless, three broad types are clearly discernible.

21

THREE TYPES OF THINKER

Differences. Some people think mostly in visual images, but they also think in auditory and other sensory images to some degree. Others think almost entirely in visual images and in other sensory images hardly at all. Still another group seldom uses visual images but thinks almost entirely in terms of other sensory symbols. Now the unfortunate thing about these three mental types is that they represent three different ways of dealing with problems, and *none can "understand" the others.*

Tower of Babel. Imagine three key executives at the head of an organization. All of them are capable, sincere, and experienced men. Jones, the president, is a visual thinker of the second type mentioned. A vital change of policy is indicated to meet a certain situation, and Jones quickly visualizes the necessary changes organically. He visualizes shifts of personnel, amalgamation of departments, reduction of certain stocks, the building up of others, and so on. Smith, the first type of thinker mentioned, is a vice president. He can see the mechanics of the plan suggested by Jones, but he is more influenced by the abstract aspects of the situation. He thinks of the effects on the personnel and on customers of breaking up and reorganizing the old familiar organization. He would prefer to go more slowly and less radically. White is a second vice president, and is not a visual thinker at all. He is of the third type mentioned.

Statistical approach. White is incapable of visualizing the changes suggested; they appear like a radical and unsupported series of changes without much underlying pattern. So he refuses to move until every aspect of the proposed changes has been supported by a mass of statistical data. He is like a blind man feeling his way by sense of touch alone, and tapping the pavement before taking each short step forward. Usually his statistical gathering and analysis builds up such a formidable barrier to progress that he remains in a rut, elaborating statistics, and becoming more entangled with them all the time. Bookkeeping takes the place of creative thinking.

Superiority. Now which of these three types is superior? The answer is: Not one of them is superior to the others. The purely visual type of thinker is a good engineer, dealing with mechanical problems in which human values do not enter very much. He can see the *mechanics* of a situation vividly, but regards psychological or humane considerations as "weakness!" He has few friends and is feared and disliked by his associates, even though he may maintain the most rigid standards of "mechanical justice" and personal integrity. He is often successful but always lonely; when he makes mistakes, they are tremendous mistakes and likely to prove disastrous. Otherwise he is limited by a steady decline. in popularity, which filters down through all his public relationships.

Lack of decision. The second type, Smith, is a more balanced thinker, but often he lacks the power of decision. He can visualize a situation clearly enough, but his visual concepts are often at variance with his feelings about a project. He makes excellent decisions, but then argues himself out of them. He possesses neither the dogmatic certainty of the pure visual thinker, nor the blissful reliance on statistics of the "White" type individual.

The statistician. This latter (White) type of person, by thinking in abstract terms, or in sounds, or movements, has to feel his way slowly and be supported by statistics before undertaking a significant move. Thus he tends to "drag his feet" at all proposed changes.

The Burden Institute. At the Burden Neurological Institute of England, where the discovery of the three types of thinking was made in 1943, it is thought likely that the visual (Alpha rhythm) type is probably inborn and hereditary, but that differentiation to some degree usually happens as a result of their conditioning experiences. Experiments with identical twins demonstrate the fact that by training or "conditioning," one type can acquire the characteristics of either or both the other types while retaining at the same time his own pattern. Creative Realism has demonstrated that by a deliberate program of training, *even large groups of mixed types can acquire a common mental meeting ground; that when this happens, a spectacular improvement in the efficiency of the group results, with a corresponding improvement in the health and happiness of its individual members.*

FRUSTRATIONS

Causes. The principal cause of unhappiness with its frustrations and failures is not that some people are deliberately "evil" or "mean," it is simply that we fail to understand each other. We cannot understand each other fully because our subconscious minds are not conditioned to compute the data supplied by others according to its intended meanings. What seems significant to one type seems insignificant to another type;

each type gives a different emphasis to the same data. So we are led further apart by every joint attack upon a common problem.

Interrelationships. In the foregoing example we pictured three executives, men of good will, capable, experienced, and honest, and bound by a common cause, and how subconsciously their efforts might frustrate each other. But multiply this situation by a board of directors, shareholders, junior executives, personnel, customers, and, yes, even competitors, multiply this again by a similar interfamily relationship of frustration which each of these people live under, and we have a picture of the situation under which probably three out of every ten of us become mental casualties. When we consider decisions being made under similar conditions which profoundly affect the lives and destiny of all of us, it is frightening.

Masked. The basic mechanisms of each individual's subconscious is masked beneath many layers of acquired social and "pretended" behavior. Not that a person is prone to deliberate misrepresentation; he simply mistakes play-acting for reality. As a child, he may indulge in a species of hero-worship toward a parent or friend and mimic this person's words, manners, and even appearance. We are all born mimics.

False personality. It is quite common therefore to find one basic type imitating the mannerisms of either of the other types. We might find a Jones type of visual thinker simulating the slow and calculating type of behavior of a White type statistical thinker, or a White type imitating the crisp, decisive mannerisms characteristic of the Jones type. We might find the Smith type imitating either. Not that any of these types are aware that they are imitating anyone or any type. The false personality, peculiar to civilized man, is the product of a behavior pattern imposed from without by environmental factors without regard to inner fitness. Its crystallization in any given individual is governed by chance.

MENTAL TYPES

Partial development. As you shall discover for yourself later, there really are no *basic* and unalterable types. Creative Realism holds that each of the types listed represents a development of one part of the mental machine—that is to say, *of the brain but not the mind*—and a slowed-down or even a suspended development of from three to five other parts of it. The newly born infant emerges but reluctantly from sleep. Potentially it has four channels through which it may learn awareness of the outside world: seeing, hearing, touching, and smelling. Perhaps the amount of fondling that a baby receives determines the extent of its tactile awareness later; by the relative quietness or noisiness of the nursery, its auditory awareness may be either developed or retarded; by the static or changing patterns of visual stimuli, its visual awareness may be retarded or developed. Such factors as these may influence the development of the types referred to.

Law of accident. Thus, our mental type is probably determined by the law of accident. The amount of time our mothers had for fondling, the relative noisiness or tranquillity of the nursery, the amount of light and movement in the nursery—these may have been some of the determining factors which brought about the completion of certain sensory circuits ahead of others, guiding the avalanche of organization within the brain into dealing with the first stimuli received and laying down a pattern of mental behavior which gives precedence to it for a lifetime. As other sensory circuits are completed, the stimuli received over them also receives attention, but it is always in the nature of mere background, as it were, to the first type received.

Meanings. Unless the mind can translate the words and visual images received into meanings relative to itself, a person is to all intents and purposes as incapable of understanding as an ape, who responds only to his feelings, lives in his feelings, and is his feelings. Yet from what has been touched upon, it becomes obvious that the science of semantics cannot help us much toward a common understanding. Semantics would be in the nature of a blind man trying to define something to a deaf-mute, for a similar barrier exists between mental types.

THE FOURTH TYPE

New way of looking at life. Creative Realism has demonstrated that regardless of the mental type to which we belong, we can each develop the more dormant interpreting areas of our brain by a series of relatively simple exercises, and by this means we are able to penetrate the meanings expressed by any of the three types of thinking patterns; but more than this, we acquire a new way of looking at life, a way that is vastly more effective and superior to that employed by either of the three types of thinking patterns already described. We become, in effect, a fourth type of thinker.

BASIC PATTERNS

The quest. The mind is a seeker of patterns. A pattern is a sequence of events in time, or an arrangement of objects in space, which can be remembered and compared with another pattern. Pattern is the opposite of chaos or randomness. One chaos cannot be compared with another chaos. The human brain is a patterned structure, and it deals with events in accordance with these basic patterns. The human mind though is capable of modifying existing brain patterns, and of developing new ones.

Plasticity. The human brain is the most plastic of all organs. Even a brain mutilated by surgery retains its resilience, and adapts itself to the stresses of environment. When a good part of a pattern is destroyed in this way, there may be some slight changes in personality, but by proper training it can be re-established. Thus, faculties simply dormant through disuse are easily developed.

Stages. In the first two chapters we offered the theory that living nature upon this planet is the physical expression of an "immaterial field" of mind which surrounds the world and has entered into a relationship with matter for the purpose of evolving a state of *objective self-consciousness*. It has moved upward in an evolutionary sense, by first entering into a relationship with matter to produce protoplasm in the form of single cells; then in erecting a wide variety of differently patterned bodies from these cells, which together would produce the conditions suitable to the most highly complex organism of all . . . the instrument of its consciousness . . . man.

ANALOGY

As it is important that we form this basic concept clearly in our minds before proceeding with the exercises, let us, by stretching our imaginations a bit, try to visualize the following:

Intelligence. Imagine that the ordinary electromagnetic field which surrounds the earth, and which makes radio and television possible, is possessed of another quality—intelligence. Imagine that it deliberately enters into a relationship with matter and that, by bending the inert stuff to its will, it forms it into tiny dipolar batteries called cells. Imagine that by forming large numbers of these tiny batteries into larger units called bodies, it can harness still more of its own electrical power. To employ this power in a wide variety of ways, it equips the bodies with many different forms of transformers; now imagine that the total effect of all these engines working in harmony is to produce a field suitable for a very complex radio station to operate in. Now imagine that the radio station is for the purpose of receiving, computing, and rebroadcasting the faint signals pouring into the ether from all the other organisms, and that by the very act of receiving, computing, and broadcasting *it acts as a controller of all the other organisms.* Imagine that in its totality this receiving, computing, and broadcasting is *consciousness.* This will give a rough analogy.

The telescope. Imagine all of the physical organisms in nature combined in the form of a four-sectioned telescope: the one-celled algae, protozoa, and so on, forming the lower section; then the more complex organisms—corals, jellyfish, mollusks, worms, and so on—forming the second section; then all the rest of the creatures up to man forming the third section; and man, unique among all the other animals, forming the fourth section.

The Fourth Section. What differentiates man from his cousin, the ape, is a special pattern which, roofed over the old brain pattern of the lower organisms, forms what is known in engineering terms as an automatic control system by feedback. The principle in its simplest form is illustrated by the thermostat which regulates the heat of a room. The information furnished by its thermometer about the room temperature is "fed back" to open or close a valve, which in turn controls the heat of the room.

Automatic control. The automatic feedback control system of a human brain, however, is a tremendously complex affair, and comprises an "analogue computer" for selecting and analyzing the data received through the senses from the outside world, and computing this in relation to data received from within the body, then in "feeding back" the answers to adjust the chemistry of the body to meet the situations posed from without.

Freedom. This automatic feedback control system takes the consciousness of man—or perhaps it would be better to say, *part of the mind of man*—out of the business of "housekeeping" and frees it to become an instrument of the highest form of consciousness.

MIRACLE MACHINE

Its complexities. To give you some idea of the complexity of the machine which you are equipped with, W. Grey Walter,* one of the world's outstanding brain specialists, estimates that could man make a mechanism as intricate as a brain cell and crowd it into a quarter of a cubic inch, he would need a factory of a million and a half cubic feet to contain the ten thousand million cells, which make up a single human brain. He estimates that could these manmade mechanical cells be made for ten cents each, the total cost would be a billion dollars, and that could the wiring connections between them be made for two cents each, these would cost two trillion dollars more. The power needed would be at least half a million kilowatts, even were transistors used, yet the miracle machine inside your skull runs on only twenty-five watts.

OUR PROBLEM

In the chapters which follow we shall use that part of our minds freed by our automatic control system to "repattern" that system to the extent that still more of our minds are freed to fulfill the purpose which brought us to birth—*the attainment of consciousness.*

---

* In *The Living Brain* (W. W. Norton and Company: 1953).

CHAPTER 4

Integrating the Subconscious

By insensible steps, the plant builds itself up into a large and various fabric of root, stem, leaves, flowers, and fruit, every one moulded within and without in accordance with an extremely complex, minutely defined pattern.

THOMAS H. HUXLEY

THE INTELLECT

Definition. The "intellect" is defined as: "That faculty of the human mind by which it receives and comprehends, as distinguished from the faculty of feeling and willing." Thus most of us perhaps have come to regard the intellect as a "conscious faculty." In reality, however, the intellect is a subconscious faculty, and *intellection and consciousness cannot occur simultaneously.* When we are wrestling with an intellectual problem, and are aware of what we are doing, we are not conscious; we are involved in our subconscious processes.

The computer. The intellect is a mechanical computing machine with only the "keyboard" protruding into consciousness. We can "push down on the keys, twist the crank," and receive a computation, but the actual processes by which the computation is made are invisible to us.

Linear thinking. The mechanical intellect works according to the principles of logic. It reduces all data to a single dimension, compares these elements one with another, arranges them into a cause-and-effect sequence and serves this up as a result.

Two plus two. Purely logical thinking can only add and subtract, and, while this is useful in helping us arrange many of the little mechanical chores of life, it can be completely misleading when applied to the process of living. For instance, two and two do not always make four from a realistic viewpoint. Two cows and two microbes in such a mathematical association would be meaningless. Even to the dairy farmer, thinking in terms of milk producton, two Holsteins and two Herefords (beef cattle) might only equal three cows.

NONLOGICAL UNIVERSE

Nonlogical man. Nature is *not* logical—and consciousness least of all—and man is the most conscious organism in nature. Therefore, inherently, man is not logical. His logical subconscious with its intellect is but a tiny built-in computing machine, and it works in that way because that is the way in which it is designed to work. It is designed to attend to just one small aspect of life, and to attempt to base our whole lives upon its findings is to limit ourselves to "flatland" and its distortions. Instead of accepting things because they are "logical," we should regard every "logical system" as having a nonlogical plus or minus; and until we can envision these by conscious experience or "intuition," we are not in a position to judge the validity of the system.

Life and logic. Life itself is not logical; it is only the human intellect that is logical. The known facts of evolution on this planet do not by any means furnish an explanation of it. The theory is valuable because it enables us to deal with many problems intellectually, and to effect improvements in our environment because our intellects are brought into a rational relationship with them. But the theory—even as an explanation of "how's"—is riddled with gaps which we plug with words instead of explanations—such words, for instance, as "mutation," denoting the changes which have taken place in some organisms, giving rise to new species. As most mutations which produced new species anticipated conditions never experienced, it is like saying that the echo happened before the sound.

Something more. To understand life then—*to actually live* in the fullest sense of the word—we must not only intellectualize, but we must be able to *directly experience* many aspects of life which do not yield themselves to intellectual analysis. And *we must be able to experience these consciously,* to know that we are experiencing them, for consciousness is indivisible from them; they are parts of the phenomena of consciousness.

THE THREE TYPES

Subconscious development. In our last chapter it was explained that all people may be divided into three main types of thinkers: the visual type, the visual-auditory type, and the abstract, tactile-kinesthetic type. It was said that the three types are probably developed as the result of accident. It is now pointed out that this differentiation of type only takes place in the subconscious development. In short, the subconscious computing machine which is being organized in the brain of the child becomes "aware" of the signals coming in over the nerves from one of the senses before it develops an awareness of the signals from the other senses. Because of this the computing mechanism is given a developmental "shove," as it were, in favor of these first type signals, and forever afterward regards them in all computations as being first in importance.

Pleasure and pain. The sensory impulses arriving in the brain are "packaged" into images and stored in association with other images in the brain cells. These associations *are meaningful in terms of pleasure and pain.* Those associated with pleasure are readily recalled; those associated with pain trigger a "warning signal" and are recalled with difficulty.

Accidental associations. Yet even as the type of stimuli first received by the brain is due to accidental influences, our pleasure and pain associations are also largely the result of accident. A child is frequently dosed with castor oil masked in orange juice. The taste of the juice and its smell becomes repugnant. If the child is the visual type, it will develop an aversion even to the color orange. Thus the whole fabric of our "tastes" and "distastes" and the readiness with which our subconscious computing machines compute certain data, while displaying a great reluctance to work with others, is woven largely by accident.

Mental pleasure and pain. Nature has guided the whole course of evolution by pleasure and pain, and these are the only measures by which the lower animals can judge an experience. In the case of human beings, however, another sort of pleasure and pain enters in: mental pleasure and mental pain.

Example. Let us suppose that a youngster is exposed to the bullying of an older child, and repeatedly humiliated by him. Let us further suppose that the older child has red hair, and a certain raucous manner of speaking. The probability is that he will forever afterward feel a subconscious aversion to people of that particular type and toward all people who express themselves in even a remotely similar manner.

Pleasure seeking. To sum up: Owing to the accidental influences of their early environment, men are divided into three different types of thinkers: visual, visual-auditory, and abstract, tactile-kinesthetic types. Each type is like a mental cripple, limping along and making intellectual decisions based mainly upon the data received from one of the five senses, with the data of the remaining four senses either played down or ignored. Furthermore, his decisions are subconsciously influenced by accidentally acquired pleasure and pain associations, which in reality have little or nothing to do with the essence of our problems. Man like the rest of the animals is a pleasure-seeking organism; he unconsciously veers toward the pleasurable and away from the painful, in a mental sense as well as in a physical sense.

AUTOMATISM

Partial consciousness. In this stage of his evolution, man is not fully conscious. Although nature has given him the brain development necessary to free consciousness, he has not yet taken possession of it. He is like one imprisoned from early childhood in the cabin of a houseboat, and, able to view only a small portion of the sea's surface through a porthole at each end, has no conception of the sky above, nor the depths of the ocean below, and so whiles away his time by inventing imaginary games. After a time, he has laboriously invented a little game to explain each change in the motion of his boat, and gradually he has come to accept these as an explanation of the universe.

The ladder. We might imagine our prisoner's deciding one day to build a ladder by which to reach a closed hatch above his head, and completing this step by step. Eventually it is done. He climbs to the top step and pushes up the hatch, then thrusts his head up into the free air. His eyes behold the vast expanse of sky above and the great heaving ocean around him, and he *experiences the real world,* which has little resemblance to the world born of his fantasies.

Partial knowledge. The knowledge gathered by the senses to be stored as memories and computed by the intellect can never be sufficiently large and all-embracing to satisfy a man's needs. No matter how much formal education he absorbs, he will always be acquiring information in one area of learning yet remain ignorant in other areas of learning to which he has not been exposed or to which he has not directed his attention. Moreover, there is a profound distinction between the acquiring, assimilation, or absorption of facts by rote and the actual involvement of experience with these facts. Mere book learning results in a knowledge of the form without an understanding of the essence. Only *conscious experience* can bring us this all-embracing understanding which enables us to truly evaluate the things of the intellect.

DUAL PROBLEM

Method. As Creative Realists, then, we have a dual problem to commence upon. First: We must devise a method by which that part of our brains called the "sensorium"—the seat of the sensations—may be developed to the point where all of the sensory stimuli—whether of sight, smell, hearing, taste, or touch—are given equal treatment and combined, as it were, into a single "supersensation." We must be able to effect this combination at will in order to understand each other, and to supply our subconscious computing machines with the best possible data. Second: We must devise a method by which our consciousness can be detached at will from its present entanglement with the subconscious, to the end that we can confirm our intellectual computations by conscious experience.

Objectivity. We shall discover, when we are able to detach our consciousness from its subconscious involvement, that there are no prejudices, no likes and dislikes, no "I want and I don't want's" in consciousness; that all of these accidentally acquired associations exist only in the subconscious; and that when they are deprived of their conscious content by detachment, they gradually fade away like weeds cut off from their roots and left to wither in the sun. Later, we shall learn to use another technique by which even the roots may be destroyed.

The key. The key to objectivity is the visual faculty. Regardless of whether we happen to belong to the nonvisual type of thinker or not, the visual faculty is the most easily controlled faculty of the mind, and the most amenable to development. Everyone dreams at times, and dreams all have a visual component. It may be faint and shadowy, *but nevertheless it is there.* When we dream and remember our dreams, we have a glimpse into the workings of our subconscious processes while these are idling. If a visual content exists in our dreams, it must obviously exist in our subconscious processes during the waking state.

Organized patterns. The visual image, however, not only exists as an essential part of all of our ideas; *it is the most essential part of them.* In short, the visual image is the element or mould by which all other sensory impressions are patterned into coherent units or symbols which can be manipulated meaningfully by the subconscious computer. Strongly organized, vividly visual images can form a pattern through which the energy of the entire brain becomes channeled—sleeping and waking— toward the accomplishment of any objective we may set for ourselves.

APE AND MAN

Detachment. In Chapter One we said that an ape lives in his feelings, *is his* feelings, and possesses nothing which can detach itself from his feelings—in short, that an ape *completely identifies himself with his subconscious images.* Attached to his images are the accidentally acquired pleasure and pain memories, and as his images take form in his mind's eye, the pleasure or pain memories trigger his emotions. Alas, most men also live in this state, at least most of the time, but unlike the apes, man does possess *something* which can detach itself from his images with their pleasure and pain memories, and not only this but this "something" can at will deliberately create images of things not present to the senses. We call this something "consciousness."

Illustration. To illustrate the possibility of complete detachment from our subconscious images, consider the following: Most brain tumors commence as a tiny growth beneath the layer of cells which cover the cortex or brain surface. By the time the growth is large enough to be found by X-ray and other techniques, it is usually too late to operate.

Seizures. One of the early symptoms is an epileptic-type seizure, and before such seizures the patients often have a "premonitory dream" or vision. So at the world-famous Montreal Neurological Clinic, the surgeons reasoned that could they find the area of the brain in each separate case which produced the warning dream or vision, they would have the site of the tumor, and would be able to remove it in its early stage.

Brain operation. A painless operation under a local anesthetic exposes the surface or cortex of the brain; then with the patient fully conscious and able to describe his experiences, the surface of the brain is gently explored with a fine wire probe which carries a mild charge of electricity. When certain small regions of the temporal lobe are touched, the patient smells nonexistent smells, hears dream music, the voices of friends perhaps, and usually these are accompanied by vivid, visual dreams like mental movies. This may be a long and involved sequence, yet all the time the patient is fully conscious and as detached as though he were observing a moving picture play in a theatre. Sometimes a point is touched by the probe at the commencement of a dream, and it will play through its whole sequence; then a point may be touched farther along, and the dream will commence in its middle. If a point still farther along be touched, the dream may commence near its ending. Eventually the area which produces the warning dream or vision is usually found, and marked; then the surgeons remove the tumor.

THE OBSERVER

Consciousness and subconscious. Now so far as we are concerned, the foregoing discussion of a brain operation graphically illustrates two things. First, it shows the conscious mind and the subconscious mind in simultaneous operation, with the consciousness detached as an observer of the subconscious processes as these occur in the same brain. Second, it illustrates the complete mechanicalness of the subconscious mind, and shows it as a sort of biological "juke-box" which will automatically play back any recording when the "right button" is pressed.

Subconscious content. As we have said before on several occasions, the subconscious and its intellect is a computing machine, and the memories stored as the result of our own experiences, and the teachings of parents, teachers, preachers, playmates, books, comic strips, radio, television, advertising, and so on, together with the pain and pleasure sensations which accompanied their gathering, are the data used by the computing machine.

Will. Will is an attribute of consciousness. What we usually mistake for will is merely subconscious desire—the craving for a particular sensation; the memory of a pleasure experienced and the desire to repeat it; or the memory of pain which followed a particular line of conduct, and the desire to avoid a repetition of it. Real conscious will is the ability to act or to refrain from acting, without reference to our pain and pleasure memories, our hopes and fears, likes and dislikes.

Development. At the present time, most of us are under the domination of our subconscious minds. Our consciousness is fractionated among the hundreds of little movies, with their pleasure and pain associations; it is locked up in the cabin of the mental houseboat and must free itself by building a ladder in order to develop real objective awareness of the world without. We build the lower steps of this ladder by taking command of our subconscious and forcing it to form and associate visual images in a nonsense series of pictures—that is, in a series of pictures which cannot be recalled by logic. Having gained power over our subconscious, while at the same time developing our visual faculty, we can gradually reverse the presently prevailing order of things and use our subconscious as a tool of consciousness.

THE EXERCISE
INTEGRATING THE SUBCONSCIOUS

The technique: Seat yourself comfortably in a quiet place, and, as you read each word, close your eyes and form in your mind's eye as clear an image of the thing suggested by the word as possible. Do not stew and worry if your pictures are not very clear at first; if you happen to be a nonvisual type thinker, at first you may not be able to form more than a hazy outline. This will improve surprisingly with practice. When you form a second picture, drop the first one completely from your mind's eye. It can only hold one picture at a time, and any effort to hold more than one will result in failure.

THE NONSENSE SERIES

Were we to read the following twenty-four words in the same manner, let us say, that we have read the words in the preceding chapters, we should have great difficulty in recalling them in their proper order. There are no natural relationships existing between them. Yet by visualizing and associating them, we can easily recall them at will, as we shall see. First, without attempting to either visualize or associate them, read them in their numbered sequence.

(1) Rabbit	(7) Rocket	(13) Lamp	(19) Barley
(2) Man	(8) Temple	(14) Statue	(20) Parade
(3) Tree	(9) Moose	(15) Book	(21) Map
(4) Bird	(10) Mountain	(16) Beggar	(22) Roof
(5) Window	(11) Snowball	(17) Pony	(23) Rock
(6) Stove	(12) Soldier	(18) River	(24) Shop

Now set the book down for a few moments and try to remember and to write down as many of the twenty-four words as possible in their proper order. You probably will not be able to remember more than five or six.

First picture. This time, visualize and associate the words in the manner described on the facing page under the heading "The Technique." For instance, as a starter, take the first word in column one: sit back, close your eyes, and form the image of a large white rabbit. . . . See him clearly sitting on his haunches with ears upright and nose twitching. He hops along then toward a . . . *man,* the second word in our list of twenty-four words.

Second picture. Man standing with his hands in pockets. Make a clear picture of this man. Visualize him as being bareheaded and dressed in slacks and a sports shirt. Don't forget to drop the rabbit completely from your mind as you commence to visualize the man.

Third picture. The man strolls over to a large elm tree, places his hand on the trunk and gazes up into the branches. Now drop the man from your mind and give all your attention to visualizing the elm tree with its spreading branches and shimmering leaves.

Fourth picture. A white bird flies out from among the branches of the elm. Now drop the tree from your mind's eye and strongly visualize the flying white bird.

Fifth picture. A house looms up ahead of the bird, which flies through an open window. Now imagine yourself looking through this open window into a kitchen. Drop the bird from your mind. In the kitchen there is a glowing, red-hot stove.

Sixth picture. A rocket falls with a thump on the red-hot stove . . . sizzles for a moment, then zooms upward through the ceiling out into the air. . . . Now watch the rocket as it traces a curving trajectory and drop from mind all else.

Seventh picture. The rocket lands with a shower of sparks in front of a white marble temple. Drop all else from your mind and visualize the temple.

Eighth picture. The door of the temple swings open and a great bull moose stalks out. Forget the temple now and clearly visualize the moose as he walks along.

Ninth picture. The moose halts and stares upward at a tall snow-capped mountain. Drop the moose now and visualize the mountain clearly.

Tenth picture. A huge snowball comes bounding down the slope of the mountain. Drop the mountain from your mind's eye, and follow the course of the snowball.

Eleventh picture. The snowball plunges in front of a soldier who is standing with his hands in his pockets. Drop the snowball from mind now and visualize the soldier.

Twelfth picture. The soldier stoops and picks up a glass lamp that stands on the ground and hurls it through the air. Drop the soldier from mind now and visualize the lamp as it hurtles through the air, turning over and over.

Thirteenth picture. The lamp strikes a statue and shatters to pieces. Drop the lamp from mind now and visualize this statue. Imagine it is bronze, of a man on horseback.

Fourteenth picture. A red-covered book falls from the statue and flutters to the ground. Eliminate the statue now and clearly visualize the book lying on the ground.

Fifteenth picture. A ragged beggar shuffles up, picks up the book, thrusts it into his coat pocket, and continues on his way. Now visualize the ragged beggar.

Sixteenth picture. The beggar halts before a beautiful black pony. Drop the beggar now and concentrate upon visualizing the pony.

Seventeenth picture. The pony snorts, rears, then gallops to the bank of a river, where he skids to a halt. Drop the pony now and visualize the river swirling along between its banks.

Eighteenth picture. On the opposite side of the river is a field of ripe, golden barley, waving rhythmically in the gentle breeze. Drop all else from mind now and strongly visualize the field of barley.

Nineteenth picture. Into the field of barley a parade of people marches behind a baton-twirling drum major. Drop all else from mind and visualize this parade.

Twentieth picture. The drum major pulls from his belt a map, unrolls it, and tosses it into the air. It is caught by the breeze and carried high into the air. Drop all else now and visualize this map sailing along on the breeze.

Twenty-first picture. The map gradually loses altitude and comes to rest finally on a red-tiled roof. Drop everything else from your mind's eye and concentrate upon picturing this red-tiled roof.

Twenty-second picture. A rock crashes down on the red-tiled roof, bounces off, and goes rolling along the street below to be brought to a halt by the door of a shop. As we combined the picture of the window with the stove for convenience, the twenty-three pictures of this series will give us a recall of the twenty-four words.

Recall. Now lay this book down, sit back in your chair and recall the pictures. Close your eyes, and relax—any excessive tension will prevent recall—then simply call up the mental image of the rabbit and follow through with the entire series of pictures. If you were careful to visualize each picture as clearly as possible in the first place, and to associate it with the next one before dropping it from mind, you will not have the least difficulty in recalling the entire series.

DIFFERENT COMBINATIONS

Effects. Now just think of the almost endless ways in which these twenty-four pictures could be combined into different associations. Think of the little narratives and dramas which could be formed of them. But think also of the effects of such combinations; if instead of being a nonsense series selected at random and without pleasure and pain connotations, suppose that each of these pictures had been accompanied by an emotional experience at the time of its forming, and suppose that when they were recalled, all of these emotions which accompanied their forming were reproduced. This is what actually happens in the automatic subconscious. The process is going on all the time—sleeping and waking—as chain after chain of images are triggered accidentally or deliberately recalled. In the waking state we call this "fantasy" or "daydreaming"; in the sleeping state we call it simply "dreaming."

Millions of pictures. Stored within the brain are not merely twenty-four associated pictures, but millions of pictures, most of which are accompanied by pleasure and pain memories. As we grow up, a sort of filtering process takes place by which the painful memories are distorted and given different meanings by associating them with other pictures taken from happier contexts. This process of distortion prevents the triggering of emotional states which might play havoc with the chemistry of the body if allowed free rein.

Worry state. It is probable that practically all of our most painful and poignant memories are de-armed by this type of distortion, but even then, that they become associated into complex chains or systems which are expressed in such traits as worry, timidity, ultraconservatism, defensiveness, and pessimism, which sap the mind's vitality and dry up its natural creativeness.

CONCLUSION

Conscious will. By the foregoing exercise, you employed conscious will to make the mechanical part of your mind jump through the hoop by creating and associating a nonrational chain of visual images, and by recalling these again into consciousness. You shall be able to recall this chain of images quite easily, even five years from now. You can imagine the permanence then of a chain of images when associated logically and backed by strong emotion. You can also imagine how such chains can be triggered by accidental happenings, and thus cause you to act, not in accordance with the reality of the situation, but contrary to the reality of the situation—even though you believe that you are being perfectly logical about it.

Intellect insufficient. You can see now why the intellect alone is not sufficient. Without a high development of conscious awareness, we are not free individuals as perhaps we have hitherto believed ourselves to be, but mere biological statistics operating blindly according to the laws of chance. Until we can separate our consciousness from the machinery of the subconscious, we are completely tied to responding automatically to the present in terms of the distorted memories of past experiences.

CHAPTER 5

Toward Consciousness

We have come from somewhere and we are going somewhere.
The great architect of the universe never built a stairway that
leads to nowhere.

ROBERT A. MILLIKAN

THE GROUNDWORK

Co-operative movement. In the preceding four chapters the outline
of the basic concept of Creative Realism was sketched. Nature was
shown as a great co-operative, *meaningful,* forward movement in time.
It was suggested that the significance of this evolutionary movement is
plain: *the attainment of consciousness.*

Parallelisms. Throughout all of nature's observable processes a series
of parallelisms seems to exist. Thus, the organization of an atom has
been likened to the organization of a solar system. It was suggested that
the development of a human body from the fertilized ovum to the adult
individual parallels the development of the body of living nature as a
whole on this planet; that even as the *purpose* behind the development
of a human being is the attainment of individual consciousness, the purpose of the evolution of nature's body is the development of consciousness.

Brain cells. Each of us expresses his consciousness through the co-
operative activity of some ten thousand million brain cells. Each of
these cells is an individual separate living unit. According to the theory
of Creative Realism, nature expresses *her* consciousness through the co-
operative action of some two thousand million human beings. Thus,
each of us is, in a sense, a single brain cell through which the consciousness of mother nature is striving to express itself.

41

The field. We have imagined the mind of nature as a "world soul" surrounding our planet much in the same way we might imagine a magnetic field surrounding an electrified, spinning metal ball. Just as a magnetic field has the capacity to arrange iron filings into a pattern, we can imagine the world soul having the capacity to channel matter (energy) into specific patterns. If we can imagine this world soul as being in the process of evolving from unconscious automatism *toward consciousness and freedom,* even as the human foetus evolves from unconsciousness and automatism toward consciousness and freedom, we can visualize the picture.

TOWARD FREEDOM

Freedom from fear. Freedom is the condition of being released from the bondage imposed by our own inhibiting ignorance. In short, *it is freedom from fear* . . . and we only fear the unknown. The unknown is that which our minds have not been taught to deal with nor to understand. We have no mental patterns established for responding to that particular thing, and so we either hide from it or flee from it. Sometimes we try to imagine what the unknown is like, and the result is a series of fantasies based upon fear, and this is called "worry," which shackles us more deeply to our ignorance than ever.

Pathology. Within the human brain, a small group of cells may turn malignant and not only frustrate the normal functioning of the mind, but, in time, destroy the brain altogether. As every principle has a dual aspect—positive and negative—it is conceivable that the opposite of the above is also true; that occasionally a relatively small group of cells within the frontal lobe of the brain attain *a higher level of consciousness* and that, when this happens, the effect also spreads and is felt throughout the entire brain.

Analogy. We have seen similar effects in human affairs. Small groups of individuals have turned "malignant" from time to time and their spreading influence, until halted by the surgery of war, has caused profound suffering and misery to all mankind. Other small groups have achieved a higher level of consciousness than the average, and their beneficent influence, spreading outward, has blessed the human race and brought benefit to all.

Personal effort. The attainment of a higher level of consciousness cannot be achieved except by individual and personal effort. By attaining consciousness we attain freedom . . . *but it is individual freedom* . . . freedom from the dreams and fantasies of our own subconscious minds. Only then may we be able to use our natural powers for the benefit of mankind, including ourselves.

PATTERNS AND PURPOSE

Evolution. Creation is the act of establishing meaningful patterns through which a purpose might be achieved. Thus, a pattern implies a meaning, and a meaning can only be unfolded by means of a pattern. Upon this planet evolution has moved forward from pattern-forming to pattern-seeking. Once a pattern was firmly established as a basis, a new level of pattern-seeking took place in which often a new pattern was laid down and then scrapped, and another new pattern tried and scrapped, and this process of pattern-seeking went on until the right one was found and then established.

The telescope again. In this way, living nature on this planet, considered as a single great organism, has established four operational patterns like the sections of a telescope: the basic section completely unconscious and automatic, the second section possessing a very limited ability to modify its existing pattern to a slight degree, the third section having far greater adaptability and being more conscious, and the fourth section, consisting of mankind, being the most conscious of all.

The pattern-seeker. Nature is still a pattern-seeker, but her pattern-seeking is now being conducted through the brains of mankind. All science is the result of pattern-seeking; all art is the result of pattern-making. Science discovers existing patterns and adapts these to his purposes. Art seeks to establish new meaningful patterns, and one becomes the inspiration of the other. Nature through man is still laying down new patterns and scrapping them as these prove to be inadequate, as we can see by the events taking place around us.

Contributory patterns. In view of what has been said, it should be clear that to succeed, every new pattern must be related to the already established patterns on the one hand, and be a projection forward into time of the basic meaning as unfolded by the already existing patterns. Any new pattern which runs counter to the basic meaning is doomed from its beginnings.

TOWARD CONSCIOUSNESS

Individual effort. No further advance toward consciousness can be made except through individual effort. All previous patterns laid down by nature were for the purpose of making this final advance possible. An individual can contribute little to the pattern of his physical body as laid down by nature. He can make the best possible use of the pattern, but that is all. His mind, however, is his own responsibility. The patterns laid down in his own subconscious can be an extension forward of nature's meaningful pattern, leading to his own higher consciousness and greater creativeness, or they can be made counter to nature's evolutionary plan and result in his own undoing.

Automatism. In our previous chapter it was shown how our subconscious patterns are accidentally acquired, and so it is easy to understand that inasmuch as our subconscious patterns are for the most part not only lacking in purpose but may of themselves actually be destructive and contrary to the purpose of evolution, they cannot bring us anything new and creative; for until we learn to rule our subconscious and pattern it according to our own and nature's meaning, we shall continue to be tossed hither and yon by the accidental happenings of our environment calling forth responses from our accidentally acquired subconscious patterns.

Difference is basic. Thousands of recordings of brain-wave patterns taken at neurological clinics and institutes prove that each of us has a pattern of mental activity that is as individualistic as are our fingerprints. This is true even in the case of identical twins. Thus, on the subconscious level each of us constructs a different pattern from the same impressions received. The element which makes us different is basic: *it is our true personality,* our very souls.

JIGSAW PUZZLES

Conflict of ideas. Our true personalities cause us to elaborate subconscious structures and interpretive mechanisms different in some degree to all others, because no living human can be self-sufficient any more than can a human brain cell be self-sufficient. A human being lives and moves and has his being as a unit of society in the same way that a single brain cell is a unit of a society. Yet if all human beings were exactly the same, man could never evolve mentally. It is the conflict of ideas within the human family which brings forth the new and the creative. At least that is the way it should be. We are all little individual pieces formed of a unity, in the same way that the pieces of a jigsaw puzzle are cut from a single piece of wood.

Competition. Subconsciously then, we are all in a sense competitive. Another person's ideas stimulate our own flow of ideas *because these are different from our own.* If our ideas are more stimulating in some respects than his, we both benefit by what may be thought of; we all benefit from this mental competition.

Meeting place. In these days of endless debate we hear a lot about finding a meeting place of minds, but in the sense that there is an intellectual (subconscious) level at which we can all view our common problems in the same way, this is a complete fallacy. The basic nature of man makes this impossible. Debate upon this level can only accentuate our differences, *and without consciousness* these differences become more sharply delineated, charged with emotion, and explode into the ultimate response to frustration—physical conflict.

Interpretations. In short, there are more than two billion individuals alive today, each of whom is equipped with a unique and individualistic interpretive mechanism. The human senses do not see, hear, touch, taste, or smell *reality;* they merely respond to certain physical stimuli. In each individual this response is slightly different. For instance, the human eye is only sensitive to a narrow band of radiation that falls between red and violet. A difference of a few hundred thousandths of a centimeter in wave length determines whether we see a thing or whether it is invisible. The same is even more true of the coarser receptors such as the nose, ears, tongue, and skin. As these sense impressions are all that the subconscious computing machine has to work with, and as each subconscious interprets the little of reality brought to it by the feeble senses differently, how could such interpretations ever agree?

INNER VISION

Objective consciousness. The only area where people can meet in agreement is in objective consciousness, the consciousness which includes the work of all individual brains who have ever lived and those which are at present living: in short, the field which forms the mind of nature, the source of all human reality, the wholeness of which every individual mind is but a tiny part. This reality manifests itself in the human brain as inner vision—a deep and detached *certainty* about a course of action, which has nothing to do perhaps with the intellectual appraisal of it.

Stimulation. When we contact another individual from this viewpoint of consciousness, we are no longer interested in the great American game of "selling" by bludgeoning the corners off every other piece of the jig-saw puzzle to fit our own. We enjoy the stimulation of every different viewpoint on the intellectual level, and realize that the greatest advantage to all will result not from a slavish acceptance of a single viewpoint, but from each individual making the contribution he is best equipped to make, and all fitting their pieces together to the accomplishment of an objective beneficial to all.

Fusion. Make no mistake, every worthwhile thing is accomplished by two or more people fusing their differing subconscious concepts into a harmony . . . as a number of different musical tones are fused into a chord. In building a home or a business or a nation, the greatest advantage should be taken of the unique and different contributions possible by each individual . . . because he is different. Recognition and respect for each other's basic differences in interpretation and the realization that these can be made valuable when applied to a consciously conceived objective, shared in by all parties, is the first principle of successful organization. This illustrates the value of "competition" as a subconscious stimulant, but its very real danger unless it is welded into a co-operative over-all project, *a project consciously conceived and consciously directed.*

FATHER OF DISCONTENT

Frustration. All of our discontent with "things as they are" and many of our secret fears, antagonisms, and hatreds are due to our naturally existing differences in personality structure. When our true personalities are denied expression and are forced to make an unnatural adjustment to the personality of another, whether that personality be a husband or a wife, a brother or a sister, a boss or a superior officer, we may achieve (by means of a false personality) an appearance of unanimity, but this is always at the cost of our own inner feeling of self-respect and dignity.

Rebellion. The feeling of inferiority generates secret hatred. This is often seen in family relationships, wherein children try to balance their psychological budgets by getting even with each other. In industry and commerce, sincere and tolerant employers are often shocked by the flaring hatred which takes form in perhaps meaningless strikes or in acts of sabotage. In government sometimes a highly placed personage will even commit an act of treachery in order to break away psychologically from a pattern of conformity which he feels has cheated him of personal expression.

PAVLOV

Conditioning responses. Around the turn of the present century, a Russian scientist, Ivan Petrovich Pavlov, conducted some original research into the causes of man's automatism. He wanted to know why apparently intelligent individuals so often behave in certain ways against their own inclinations and wills: in short, how purely involuntary behavior becomes patterned into us.

Pavlov's dogs. At first Pavlov used dogs as his subjects. Whenever he fed the first batch experimented with, he would ring a bell. After a time it was found that when a bell was rung, the dogs' mouths would water even if no food were forthcoming. By flashing a light at other dogs and then striking them with a whip, the animals would learn to cower when the light was flashed even when they were not struck afterward. Later experiments were continued with human beings which seemed to confirm his theory that all behavior is the result of external conditioning.

The slave state. Pavlov's experimentation laid the scientific groundwork for the modern slave state, but worse still, the cult of "behaviorism" fired the imagination of anthropologists, sociologists, and other scientists in the free countries. The colleges and schools became conditioning mills in which individuality was deplored and all were required to respond in the same way to the same stimuli. Research became fractionated, so that as a result each worker was confined to the exploration of a single isolated fragment of a subject until we became a race of specialists. Each learned in a single phase of life but remained profoundly ignorant of all others. This deepening ignorance brought with it deepening fears and as the conditioning mills continued to grind all individual patterns into standardized and interchangable cogs, our true personalities became more and more hampered in the expression of their innate possibilities. The tremendous increase in mental illness is one of the results of this standardization.

Pavlovian behaviorists. To "interpret" is to explain the meaning of a thing in terms of another thing. The Pavlovian behaviorists hold that *man has no basic meaning to which other things may be interpreted.* They hold that man is just a very complex organism that has evolved accidentally from the simplest organisms, and who has now become capable of reacting to external stimuli in a very complex way. Therefore, they reasoned, *any illusion could be conditioned into children as a basic meaning, and, if this were done properly, this illusion would act as an automatic interpreter for all other things.*

Insanity. We occasionally see the above principle demonstrated by an insane person suffering from a basic illusion that he is Napoleon or some other great historical figure, and then interpreting all events as though he actually were Napoleon. We have seen a whole nation conditioned in a similar ridiculous illusion that they were a master race, and the cost of destroying that illusion has been a heavy one.

SUMMARY

DISCOVERING BASIC REALITY

System of training. The only hope for mankind rests in the development of a system of training which will enable each individual *to find the basic reality within himself, and to develop it through creative individual expression,* in harmony with the meaning of living nature of which he is a part. Regardless of all the "Rube Goldberg concepts" of physical science, and the delight of the childish mind in weird and wonderful mechanical gadgets, mankind is still in its infancy and had science existed fifty million years ago on this planet, no scientist by any stretch of his imagination would have been able to envision the realities of today, any more than the scientist of today is able to envision the realities of fifty million years hence. Science is the art of discovering the patterns already laid down by nature, of finding "how" it was done. Creative Realism is the art of exploring "why" the pattern was laid down, and through an understanding of the "why" helping those interested in the subject to discover their own individual patterns and to relate these creatively to the great "over-why" of nature.

Natural personality. To interpret realistically the meanings of events, we must find the reality within ourselves. Pavlov's "conditioning" works by *perverting* this basic reality—by substituting an illusion for reality—by which other things and events are automatically *misinterpreted.* To find the reality within ourselves we must retrace our steps in imagination and consider the "natural personality" that each of us was born with—the personality endowed with a unique set of possibilities or "talents," some of which perhaps we were able to unfold or further develop but many of which were repressed and frustrated by the "conditioning" of our environment.

BRAIN WAVES

Distinctive pattern. Extensive E.E.G. (electroencephalographic) studies carried out at the Burden Neurological Institute in England, and elsewhere, show that even in earliest infancy and throughout childhood, the individual differences in brain rhythms between children are striking. Each has a distinctive pattern of his own. According to Creative Realism, this basic pattern of electrical activity is ordered by the basic pattern of the individual field, or soul; in short, it is channeled by the individual structure of the soul in much the same way as electromagnetic waves are channeled by the structure of a physical field outside of the body.

"Paradise Lost." Usually, between the ages of 10 and 11, although sometimes a year or two earlier or later, the typical brain rhythms of childhood undergo a change of pattern, and gradually take on the character of the rhythms typical of the civilized adult. This (in the view of Creative Realism) marks the end of the development of the natural or "true personality," and the commencement of a "false personality," destined to absorb more and more of the natural élan of living in patterns only remotely related to the great over-all creative pattern of nature.

Grafts. We might imagine this "true personality" as a straight young sapling capable of naturally growing and supporting a certain number of its own natural balancing branches. But instead of being allowed to do this, a system of "Pavlovian" grafting takes place, by which the young trunk is forced to support and to nourish with its sap, a mass of branches cut from other trees and foreign to its true nature. Thus, in yielding a crop of strange fruit it loses its own identity even as the grafted branches lose their identity. Illusion replaces the childhood sense of identity and the growth of the true personality is arrested in favor of an artificial, smirking, yammering robot personality.

Learning. Children are interested in different subjects, naturally. Thus, under the observation of trained kindergarten and elementary school teachers, not to mention the parents, it should be quite possible to discover a child's natural aptitudes and to plan his education so that these may be given the fullest possible expression; but even this will be fruitless unless the child is helped to deepen his understanding of reality and to develop his consciousness.

THE QUEST

Conscious perception. Search as we will, we can never find the reality we all hunger for in the conditioned illusions of our subconscious, nor in our intellects which are oriented to these illusions. We may only find reality by becoming conscious of it—through direct experience. To experience reality directly, we must return to the task of developing the instrument of conscious perception abandoned by us in childhood—the true personality.

Mutation. The story of the "prodigal son," beautifully told in both the Christian and the Buddhist sacred writings, illustrates a deep truth. No matter for how long we have "eaten husks among the swine" after squandering our birthright, we can still return to our "father's house" in consciousness. Nor will this return be a mere retracing of the steps, but we shall bring back with us the experiences and the intellectual gains, hard-won through our bitter wanderings. Could all humanity become just occasionally conscious of the reality of the great mind of nature by which we are all linked in a common brotherhood, the effect would be to bring about a spiritual mutation in conscious evolution, as dramatic as the one which isolated our ancestors from their brothers—the great apes.

CHAPTER 6

Three Phases of Development

It is said that "to enter the kingdom we must be born again" . . . but before we can be reborn, we must die. In order to die, we must live. In order to live we must awaken to life, and in order to awaken we must realize that we are asleep.

THE LAMATSPANG CUSHOG

REALITY

Unity of experience. Reality is not something which can be taught. It is something which must be experienced—and experienced as a unity. When we examine its fragments intellectually, we "shatter the mirror" of our consciousness, and so the very act of intellection excludes consciousness. Not that intellection is a bad thing in itself; it is an extremely useful tool when used as such, but it should not be confused with consciousness. Fragments of reality taken out of their context and examined intellectually become distorted by the very act of observation, for interpretation is part of observation, and we each interpret the same things in different ways.

Reflection. Neither can reality be contacted by reflection or meditation. When we reflect about life, we merely re-examine the stored photographs of past events. The moment that has passed has forever passed, and so with it has passed the concatenation of events recalled with the photographs. These can never return in exactly the same way and in the same groupings.

Conscious experience. The photographs taken by the senses in this respect were out of date even before they were developed and filed in the

51

brain cells. Conscious experience means *to be vividly aware of life as it is happening* as contrasted to *dreaming about it after it has happened.* It means to "reach out into it" with the true or natural personality and to feel a living part of it, to sense its overtones of drama, the depths of its beauty, the warmth of its humor, and to sense the wonder of its majesty. It means to feel all this, and far, far more as a single impression, something in the way that a gay and happy child seems to experience it.

CONSCIOUS-WILL

Creative vision. "Consciousness" and "will" are one and the same thing. To try to make this clearer, what we usually call "will" is an impulse generated by an emotionalized desire. The desire is usually based upon our wish to impose a project or plan that is satisfactory to ourselves upon others, who may be reluctant to accept it. We want a certain course followed, and we do not want any other course. The whole thing is bound up usually with narrow egotism and seeks our own advantage at any cost. In conscious-will, on the other hand, there is no personal ax to grind. Our vision enables us to see something which should be done, simply because it is the creative and right thing to do, and so we do it, feeling in return the sense of "worthwhileness" and satisfaction which follows every truly creative act.

MODERN TECHNIQUES

Visual selectivity. Certain electrical rhythms of the brain called "Alpha rhythms" have been associated with visual selectivity. Usually, when a subject sits back and closes his eyes, the electroencephalograph (E.E.G.) records a clear pattern of these Alpha waves. If the subject is asked to visualize an object, the Alpha waves cease. The inference is that these waves act as a scanning apparatus, something like subconscious radar, which selects specific images to be compared with other images for relative meanings. Although short bursts of Alpha waves are common in children, it is rare that well-defined Alpha patterns are found before the age of 10 or 11.

Imagination. Absence of Alpha rhythms in adults is known to be associated with vivid visual imagination. But when we experience a flash of true consciousness and try to describe it afterward to another, we find ourselves thinking of it in terms of an *illuminating and generalized moment of imagination*—like a flash of lightning which lights up for an instant an entire countryside on a dark night, as contrasted with the usual process of imagination which operates like the headlights of our automobile, merely picking out the objects in the road ahead.

Imagination-consciousness-will. We might think then, of the true, natural personality, as normally expressed in childhood, as being endowed with a state of consciousness-will that is to all intents and purposes the same as a *generalized* state of vivid visual imagination.

NARROWING HORIZONS

Change. As the brain of a child develops then, the subconscious computing machine commences to organize under the action of its intellect. As a consequence, the type of consciousness enjoyed by the young child undergoes a change. It becomes narrowed down as more and more of it becomes introverted and specialized, until all that remains of the once vivid generalized imagination is the narrow beam of the scanning apparatus as expressed in the Alpha waves.

Introversion. In the above secondary phase of mental development, the consciousness becomes absorbed in its own organization and is splintered among the symbol-images stored as memories. It creates a false world within, ruled by fantasies, produced by the splintered imagination toying among the stored symbols. Gradually a false personality, oriented to this false world becomes organized, and a tight cocoon of unrealities and pretenses is woven around the true and natural personality to prevent its expression.

The third stage. The behaviorists of the Pavlov school consider that the development of this secondary phase is the end to be achieved. When they speak about the integration of the personality, they have reference to the organization of a false personality, oriented to the illusions drilled in from without, and interpreting all experiences in relation to a main illusion deeply conditioned into the child's mental structure from its earliest moments of consciousness. Thus, Pavlov's "civilized man" would be a completely subconscious robot, reacting in the manner ordained to all stimuli, whose only conscious experience would be the indirect one obtained through the narrow "scanning mechanism" of his intellect which registers in the Alpha rhythm. As we shall discover, however, this secondary phase of mental development—the elaboration of the subconscious and its intellect, through the introversion and fractioning of the consciousness of childhood—should be but the prelude to a third phase of mental development—the phase which gives to life its meaning.

TRANSCENDENCE

Slow evolution. The methods used in the schools and colleges for intellectual and subconscious development represent a slow evolution of the process of learning by imitation common among all animals. Nothing really new has been added to it. Of course, numerous new subjects have been added to the curriculum, but the process is still learning by imitation, for that is the only way in which the subconscious can learn. Of itself it cannot *originate* anything. It is simply a computing machine which must be taught how to compute, after being supplied with data. To become "conscious," however, the mind must be taught to *transcend* the subconscious, to rise beyond the intellect, and to contact reality by *direct experience.*

Religion. Even as the method of teaching by imitation has been used by man from his beginnings to prepare his children to cope with the physical problems of the environment (intellectually and subconsciously), another equally ancient method has come down to us *for the teaching of consciousness.* We call that method "religion." Wherever the early explorers went and found human beings, they found them worshipping their creative source by means of some sort of traditional religion. Prayer and ritualistic ceremonies were aimed at stimulating the minds of the worshippers *to reach for a greater reality beyond their personal selves.*

Dynamics. Some sort of invocation or prayer addressed to a super-human power was always considered to be the dynamic element of these primitive religions, and the prayers were always aimed at achieving a certain result, such as healing the sick, bringing rain, or defeating an enemy. Such was the "parapsychological medicine" used by Indian shaman, African witch doctor, South Seas kahuna, and Tibetan gom-chen alike. In fact, we see the formalized and attenuated shadows of these magical techniques in our church services of today.

INCOMPLETENESS

Contacting reality. The fact is, unless we are able to contact reality—the great creative overmind of nature—through conscious, direct experience, we all suffer from a sense of *incompleteness and insufficiency.* This feeling of being unable to do a vague "something" that we feel we should be able to do is disquieting and led the early religionists to the concept of "original sin" as an explanation. During the last century, Sir James G. Frazer, a British anthropologist, after a profound study of such records as were available about the magical rites and religions of primitive peoples, wrote *The Golden Bough,* which suggested in effect that all of these systems, developed and practiced by mankind from its beginnings in every isolated corner of the world, were merely the product of ignorance.

Scientific acceptance. Frazer's hypothesis, despite the incredible inaccuracies upon which it was based, offered a psychological escape from this feeling of "incompleteness," or, as the religionists put it, "the taint of original sin," and so it was eagerly seized upon as a negative argument against the existence of an unknown creative source.

Frazer's interpretation. From what has previously been said in this book, it is clear that Frazer's hypothesis was a purely intellectual-subconscious computation, based not upon *his own direct experience in consciousness* but upon the incomplete sensory observations of others. His theory, in other words, was an interpretation made by his own subconscious conditioning. Before writing *The Golden Bough* had Frazer lived for a dozen years among say, either the New Zealand maoris (of that day), or the Celonese fire walkers, the whirling dervishes of North Africa, the Hopi Indian snake-dancers (who have brought rain to the desert without fail on every occasion of their dance for at least 300 years), or the Tibetan lamas, had he seriously undergone the necessary disciplines, and then directly experienced the phenomena produced, by means of his own consciousness, there would have been no *Golden Bough.*

Deconditioning. The foregoing is set forth at some length because once a concept has been conditioned into the subconscious, it acts as a part of the interpreting mechanism, and may prove a block on the road to consciousness unless "deconditioned" by the acceptance of a superseding concept with a greater content of reality. All atheism, materialism, and cynicism are due to subconscious conditioning in fallacious concepts, and a consequent absence of direct conscious experience.

SUMMARY

Three phases. The human mind then should normally develop in three phases: first, that phase which organizes the physical body from a single cell; second, the intellect-subconscious phase; third, the conscious phase. The first phase operates according to its own innate pattern of knowledge. The second phase develops as the result of conditioning by imitation. The third phase—consciousness—develops only as a result of a personal and individual effort to directly experience that which transcends the self. Thus, the first phase of development occurs automatically; the second phase, semi-automatically; and the third phase does not take place at all, except through personal effort.

APPERCEPTION

Definition. "Apperception" has been defined as: "Perception of one's own mental processes; self-consciousness" (Cassell's *New English Dictionary*), and the first step toward consciousness is the development of apperception as the usual and ordinary state of mind during the waking hours, as contrasted to the usual and habitual state of waking-sleep in which most of us live at present.

Experience of self. Yet even the development of a habitual mental state of apperception is only half of the feeling—by direct experience—of self-consciousness, and self-consciousness is only a half-way point toward the attainment of consciousness. Apperception is a feeling of one part of our mind observing the other parts in action—one part becoming set apart as an observer of the other parts, as it were. Self-consciousness, on the other hand, *is a feeling of identity with that observing part,* a feeling of realness, a sense of unique personality, a knowledge or direct understanding, which mere words cannot convey, that *This is I,* and that which is being observed is "not I" but just the machinery that is being used by this real "I." Those of us who have had the experience of military training know the feeling of mild shock and momentary wonder which comes upon hearing ourselves directly addressed by name when on parade—a sudden feeling of being segregated from the anonymous hundreds of men who make up the battalion. The realization of self-consciousness comes to one something in the same manner.

Integration. Our problem then is to withdraw the "splinters of consciousness" from among the symbol-images of the subconscious, to integrate it again as a separate, functional phase of mind as it existed in childhood, except that now it is not only able to perceive directly and respond to the perception, it is able by virtue of the subconscious machinery it has organized to process its perceptions into coherent ideas, and to pass these along to others or to turn them into physical realities as it wills to become incorporated into the patterns of modern living. To make this integration permanent we must be prepared to work at it consistently for a considerable period of time.

EXERCISE
DEVELOPING SELF-AWARENESS

Pause right now, sit back in your chair, and silently repeat to yourself the following words:

"This is I [your name] sitting in this chair, in this room, and I am completely aware of my own personality, apart from this room, from this chair I am sitting in, and from these words that I am repeating to myself."

Now drop the words from mind altogether, *but try to maintain the mental state suggested by them.* Try to "feel" the reality of your personality in that portion of your brain behind the forehead.

PRACTICE

At first you may only be able to hold the consciousness together for a minute or two before it breaks apart again like a ball of quicksilver and rejoins the subconscious. If you consistently practice this exercise in self-awareness on every possible occasion, however, a permanent integration of the consciousness will result, and you will be able to remain in a state of self-awareness for as long as you wish to do so.

WORDLESS CONSCIOUSNESS

Remember, consciousness itself is wordless. The moment words are thought of, consciousness disappears. Words are subconscious symbols, but consciousness is an extremely alert state of vivid awareness and it has nothing to do with words.

CATAPULT

The idea therefore is merely to use the words as a sort of catapult with which to launch the state of consciousness, but leaving them behind as you soar into self-awareness, maintaining yourself in that state by a wordless effort of will alone.

ADAPTING

You can, of course, vary the "catapult words" to suit the occasion. For instance, in walking, you can say to yourself: "I am fully aware of myself and am objectively observing these people I am passing." You will be amused to notice that most of the passers-by are sound asleep, some smiling in their dreams, some scowling or muttering, but all totally unaware of themselves and but very dimly aware of their surroundings. They are for the most part completely immersed in the fantastical world of their own subconsciousness.

CHAPTER 7

Conscious Integration

The perfect way knows no difficulties because it refuses to make preferences: Only when it is freed from both hate and love does it reveal itself fully and without disguises.

SENG-TS 'AN

CONSCIOUS INTEGRATION

Silence. At first, when we practice the exercise in "self-awareness" given at the end of Chapter Six, we are likely to be somewhat disturbed by the fact that when we are in a state of alert, self-remembering consciousness, we apparently stop thinking. This is just an illusion, however.

Yammering. The stray words, disjointed sentences, imaginary conversations, snatches of music, and so forth, that we are ordinarily aware of, are distinctly *not* thinking. This "yammer" has nothing to do with the actual processes of subconscious computation; it is simply "noise" or static which prevents the proper working of the subconscious.

Release. The subconscious is only released to do its most effective work when we are completely oblivious of its functioning. That is why many of our best ideas pop into our minds fully fledged after a sound night's sleep. Sometimes this happens also after a game of golf, or some other activity in which the consciousness is kept in a state of alertness and so prevented from interfering with the work of the subconscious.

Objectivity. Consciousness is a state of alert mental awareness of what is happening in the world around us. It is purely *objective* in nature. Subconsciousness, on the other hand—and as the word implies—is subjective in nature. Its business is to correlate the events which happen

59

inside the body with the events which happen outside of it. Subconsciousness cannot of itself have any direct knowledge of what is going on outside the body. It must depend upon the consciousness for such information. When the consciousness is introverted and fractionated, it cannot supply this information. It substitutes daydreams and fantasies for real events. In attempting to maintain a correlation between the chemistry of the body, and these substitutes for real objective events, the subconscious is hampered and frustrated and the energy control mechanisms of the body are thrown out of balance. This prepares the ground for every form of disaster and disease.

Opposition. The student of Creative Realism can expect tremendous opposition from his own false personality in practicing the exercises of conscious integration at first. It will defend its present practices of daydreaming and fantasy weaving as being in no way undesirable and it will cling to every aspect of it as an opium smoker will cling to his pipe. The very assertion of the will in the practice of the exercises, however, is an essential part of the exercise.

AWARENESS OF SELF

Quieting the subconscious. The state of self-consciousness or awareness of self is completely strange to most of us. When the yammer of the subconscious is stilled, the sense of wordless awareness of self and of the world around us is almost as startling as the silence we experience when we step outside a boiler factory and close the door behind us. *The art of living consciously must be learned.* It entails the organization of a control mechanism within the brain; a scrapping of old patterns of mental behavior which have served their day in favor of a new pattern— a pattern through which the true or natural personality may function in consciousness, as an observer, like the "Deos" of Aristotle, free from reaction with the observed.

Imagination. We spoke before of the consciousness of childhood being similar in nature to a generalized state of vivid imagination. We might use as a somewhat inept analogy a beam of light with an extremely wide focus, lighting up foreground, middle-distance, and background *as one extended "here and now."* As this state of consciousness becomes introverted through subconscious organization, the "beam of light" becomes not only narrower, but also dimmer, until it does not light up the "here and now" at all. To the adult, there is no *now;* there is only yesterday and tomorrow. He lives in a vacuum between those two points touched by his faint and narrowed beam of consciousness.

The synthesizer. Now the difference between the generalized and vivid state of consciousness of childhood and that of an adult *who has achieved self-consciousness through planned self-evolution and systematic exercising* is this: The generalized imagination of childhood manifests as "fancy" while in the advanced adult, it not only conveys a wide and penetrating awareness of life as it is happening but, by nature of its indwelling will, it may also act as a "synthesizer." That is to say, it can at will draw all of the diverse elements of a given situation together into a series of images and project these as a pattern for future action.

Fancy. It would seem that all living things share to some degree in the type of consciousness exhibited by the human child. We can see "fancy" at work in the gamboling of young animals at play; in the clowning of penguins and "booby-birds" and even in the antics of some insects. In fact, it would seem that this state of generalized consciousness exists *independently of the living things,* and that these latter are able to "tune in" to it by means of natural resonating mechanisms, just as we may tune in our radios to those programs which suit our fancy of the moment. Our radios have nothing to do with the broadcasting of the programs, but they enable us to share in them.

THE HYPNOTIC STATE

Purest form. Writing in the *Journal of Clinical and Experimental Hypnosis* (Vols. 1-3) Dr. Jerome M. Schneck of the College of Medicine, New York University, advances the theory that the "hypnotic state" exists in its most pure form when "conscious thinking" is eliminated, and contact with (awareness of) the environment (as an individual) is so reduced that the awareness of time, place, and person is absent. The conclusion he puts forward is that probably all biological forms live to some degree in this state.

The ocean of mind. Creative Realism goes further than Dr. Schneck does and asserts that all organisms *naturally* live in the so-called "hypnotic state," that this state is not something unusual, but that, on the contrary, the state of consciousness is unusual. Let us return for a moment to our basic hypothesis of the mind of nature surrounding this planet like an invisible ocean or field. And let us imagine a certain analogy, which, of course, could only exist in a figurative sense:

The fishes. In our familiar watery ocean, different organisms prefer to live at different depths. Living things have been dredged from the ocean floor at depths where the pressure would be great enough to crush a steel hull like an eggshell. No ray of sunlight penetrates these great depths, and many of the denizens provide their own "headlights" as do the glow-worms and fireflies on land. We shall imagine man in his evolutionary progress as being like a fish, struggling upward toward the sunlight of consciousness on the ocean's surface. It would be a slow process, for he would have to adjust to the different pressures and conditions imposed by the different levels, but we can imagine him eventually arriving at a depth where the waters are lighted by a diffused glow of sunlight from above.

Comparison. In comparison to the faint firefly gleams occasionally seen on the lower levels, this light would appear brilliant, but were he to rise to the ocean's surface and by a tremendous effort leap clear above it for a moment, he would experience a dimension so different from that of his familiar depths that he would be at a loss to even think about it himself in meaningful intellectual terms. Now imagine that by repeating his leaps into the sunlight of consciousness he could learn to glide like a flying-fish and so gain a greater understanding of this new dimension.

Water. To continue the analogy: The body of a fish is mostly seawater. The cells which form it are watery spheres in which protein molecules are suspended with aggregated particles of nutrients, and so we might say that the fish is formed of the ocean and that it moves in the ocean and that it is to all intents and purposes a "specialized part of the ocean," completely dominated by the currents and pressures and by the chance-born movements of other "specialized parts" of the ocean, some of which it devours as food and others of which seek to devour it. The level of *self-awareness* is nil. There is nothing within it which says "I." Yet experiments have demonstrated that a fish is capable of learning certain simple things.

Higher levels. Now we shall imagine that this capacity to learn increases as the fish ascends to higher levels; that when it finally ascends to live in the area near the surface illuminated by the sun's penetrating rays, a new development of its nervous system takes place, like a bud opening in the sunshine, and that this develops into a "subconscious stratum" designed eventually to correlate the conscious perceptions of the new dimension, with the unconsciousness of the organized bit of sea-water that is its physical body and through it to extend the influence of consciousness in that dark and savage dimension.

ENERGY SYSTEMS

Invisible field. We might imagine then, the mind of nature operating as an invisible "field" within the waters of the ocean as it operates within the atmosphere above, and we might consider fish to be a type of specialized "energy-system" organized by the mind of nature from elements existing within the great generalized energy-system called the ocean. Considering organisms in this light, as specialized energy-systems, designed for specific purposes, we know that the purpose of the little organisms called plankton "eat" nitrogen, and by the process of digestion, this nitrogen then becomes fixed and available as the nitrogen fraction of protein to be built into the bodies of the fish which live on the plankton.

Equilibrium. Expressing this in terms of equilibrium, we might say that all living bodies are energy systems, which strive to maintain themselves in a state of dynamic equilibrium. As soon as this dynamic equilibrium becomes upset, the organism feels a "need." In the case of the plankton, for instance, we might think of such a "need" stimulating a hunger for more nitrogen. In the case of some larger fish, we might think of an upset in equilibrium expressing itself as a hunger for plankton, and in the case of still other fish, expressing itself as a hunger for the fish which ate the plankton, and so on.

Restoration. Thus, in a sense, all behavior of living things in the unconscious and subconscious aspects of evolution is motivated by (1) an upset in their equilibrium as energy-systems, and by (2) the efforts to restore this equilibrium felt as a need or a hunger. In the purely unconscious organisms such hungers are probably limited to food and procreation.

Tooth and claw. Regarded in the foregoing sense then, what has been described by the poets as "the rule of tooth and claw" in nature is nothing more than one part of nature being devoured by another part of nature in a continuous process of change, or metabolism, within the great body of nature itself. Certain nutritive materials organized into energy-systems by "organizational cores" or "souls" formed with the field that we have called "the mind of nature" are broken down, then built up into other energy-systems, while the "organizational cores" or "souls" return again in eggs to organize new energy-system bodies. Nothing is lost.

Eat and be eaten. So we may say that there is neither gain nor loss in an individual sense in the process of eating or being eaten. Therefore, just as directive mechanisms exist within the limited field of a human body, which bring consuming organisms such as antibodies into a relationship with their prey, such as invading bacteria, there seems to be certain invisible mechanisms within the body of nature which perform the same sort of service. We might suppose that a lack of equilibrium in a fish's body trips something in the nature of a "scanning mechanism" which leads it to the means of re-establishing the equilibrium. In short, the energy-system of the fish-body is led to its prey by some sort of natural scanning apparatus; then it is able to capture it by exerting a force similar in nature to the force exerted by a negatively charged atom which reaches out and captures a free electron.

TELEOLOGY

Purpose. If we think of the great body of nature as being shaped, under the influence of its all-pervading mind, toward the end of consciousness, it would follow that this purpose or end would be known by a directing phase of the mind of nature. We might think of this directing phase *as being more conscious* than the phases of mind being directed, than those phases forming the "organizational cores" or "souls" of the swarming organisms of which the great body is composed.

Prediction. To know the end and the purpose would be to know the future. The past cannot be altered; the present has grown out of the past and it is too late to alter it; only the future is plastic and pregnant with possibilities. So to form a *purpose*—to aim at a specific target in the future—*is to be better able to predict the future* than a less conscious organism, chained to responding automatically to the stimuli of the immediate present, or better able to predict than the dead past was able to do.

Direction. Mere prediction would avail little without the power to direct events into fulfilling the purpose. Therefore we might assume that the conscious level of the mind of nature is charged with purpose, is able to predict the future course of events, and can predict because it is able to direct all elements within its scope toward the production of the events desired. The ability to direct events would involve will. Perhaps this is what was meant by the ancient prophets when they adjured their followers to "obey the will of God."

Will of God. If our basic hypothesis is valid, then the more conscious stratum of the mind of nature would find expression through the most conscious stratum of the most conscious organisms within its body—through the conscious mind of man—and the will of nature (or God) would express itself through the wills of the most conscious humans. Thus, the more conscious organisms in nature would have a certain directive power over the less conscious. This is demonstrated, of course, by the fact that man has subjugated and brought under his control most of the less conscious organisms in nature, and the more conscious human beings automatically exercise a degree of control over their less conscious brothers in business, politics, science, and the arts. It is the natural order of things that the more conscious shall always exercise control over the less conscious.

Definition. The lesser conscious must always be receptive to the more conscious. Thus, the "hypnotic state," as it is called, is the condition in which all except the most *highly* conscious human beings naturally exist. It is a psychological state of anticipation in which the brain rhythms are sweeping the fabric in a shimmering procession in search for significance; it is a state of constantly speculative expectancy, in which a clear-cut suggestion is eagerly seized upon and put into execution, regardless of its source.

MECHANISMS OF CONSCIOUSNESS

Extrasensory phenomena. Dr. J. B. Rhine of Duke University, Durham, North Carolina, and many other scientists in Europe and elsewhere have demonstrated that the power of consciousness is not limited to its effects produced within the human brain. Telekinesis, telepathy, precognition, and other extrasensory phenomena are well-established facts.

Splintered consciousness. As we have before said, the mind of man in its totality embraces the three phases expressed by the mind of nature: the unconscious, the subconscious, and the conscious. At present, his consciousness is splintered and trapped among the memories of past events stored in his subconscious. When we are able to extricate our consciousness—and to integrate it even temporarily—we automatically gain considerable power over the subconscious and unconscious phases of mind within our own bodies. The extraordinary effects which can be produced by autohypnosis are evidence of this. When we are able to permanently integrate our consciousness as a "conscious mind," then it is probable that we shall be able to know "the will of God" clearly and unmistakably and, knowing it, be able, by co-operating with it, to easily perform creative works far beyond the possibilities of subconscious man.

Practice. The attainment of consciousness is the highest objective that a human being can aim at in his present stage of evolution. In fact, it is the only truly worthwhile objective that a human being can aim at. Consciousness is the "Kingdom of Heaven" and when that is attained, "all other things shall be added." Let us then make this *our purpose as human beings,* for this purpose is also the purpose of the mighty power which formed our souls in the first place. We shall be assisted in fulfilling it by all of the creative forces of nature. If we only persist, and practice the techniques here given without weakening in our purpose, we shall attain it.

CHAPTER 8

Knowledge and Understanding

Man that is in honour, and (yet) understandeth not, is like the
beasts that perish.

PSALM 49:40

THE PROJECT

Objective exercises. The mental work we must do in conscious integration falls under two headings. First, there are the objective exercises, commencing with the one given in Chapter Six under "Apperception" and "Experience of Self." It is suggested that the student practice
this exercise many times daily for about a month before adding the
exercise given in Chapter Eleven for intensifying and vivifying the state
of objective consciousness by means of the combined sensory impressions.

Reconditioning the subconscious. Under the second heading falls the
work we must do upon our own subconscious. By reconditioning our
subconscious to work on a basis of reality instead of fantasy, and by furnishing its computing machine with fresh stock of information to assist
in its computations, we furnish it with the materials it needs in order to
perform its best work. Some of this work is accomplished by studying
the contents of this book, and by trying to form visualized idea-chains
of the material set forth, after the manner given in the visualizing and
associating exercises in Chapter Four. Finally, we lock all of this subconscious machinery together by *instilling understanding*. We use the
method of autohypnosis to train the mechanism of our nervous systems
to make the truest interpretations (in terms of consciousness) of the impressions which come to them as is possible.

UNDERSTANDING

Definition. *Understanding* is the product of consciousness. Understanding means *knowing* the purpose, or the "why" of things, as contrasted with mere belief which may be based on purely intellectual-subconscious data and have nothing to do with realities. Any "belief"—however absurd—can be implanted in the subconscious of a person by simply reiterating a statement over and over again "as if" it were true. We see this technique used in advertising, in propaganda, and, in fact, it is used in all human communications to some degree. Without *understanding* we are completely at the mercy of these impressions which are imposed upon us from without, and *without consciousness there can be no understanding.* A statement is accepted by our subconscious "as if" it were true, and our subconscious automatically responds to the statement "as if" it were true.

Self-observation. The subconscious is like a blind man who must find his way under the direction of the consciousness, the only part of the mind having vision. When the consciousness is fractionated and splintered in the subconscious, it cannot give this direction; it can only supply pseudo-realities or fantasies instead of vision. Therefore, the first step toward understanding is to realize the "why" of our own subconscious processes through self-observation. Most of the schools of Eastern psychology consider these exercises as basic. In Tibet they describe it as separating the "I" from the "not-I." In our Western terminology it would be better to regard it as separating the consciousness (the observer) from the subconscious (the observed). Try to visualize a clear sequence of pictures from paragraph to paragraph as you read onward.

INDIVIDUAL LIFE

Control centers of the subconscious. To understand the control centers of the subconscious, let us commence by thinking of the miracle which takes place when a child is conceived. By the union of a male and a female cell, *an unknown vital energy* takes possession of the tiny bit of protoplasm. We may think of this unknown vital energy as stemming from the rapidly expanding, directive action of the *individual field* or *soul.* The fertilized cell divides into 2 cells, then into 4, 8, 16, 32, 64, and so on, until there are millions, then billions of cells, each one assigned under the direction of the individual soul to a place in a structure, designed to perform a specific function. *The development of one of the first four cells is retarded,* however, and this will later divide into the sex cells, of which we shall speak later.

Foremen. Immediately the organization of each structure in the "body to be" is delineated; a group of cells are specialized to control and supervise the activities of all the other cells forming the structure. We might think of these control groups as being in the nature of foremen, who preside over certain operations in a great factory. When a number of structures are organized with foremen properly installed, other control-groups of cells are specialized as "superintendents" over a number of the foremen. Their work is one of co-ordination.

Chain of control. And so a chain of control is built up which leaves no cell group in the body to operate at random. Before nerves can function, they must grow where they will be wanted; they must make the right connections, and so on; and all this is ordered and directed by the organizing field we call the soul.

CONTROL CENTERS

Intermeshed system. Every activity of the body is regulated from the subconscious level by six mental control centers. Each of these main centers in turn exercises authority over numerous subsidiary control centers and reflex mechanisms and these over still lesser centers and so on right down the line until we come to the individual cells. Through these "intermeshed" control centers, the subconscious correlates the activities of the body with the events occurring outside of the body, as perceived by the consciousness. When the consciousness is splintered and introverted, as we have said, it substitutes fantasy and daydreams for the real events of the outside world.

Six centers. The designation of the six control centers is somewhat arbitrary, inasmuch as each brain is an individual instrument. In general though, the regulating centers are delegated to the lower brain to free the upper brain from the menial tasks of the body that it may become the seat of consciousness. The six mental control centers then are: (1) the instinctive center, (2) the moving center, (3) the intellectual center, (4) the sex center, (5) the emotional center, and (6) the imagination center.

Self-observation. In the exercise of self-observation which follows, it will be necessary to catalog the various impulses arising in the mind, by the centers to which they belong; so we shall give a brief explanation of the functions of each of the six centers now to help us do this.

THE INSTINCTIVE CENTER

Control of the unconscious. We might think of the mind of man, as it evolves under the influence of the expanding "field" or "soul" following conception, as recapitulating the four developmental stages of the mind of nature as a whole upon this planet. In short, we may think of it as being in the nature of a four-sectioned telescope, the next succeeding "joint" or section emerging and pushing upward when a lower section has grown to its greatest height. We might think of the lower section of this individual telescope as the unconscious mind, and consider that it is under the control of the instinctive center.

Functions. The instinctive center then controls all of the "natural processes" we were born with. The unconscious mind, intent upon producing the child to be, would be helpless unless it could draw upon the "know-how" previously learned; we hold that this knowledge exists as an organization of the field or soul and that the unconscious mind simply executes this pattern. When it has proceeded to a certain point, the instinctive center unfolds as a control center. The instinctive center then controls digestion, assimilation, elimination, repair, resistance to disease germs, and all of those instinctive and "unlearned" patterns of behavior observable in the newborn child.

THE MOVING CENTER

Controls body action. At birth the infant is capable of only a few spasmodic movements in addition to the grasp and sucking reflexes. All of the important co-ordinated movements of the muscles must be learned by experience, by repeatedly imitating the movements of others. Gradually, in the so-called precentral convolution of the brain, approximately a million cells are organized into a sequence representing the muscles and limbs of the body; nerve connections are established between these cell groups and the muscles and limbs they represent, and through this physical machine, the mental moving center operates to control the actions of the body.

THE INTELLECTUAL CENTER

The computer. The intellect, with its subconscious computing machinery and information storage, does not become developed as an effective instrument until the child has reached the age of around ten or eleven years. That which we sometimes think of as "intellectual development" later in life is due to the increased fund of information stored. The actual machinery of the "computer" undergoes no radical changes after adolescence.

Meanings again. The information stored as memories is all-important to the work of our intellectual computing machines. This information is not stored according to type, as books are stored in a library; it is stored according to *meanings.* All "meanings" are produced by associating "sensory signals" from the outside world and from within the body, with stored memories which we believe to be of basic importance. We interpret, in other words, all signals which come to us, according to a chain of stored images, which represent our basic beliefs (or lack of basic beliefs) about ourselves and life in general. As most of these basic beliefs have been instilled into us during childhood, *they are not the result of our own conscious experience,* and are therefore not likely to be based upon reality. Yet our subconscious computing machines have no way in which to test their reality; they must accept them uncritically and act "as if" they were true. These uncritically accepted basic beliefs form the shoals upon which the good intentions inherent in all human relationships founder. *Could it be possible for all men to verify their basic philosophies of life by conscious experience, the millenium would be ushered in.*

THE SEX CENTER

Controls sexual mechanism. It was previously mentioned that at conception, one of the first four cells of the "body-to-be" is retarded during the first hour of growth, and that later, this retarded cell divides and redivides the same as the other cells, but that all of its descendants become sex-cells, and go into the organization of the sexual mechanism. Thus, we might say that one-fourth of the tremendous potential creative power stored within the fertilized ovum is later released as sexual energy.

Inhibitory influences. Ideally, while the cells of the rest of the organism are rapidly multiplying, this is supposed to exert an inhibitory influence on the creative power of the sex cells. It would seem that while the tremendous creative activity of body-building is proceeding at full spate, the creative power of the sex center is inhibited; when the process of body-building begins to slow down to some extent shortly before adolescence, the creative activity of the sex cells swing into action and the "sex control center" rapidly organizes. In the light of the tremendous energy released during the developmental stage of the sex mechanisms, the wisdom of the primitives in exercising controls through taboos and of the religionists in training their children in techniques of prayer, meditation, art, literature, and music, by which these great pressures would be released creatively or "sublimated" automatically when the stresses arose, is apparent.

The rooster. Contrary to the hear-say drivel collected by naive professors from spoofing undergraduates and paraded under the banner of "science," such as some recent reports on the "sexual conduct of the human male and female," the average decent individual does his or her best without adequate know-how to channel creatively this great and potent energy-system, which tends to seize control over the other mental centers and to dominate our lives to a surprising degree. The "sexual conduct of the human male" (according to this writer's forty or forty-five years of adult association and observation of the species) is not of the licentious variety set forth in the "Kinsey Report." It is in the swaggering, strutting conduct by which man tries to impress the other sex that he is really something extraordinary in the way of a prospective father. It is the mental conflicts caused by the various centers resisting the efforts of the sex center to assume control over the entire personality.

THE EMOTIONAL CENTER

Controls body's reserves of energy. To form the picture clearly, we shall for the moment lay the personality factor aside, and consider the human organism as a great engine for the collection, transformation, and distribution of energy. We should remember that food, water, and oxygen are processed within our bodies into the different forms of energy used by it in the performance of its work, such as caloric and bioelectrical energy; then, of course, there are repair and replacement needs to be met from the nutritional intake as well.

Storage batteries. Bioelectrical energy is generated by the cells of the body, and the excess is collected by strategically situated neurons, and carried to masses of nervous tissue (plexuses and ganglia) for storage. It is from these great storage batteries that the energy is drawn and distributed over the immense network of its nerves to keep the body functioning. The largest "storage battery" is one we are all familiar with—the solar plexus.

The engineer. The emotional center presides over the body's reserves of energy. We might think of it in terms of an engineer seated before a panel in a control room of the brain. When any of the other centers need extra power, we might imagine that a red light blinks on the panel, and that the engineer throws the necessary switches, which close the circuits necessary to throwing the reserve to the center which sent the signal. This immense surge of power often causes an elevation of the blood pressure, rigidity of the muscles, and so on, and, if this be sustained over too long a period of time, damage may result.

THE IMAGINATION CENTER

Core of consciousness. We must think of the imagination center as being the "core" of the consciousness. Just as a seed, when it begins to grow, first pushes down rootlets into the dark soil, then unfolds a tiny shoot to the sunlight, the consciousness (as we have before stated) is at present mostly rooted in the dark and sunless world of the subconscious. Ultimately, it will, by virtue of its direct perception of reality, call the tunes which all of the other centers must co-ordinate in playing, but at present its efforts are limited to fantasies and daydreams, which it substitutes for realities.

EXERCISE IN SELF-OBSERVATION
INTEGRATION OF CONSCIOUSNESS

Will into action. Within the imagination center there resides a whole constellation of unsuspected powers which shall unfold naturally as the consciousness becomes integrated, but perhaps the most important of these is the will. By the following exercise of self-observation, we call the will into action. It is repeated now, that the *will is only exercised in detachment.* Tension is the enemy of will. In self-observation we calmly and unemotionally observe the processes of our own minds in action. We do not try to alter these processes; they will correct themselves automatically, eventually, when we learn to detach ourselves from them and to observe them at will.

DIVIDED CONSCIOUSNESS

Detachment. The idea is to separate ourselves (figuratively) from our own mental processes and to observe them. We will have the extraordinary experience of living in one part of our imagination, as it were, while watching another part of our imagination, weaving fantasies, just as did the man undergoing the brain-exploration operation mentioned in an earlier chapter. We shall find this difficult at first, except upon occasion when our emotions become aroused in a debate or an argument, when we can sometimes quickly detach ourselves and hear our own voices and listen to our own often absurd vociferations with something of astonishment.

SORTING

The centers. Through practice, we have attained proficiency in the art of detaching our consciousness from our subconscious processes while observing the latter in action, our next step is to try to determine the centers to which the various impulses belong, as these arise. It is interesting to note that there seems to be a continuous effort on the part of the centers to shift responsibility to each other, and this is particularly true of the intellectual center.

Examples. Each of the centers has control over certain specific powers and functions, but it is limited to those and it cannot properly do the work of any other center. When we see an acrobat or a trained athlete in action, we are witnessing a highly developed moving center at work. Yet such a man may be retarded in development so far as his other control centers are concerned.

CORRECTIVE MEASURES

Immunity. An individual may have a highly developed instinctive center; with a wonderful appetite and figuratively able to digest nails, he may be able to adjust swiftly to temperature, altitude, and exertion; he may be practically immune to disease; and yet he may be practically a moron so far as his intellectual center development is concerned and be clumsy and poorly co-ordinated so far as his moving center development is concerned.

Toward even development. We have all seen the occasional individual with a highly developed intellectual center, and a sickly, weak body due to an underdeveloped instinctive center, and with the jerky, hesitant movements indicating an underdeveloped moving center; and so it goes. In fact, probably not one person in a million attains anything like a perfectly balanced development of all his control centers at present.

Observe six centers. From now onward, then, spend a few minutes several times each day in observing the work of the centers, trying to determine to which center each operation belongs. In eating for instance, we know that this operation belongs to the instinctive center, aided by the moving center. In writing a letter, the work belongs to the intellectual center, again aided by the moving center. In social affairs, we have usually the moving center (vocal mechanism), imagination center, with perhaps the sex center also assisting.

Imagination as creative force. In the working of the centers, all are continually bidding for an "assist" from the imagination center, and this is dragged hither and yon between them. When we attain conscious detachment, this is reversed, and the imagination with its component will *becomes the master* instead of the servant of the other centers. This makes the difference between idle and unproductive daydreaming and conscious creativeness.

CHAPTER 9

Resolving Inner Conflicts

> When the mind becomes conscious, it sees that neither negation
> nor affirmation applies to reality, but that truth lies in knowing
> things as they actually are.
>
> MAJJHIMA NIKAYA

COPING WITH CHANGE

Accumulating data. The process of visualizing and associating sensory
impressions with other stored memories is probably the natural method
by which all of the vertebrates accumulate the data necessary to cope
with the changing environment. The exercise given in Chapter Four
illustrates the ease with which an indelible record of the *outer* events
accompanying each separate experience is made, but such a record
would be of little value, unless there were filed with it a record of *the
meanings* of the experiences relative to the individual.

Inner circumstances. Thus, attached to each memory or sensory impression received from without, there is another memory of the *inner
circumstances* which attended the experience: a memory of how we
responded to it emotionally and the result of this response. If it were
satisfactory, the entire memory-image is what we term "pleasant"; but if
the response were unsatisfactory, the recall of the memory gives us an
"unpleasant" sensation.

Avoidance of pain. Pain and satisfaction are the goad and the lure
by which all organisms in living nature have been guided upward on
the evolutionary path. To avoid pain and to seek satisfaction is as
natural as it is for us to seek food when we are hungry. In such a case

77

we move away from the pain of hunger toward the satisfaction of eating under the domination of our instinctive centers with the assistance of some of the other centers.

Memory-analogues. Now, of course, there is little actual resemblance between the human world of blue skies, perfumed flowers, green trees, and murmuring waters, and the actual impalpable *physical* reality of the universe, which consists of a colorless, soundless, tasteless, odorless play of vast and unimaginable forces, only describable in such mathematical terms as space-time, mass-energy, and so on. The human senses abstract such of this physical reality as they have need of, and by the magic of their transforming mechanisms, create from them a mental world of color, sound, odor, taste, and feeling. To other species of animals with different kinds of nervous systems, the world of course is different. An analogue is a similitude of relations. So long as our colorful world of sounds, sights and smells conforms to the actual soundless, colorless reality of the physical world, we are immensely richer owing to the analogue we have created.

Elaboration. As our human world within our brains becomes more and more elaborate and complex, a new kind of pain and a new kind of satisfaction gradually replaces the purely physical pain and physical satisfaction of the lower animals. This is mental pain and mental satisfaction.

Difference. Now there is a qualitative difference between mental and physical pain and mental and physical satisfaction. Mental pain and mental satisfaction can occur *without reference to a physical situation,* whereas physical pain and physical satisfaction are purely physical sensations. When we come into physical contact with a hot stove, we feel physical pain. When we read of the death of a friend, we might feel mental pain, even though he is thousands of miles distant from us; in the first case, the pain is a result of the sensation. In the second case, *the sensation is the result of the pain.*

Animal and man. Thus, we might imagine that an animal feels pain when it is injured, and it files the memory of that pain along with the sensory images which accompanied the injury. When faced by a similar concatenation of sensory stimuli, it reacts to avoid a repetition of the painful experience. It flees if possible. If it cannot flee, it responds with fury to destroy that which threatens pain. Man tends to duplicate that process in a mental way.

FREUD'S FINDINGS

The superego. Freud concluded that within the human psyche "there exits a faculty that incessantly watches, criticizes and compares, and in this way is set against the other part of the ego." Creative Realism regards this so-called faculty as the true personality, the observer of the self who will ultimately evolve into consciousness, but who at present lives in the twilight zone of preconsciousness, in the state of suspended development before referred to. If an idea is painful to this "censor," he thrusts it back into the subconscious computing machine from whence it emerged; but should the center to which it belongs call upon the emotional center to try to force it through into actuality, despite the veto of the real personality, a conflict ensues, and the mental pain of this conflict is translated into physical sensation, sometimes with disastrous results to the nervous system and the mental mechanism.

Uncovering repressions. Freud's system of psychoanalysis has for its aim the leading forth of such repressed unpleasant memories, and the re-grouping of the false personality of the emotionally ill person. He proposed to do this by helping the patient uncover such repressions, and to examine them in the light of objective consciousness, when their power to work damage disappears.

False personality. The false personality, however, is woven of lies, pretenses, hypocrisies, and fantasies. It is the psychic robot built up of artificialities to deal with the pretenses, lies, and artificialities of civilized existence, and this is the "privileged sanctuary" into which all banished ideas escape in the hope of gaining by indirection what cannot be obtained directly. This false personality will defend its "refugees" with every device of lie and subterfuge at its command. Hence, there is always a clash of wills between patient and analyst during the early stages of the therapy, and, even if the therapy is successful, a dependence on the analyst often develops which is as difficult to overcome as was the former neurotic condition.

CREATIVE REALISM VS. PSYCHOANALYSIS

Substitute for consciousness. Creative Realism holds that although psychoanalysis is often helpful and sometimes necessary as a first step in other therapy, the fact remains that the consciousness of the analyst is substituting for the patient's own consciousness. Therefore, the patient gains nothing permanent from the therapy except a temporary release of the conflict incidental to the repressed material. The mastery of *his own* subconscious processes is not strengthened but weakened, and he is left wide open, as it were, to other experiences which may cause the same sort of trouble that the analyst relieved him of.

Integration. Creative Realism holds that a properly integrated individual is one who has attained objective consciousness, and the control which automatically follows the attainment of objective consciousness places his true personality in its proper relationship to all inferior aspects of his psyche or mind. His consciousness is elevated to its rightful position of mastery and his subconscious falls into its proper position as a faithful servant.

Power of fantasy. Within the false personality the introverted and splintered consciousness with its imagination and will create the phenomenon of fantasy. Fantasy is the faculty of inventing or forming fanciful images. Fanciful images are in the nature of hallucinations, and a hallucination is an *apparent* sense perception or appearance of an object, arising from a subconscious disorientation to reality. In extreme cases, where the power of fantasy rules the whole personality, we say that the victim is "insane."

Effects of fantasy. This power of fantasy is a stick of dynamite that we all carry in the subconscious stratum of our minds. It is the "make-believe consciousness" of the false personality, which "borrows" the sense perceptions stored as memories, and acts "as if" these were actual present happenings. From these second-hand images it weaves dramas, comedies, and sequences which have no basis in reality, but these trigger the same physiological responses as they would were they actual happenings. Since these happenings can be "tailored to suit the whim of the moment," there is a strong tendency within the false personality to retreat into the make-believe world of its own creation whenever the problems of the world of reality become irksome.

Element of hypnosis. In hypnotic trance states, the hypnotist takes temporary command of the subject's false personality, after lulling the true personality—the "censor"—into quiescence, and those who have witnessed a stage performance by a skilled hypnotist can well realize the tremendous influence this false personality with its powers of fantasy can wield over the whole organism. The subject will accept the most absurd suggestions "as if" these represented reality. He can be made to go through the most absurd antics, carry on conversations with nonexistent people, play with imaginary animals, row a nonexistent boat on an imaginary ocean, and so on.

Influence over organic functions. It is a well-demonstrated fact that hypnosis can exert a controlling influence over circulation, metabolism, and certain endocrine reactions, and that, in fact, many organic functions can be easily affected by hypnotic suggestion. We know that the heartbeat can be accelerated or slowed down by suggestion; that anesthesia can be produced; that blood pressure can be increased and the circulation almost suspended in the deeper trance states—all at the command of the hypnotist *who is temporarily substituting for the subject's own conscious, true personality.* Needless to say, considerable benefit may derive from the proper use of hypnotic techniques, *administered by a properly qualified psychiatrist specially trained in hypnology.* Like psychoanalysis, however, no *permanent* benefit can come unless the subject's own consciousness can be induced to enter into the same relationship with his subconscious, as was entered into by the consciousness of the hypnotist.

Autohypnosis. The ideal method of bringing the false personality to "heel" is the technique of deliberately applied autohypnosis. In this the student, after much practice of the technique of apperception and identification with his true personality, after much self-observation and study of the work of the control centers, lays out an objectively conceived program for weaning the false personality away from its preoccupation with fantasy, and then deliberately implements this program by autohypnotic suggestion, with his *own* consciousness playing the part of hypnotist. Much more of this later, however.

Spontaneous-hypnosis. The point to remember now is that whenever we find ourselves indulging in fantasies, or daydreaming, we should realize that we are in a state of *spontaneous self-induced hypnotic trance.* In this state, we accept the lying suggestions of the sensation-seeking false personality as realities, and the entire fabric of our subconscious control mechanisms responds accordingly.

Shift of emphasis. One of the most striking characteristics of the hypnotic state is that the normal significance of the usual pattern of events may be easily shifted by suggestion to insignificant details which may be exaggerated to any extent according to the hypnotist's fancy. Thus, *the inner circumstances filed with the memory-images may be changed at will by the hypnotist's suggestions,* and even though the senses were to faithfully record the outer happenings, the sorting of these for significance and the arranging of them into logical patterns may be so changed that the subject is to all intents and purposes living in a different world from that of the waking individual. Despite the fact that his eyes are open, and that he may carry on an intelligent conversation with the hypnotist, *he is living in a world of dreams* as fantastic as that world we imagine when we are asleep and dreaming in our beds.

THE STRUGGLE

Combatting spontaneous hypnotic suggestion. As pointed out before we spend most of our lives in a state of spontaneous hypnotic sleep. The fact that this is *unintentionally* self-induced makes it much more dangerous to ourselves than would be the case if we had deliberately submitted ourselves to the control of a hypnotist, for whereas it might be presumed that the hypnotist through his training would have some understanding of, and respect for, the wonderful mental machine he was manipulating, the hypnotic suggestions that we unintentionally give ourselves are mostly based upon *our craving for physical sensation.* Were it not for our long-suffering *true personalities* and their continual struggle to preserve the real and the true within us through exerting a censorship over the fantastic ideas of our false personalities, produced by spontaneous hypnotic suggestion, mankind would have long since destroyed itself and vanished from the earth.

Return to reality. It should be fairly obvious to those who have read this far that a return to reality by the individual is becoming increasingly difficult. To an increasing degree the processes of education are ignoring the development of the individual as a thinker. They are concentrated upon conditioning him into a blind acceptance of a set of scientific and political dogmas, and literacy is construed as the ability to read and to understand instructions.

Communication. Communication is becoming more and more a one-way affair, from the top downward, and the individual who dares to differ and to talk back receives short shrift. It would seem that the vast bulk of humanity is becoming moulded into a great subconscious mind, incapable of direct perception, living in its fantasies, and utterly dependent upon the suggestions of a comparative few more highly conscious leaders. Perhaps to some degree this is as nature planned it, and the "classless society" of the socialists is a myth, for it would be a subconscious society, an imbecile society, wallowing in its self-created fantasies and completely disoriented to the basic realities of nature.

Oft-stated facts. In this book the essential principles of Creative Realism have been stated in a number of different ways. To some this may seem like needless repetition, but it is necessary to explain these principles from many angles in order that the reader may truly make them his own. The average individual dreaming before his television set, or receptively sitting before his radio, has to some extent lost the ability to exert the degree of self-mastery needed to explore a concept that is new to him. By approaching the basic facts from a number of different angles it is hoped to make understanding of a complex subject simpler; by supplying a wide variety of data bearing upon the philosophy, the subconscious computing machine of the reader is in a better position to help.

SUMMARY

TWO ASPECTS OF REALITY

To recapitulate what has been said in this chapter then, we might consider that so far as we are concerned, there are two aspects of reality which must be considered. One aspect is the colorless, lifeless, soundless, elemental reality of physics; the other is the warm, pulsing, beautiful reality of living nature. The qualities attributed to nonliving nature do not reside in those objects; *they are constructions of the mind of the beholder;* they would not exist without a mind to observe them.

IDEALS

The ultimate reality of the physical world will, of course, never be explored by the intellect of man. The reality of living nature though *will be because it is accessible through direct conscious experience.* We shall, of course, never be able to experience it through the intellect. Only the physical mechanisms constructed and used by mind may be measured and weighed by the intellect. Thus, though the intellect may serve as a pointing finger to direct, conscious experience, the latter must be plunged into by the consciousness as a single, whole, perception; one may measure a cup of water drawn from the ocean, weigh it, analyze it in the laboratory, and so on, but all of this intellectually acquired information would have little bearing on the actual experience of plunging naked into the ocean. Conscious experience is something quite different from intellection.

SELF-EVOLUTION

At the present time most of us pass our lives in a state of hypnotic trance. We dream dreams and believe these are real. We attribute qualities and motives to others and act "as if" these were true, but, in fact, they only exist in *our own* subconsciousness; they are products of our dreams. To escape from the slavery imposed by our subconsciousness we must become conscious. There is not escape from sleep save through awakening. This may be accomplished through a natural process of self-evolution.

TRUE SELVES

The means of our salvation rests in the development of our true personalities. When our true selves emerge into consciousness, our whole relationship to life becomes changed. We recognize ourselves as units of the consciousness of nature, and a sense of reality and certainty replaces the harried dreaming of our former subconscious state. *By direct experience we know the truth, and the knowledge sets us free.*

ULTIMATE TRUTH

We can never know the truth about anything until we know the truth about ourselves, and we can never know the truth about ourselves by mere intellection. We may only learn this ultimate human truth by direct conscious experience. Every step forward in consciousness destroys a little more of the fantasy and fiction within ourselves; every step forward brings the lower aspects of our minds a little more under the control of our true personalities and weakens the hold of the father of lies within us—the false personality.

CHAPTER 10

Mind and Matter

A lay disciple came to Hui-k'e and said: "Pray, master, cleanse me of my sins." "Bring your sins here," said Hui-k'e, "and I will cleanse you of them." After a silence, the layman said: "As I seek my sins, I find them unattainable." "I have then finished cleansing you of them," said Hui-k'e.

TAO-HSIN

REALITY VS. THE EMOTIONS

Happiness. Realities cannot cause either happiness or unhappiness. Objective facts in themselves have nothing to do with the emotions. All of our joys and sorrows are products of the psychical structure we call our minds and are due to the particular fictions we build into them, which prevent our objective approach to the world of reality.

The "split." Let us return again briefly to a consideration of the point we made in discussing the brain exploration technique. We said that it clearly demonstrates two phases of the mind in simultaneous operation. First, there is the subconscious phase, set in motion by the touch of the surgeon's probe, and second, there is the phase of *consciousness* by which the patient is able to observe the first phase—the subconscious —in action.

The imitator. The entire content of the subconscious has been fabricated from impressions which have come to us from the outside. It is an intricately woven mass of symbols representing pictures, smells, sounds, tastes, and tactile sensations, each of which has some sort of an emotional connotation and is capable of tripping a response in the emotional center. Not all of these emotional connotations are the result of direct personal experience, but many are caused by our imitating the feelings of others about certain things.

Conditioned responses. By imitating we learned to walk, to talk, to read and write, to dress ourselves, to feed ourselves, and to like or dislike certain foods, music, and people. By imitating we acquired our religion, our politics, and our professions. Many of the things we acquired in this way are, of course, indispensable. They represent the cultural heritage of our race. But alongside them exists all the trash of superstition and prejudice which also have been acquired by imitation right down the line from our primitive beginnings. These cause us endless trouble.

MIND AND MATTER

The human body. We said before that in common with all other matter, the human body resolves itself into the electrical. Electrical charges move toward or from each other; they group themselves into atoms which can be broken down and reassembled. Atoms in turn become grouped into larger systems called molecules, and these are arranged by the mysterious life force into the complex systems which make up living cells.

Tape recorders. Just as the magnetic impulses of a tape recorder cause a grouping of the molecules of the tape into patterns which reproduce the original sounds transmitted by the magnetic impulses under the right technical conditions, so the molecules of the brain cells are grouped into patterns by the impulses carried to them by the central nervous system. These recorded impressions become organized into larger systems called "ideas" and these again into complex idea structures or "complexes," as they are called. This type of information storage is permanent and can be played back at any time *until the trace is purposely erased by some newly inscribed molecular pattern.*

Accuracy. All of our actions are based upon the assumption that the information stored in the subconscious is accurate, and, of course, so far as the actual memories of sights, sounds, smells, and so on, are concerned, we know that at best these are only dim and partial impressions. But it is in the *interpretation* of the impressions that the greatest error enters, and fantasy takes the place of reality. So long as the consciousness is inextricably entangled in the subconscious, substituting fantasies and daydreams for outer realities, our interpretations cannot be anything else but fantastic.

TWO SYSTEMS

Sending and interpreting impressions. We might consider then that our nervous systems operate as a dual system. One of these conveys impressions to the brain cells for storage and the other system simultaneously interprets the impressions. While a man is unconscious, swarms of stimuli are still being received in his brain, but he cannot interpret them; and being unable to interpret them, he cannot react to them.

Brain areas. Those areas of the brain's cortex which act as receiving stations for vision, hearing, speech, and so on, and which can be set into motion by the surgeon's probe, are not naturally the seat of consciousness but merely terminal stations where sense impressions are sorted and stored under the control of the analogue computer we have called the subconscious mind. Any or all of these centers can be destroyed without abolishing consciousness.

The diencephalon. The latest experimental evidence indicates that the area most essential to consciousness is the diencephalon, a compartment situated below the cortex of the brain. In it is the "arousal center" which controls the fluctuations of consciousness as in sleeping and waking, and it has been shown that even if all the main sensory systems of nerves be cut so that no stimuli arrive at the sensorium, we still sleep and wake in the normal sequence if the diencephalon is not interfered with. The diencephalon is with its "arousal center" situated in what is known as the "reticular formation" of the brain made up of relatively small brain cells and outside the main pathways for motor and sensory stimuli.

Reticular formation. This reticular formation extends downward from the diencephalon throughout the entire length of the central nervous system. Without going too deeply into neurology then, we may assume that within our bodies we have two "mental" systems in continual and simultaneous operation. One system gathers the stimuli and the other interprets it.

"Arousal center." It has been known for some time that the upper portion of the reticular formation facilitates activity in the brain and spinal cord, while the lower portion inhibits activity. Recently the arousal center was found in the upper portion, and it has been demonstrated that this center acts upon the entire cerebral cortex at the same time. In contrast, each single sensory system influences only a limited area of the cortex.

Housing of consciousness. The reticular formation then, perhaps with the diencephalon as its executive headquarters, appears to be the physical housing of the consciousness; the consciousness should be the perceiver of truth and reality eternally at work within us; strangely enough, however, proof that this "perceiver of truth and reality" can be perverted is easily obtained.

HYPNOSIS

Definition. Hypnosis is defined as a state during which the conscious mind, in accord with the subject's acceptance of the presented idea, is either in total or partial abeyance, and during which the motivating influences of our psychophysical existence can be directly stimulated or inhibited by the hypnotist. Trance puts the conscious personality in complete abeyance, so that the subconscious, no longer under its screening influence, becomes immediately accessible to suggestion.

Deep trance. What happens in trance is that by means of suggestion the "arousal center" is caused to withdraw its component of *awareness* or consciousness from the cortex and the rest of the subconscious mechanism—to retreat temporarily into itself as it were, yielding for the time being the functions of censorship and interpretation to the hypnotist. Thus, only the "arousal center" the "switch of consciousness" is affected and all of the reticular mechanism of interpretation is left functioning and under the control of the hypnotist. This applies in the fullest sense only to the deep trance state or somnambulism, as it is called.

Phenomena. While in the above state, it can be suggested that the subject is going to smell a beautiful perfume and the hypnotist holds a bottle of ammonia to his nose which is inhaled with great enjoyment. Then the hypnotist holds a bottle of perfume under the subject's nose with the suggestion that it is ammonia and the subject coughs and strangles for breath. The subject is given a glass of water with the suggestion that it is whiskey and the subject will drink it and exhibit all the symptoms of intoxication; but if a glass of whiskey be given him with the suggestion that it is alka-seltzer and will sober him up, he will drink it and become sober.

Talents revealed. There are many well-authenticated instances on record wherein people with a little natural talent have been able to produce high-quality creations under hypnotic influence. One such case is quoted in James Coates's book *Human Magnetism* (Nichols & Co., 1904). When the famous Jenny Lind was singing in Manchester, she was invited by Dr. James Braid to hear the performance of one of his hypnotized subjects, an illiterate factory girl without any formal voice training. This girl in the hypnotic state followed the Swedish nightingale's songs in different languages, both instantaneously and perfectly, and when Jenny Lind extemporized a long and difficult chromatic exercise, the subject also imitated it with perfect precision, although in the ordinary waking state she was unable even to attempt such a feat.

Latent possibilities. While not everyone possesses the same natural endowment of talents and inherent possibilities, of course, it is certain that we all do have latent talents and possibilities which have never been unfolded. Talent in such diverse fields as dramatics, music, painting, mathematics, all manner of athletics, have been discovered and assisted toward development by hypnotic techniques. It is a question of training the interpretative faculty to interpret "perfume as perfume, whiskey as whiskey, and water as water."

The fountainhead. The fountainhead of reality within us is the consciousness. So long as it is diffused throughout the subconscious, however, and engaged in creating fantasies, it creates a pseudo-reality in which to live that has nothing to do with the real thing.

SUGGESTIBILITY

Nine stages. Some experts have divided the degrees of hypnosis into as many as nine stages, ranging from slight hypnosis to catatonic trance. In slight hypnosis the subject can hear all that is going on around him, and he feels that he can terminate the condition at will, but somehow he never seems to want to. The proof of his condition lies in his response to posthypnotic suggestion, which in many cases is as effective as though he had lost consciousness. The deeper the stage of hypnosis, of course, the more complete is the response to suggestion.

Suggestion and interpretation. Now suggestion, as we have said previously, acts directly upon the mechanism of interpretation. The skin of a subject may be touched with a pencil, but if this is accompanied by the suggestion that the pencil is a red-hot iron, a blister will form on the spot touched. On the other hand, by a different suggestion complete anaesthesia can be produced and a needle can be thrust into the tissues without producing a pain reaction.

All subjects. It might be said that unless we happen to be in a state of self-remembering consciousness, we are all continually in varying degrees of the hypnotic state. That is why the suggestions pouring in upon us from our environment have such a profound effect upon us. We are "conditioned" like Pavlov's dogs into interpreting phenomena in all sorts of fantistic ways. Furthermore, as much of this suggestion is conflicting, it tends to set up conflicts within the interpretive system, often reducing us to a perpetual condition of chronic harassment or indecision and worry.

AUTOSUGGESTION

Overcoming neurotic symptoms. We shall take up the subject of autosuggestion in more detail in a later chapter, but now it is well to understand that besides being exposed to the continual barrage of suggestions from without, we are also exposed to our own negative suggestions. We have a little difficulty with a thing, and we either decide that we cannot do it or that we "don't like to do it." If this suggestion is accompanied by emotion, as it usually is, it is accepted by the interpretive system and we develop an "allergy" or some other neurotic symptom whenever we are exposed to that particular thing.

The false personality. Thus when we speak of the false personality, we refer to this whole complex structure of interpretations or "meanings" of phenomena, impressed upon the reticular formation of our nervous systems from early childhood by means of imitation and suggestion. What we believe, how we think, what we can do, and what we are, is not based upon our natural heritage of possibilities, but upon these numerous and often conflicting interpretations. The executive headquarters of the false personality is, of course, the subconscious mind.

True personality. Were we *bound* to live our lives out entangled inextricably in the conflicting complexes of our false personalities, then being would indeed be a curse, for conflict means suffering, and locked within the prison-house of the subconscious we should be doomed to the torments of worry and fear by day and tortured dreams by night. But we are not so bound. With persistence we can pick the lock of our prisons and walk into the sunshine of consciousness as true personalities.

RESOLVING INNER CONFLICTS

The problem. We breathe life into our inner conflicts because we are *conscious of them and not of ourselves.* As was pointed out earlier, our consciousness is introverted and divided among the conflicting interpretative mechanisms of our subconscious. If we withdraw the "breath of life" from these conflicts by integrating our consciousness as true personalities, conscious of ourselves as true personalities and of the world of realities outside ourselves, the conflicting splinters of consciousness are merged into a harmonious whole and our interpretative mechanisms fall into a harmonious *natural* pattern, like that observable in a young child.

Instead of our psychical resources being squandered in fratricidal internal conflict, these become available to us for creative work. Our consciousness enters into the same relationship with our interpretative mechanisms as that entered into by the consciousness of a hypnotist with the interpretative mechanisms of his subject, only instead of a stream of relative suggestions, our consciousness gives *one big suggestion based upon reality,* and the interpretative mechanisms fall into the natural harmonious pattern which interprets according to the laws of nature and reality. This occurs naturally once consciousness is attained; we then become "whole men."

Proof. Proof that the consciousness is capable of self-control and self-development is easily obtained. It was pointed out in this chapter that the arousal center controls the normal fluctuations of sleeping and waking, of consciousness and unconsciousness. If we, at bedtime, determine that we shall awaken at a certain unusual hour, ordinarily we shall do so. At the precise time determined upon, the arousal center will flood the brain with consciousness. This simple experiment is profoundly significant, for it proves that although we are, as subconscious individuals, bound to our environment as automatically responding machines, our consciousness is possessed of freedom and self-determination.

Will. Usually when we speak of the will, we think of a force acting only by tortuous effort, characterized by outthrust jaw, beetling brows, and clenched fists. The opposite is true, however. The will is an integral function of the consciousness, and it operates as effortlessly as does the hand of an engineer on the throttle which sets a train into motion. When we decide to awake at a certain hour, it is an act of will. When we decide to either do a certain think or refrain from doing a certain thing, again it is an act of will. An act of will is when the consciousness, in control of the six mental control centers, directs the entire output of our energy toward the accomplishment of a preconceived objective.

Desire. What is usually mistaken for will is simply desire, and desire is usually the product of the false personality and its conflicts. The personality which desires freedom, yet demands security; which craves gratification, yet wishes to be socially respected; which wants the privilege of hating others, yet the love of others for itself. Obviously desires arising from these conflicts are mutually exclusive and can know no gratification.

SUGGESTED EXERCISE
DEVELOPING THE WILL

It is suggested that the following daily exercise be incorporated into the routine of living. Eventually it will become a habit which can be extended to cover most of the daily activities. It is an exercise for the development of the will.

REFLECTION

Shortly before bedtime, go into a room where you can be alone and undisturbed. Seat yourself comfortably, relax, and then, commencing with your present, by a chain of visual images lead yourself backward through the day's activities until you arrive at the moment when you got out of bed in the morning. Reflect upon these activities. Be completely honest with yourself and try to recall three things which you should have done but which you did not do. Write these things down. Next, find three things which you did, but which you should have refrained from doing. Write these down also on the other side of the paper.

THE FOLLOWING DAY

The following day commence with number one on the "should have" side of your list, and, putting yourself in the self-remembering state, calmly, systematically, and ruthlessly do the thing. Follow up with the next two items on your "should have done" list and complete them in the same manner. *So long as you are conscious* you shall not have the slightest difficulty, because in consciousness there are neither likes nor dislikes. These belong to the false personality and are the results of suggestion, as explained before. It is only when we become subconscious—withdraw inside of arousal centers—so leaving ourselves either in the "suggestable state" or subjects of posthypnotic suggestions received before, about the things in question, that we experience "likes" and "dislikes" and violent aversions to certain things and people.

AWARENESS

Consciousness is a state of *objective, alert awareness* and if that state is maintained, the subconscious computing machine may be relied upon to come forward with any desired information when its computations are required, and without conscious interference these will be fully fledged and untrammeled by doubts and qualifications.

REFRAINING

After completing the three tasks described, next commence on the task of refraining from doing the three things which you enjoy doing but should not do. Deliberately expose yourself to their temptation in the self-remembering state, of course; then just as deliberately reject each one in turn.

THE EASY WAY

You will be amazed at the ease with which you are able to perform the above feats, so long as you remain in the self-remembering state.

CHAPTER II

The Superimpression

For now we see through a glass, darkly; but then face to face:
now I know in part, but then shall I know even as also I
am known.

I. CORINTHIANS, 13:12

MIND OF NATURE

Functional units. If we think of ourselves as being functional units
of nature's mental mechanism, it is clear that we must be bound by
natural law to our normal function, just as is everything else which lives.
To live is to do work, work which contributes in some measure to the
physical or mental life of the great organism that is nature.

Fulfillment. Within a human body or brain, a cell could only attain
fulfillment if it were able to function perfectly. Imperfection of function would cause a disequilibrium, and the greater tides of the body's
living processes would flow around it, leaving it in isolation to die and
be eliminated as useless to the body's economy.

Unhappiness. Anything which stood between the cell and its normal
function then would be cause for illness, deprivation, and unhappiness.
Now let us consider the life of a single cell within a human brain—say a
cell of the "arousal center" of the diencephalon. The activities of such
a cell must be divided into three separate phases.

Three phases. First, there must be an unconscious and automatic phase
to attend to the maintainance of the cell's structure and to attend to all
those subtle processes by which the nutrients supplied by the body fluids

95

are converted into chemical and electrical energy. Second, there must be a phase which adjusts the cell's energy output to the fluctuating needs of its third phase—this third phase being consciousness. Consciousness is the end contribution of the cell to the mind as a whole. It is the only reason for the cell's existence. Without the means for fulfilling this function the life of this cell would be meaningless.

ANALOGY

The block. Returning to our analogy of a human individual in the role of a single cell of the "brain" of nature, it can be easily seen that the block between man's fulfillment of his real function and the energy output of his body is his malfunctioning subconscious mind.

Will. We have already said that will is a natural component of consciousness. Will is the assertion of the real self—the true personality—and the true personality is consciousness. We gave an example of how the will, by a mere assertion that it will awake at a certain hour, can arouse itself at the predetermined moment without assistance from other sources. This demonstrates the will's independence and autonomy. The mere positive assertion of a purpose is sufficient to set into motion those lesser forces needed to carry it out.

Genesis. In Genesis, we are told that creation is the result of a similar series of willed assertions by our creator, and perhaps the ancient author of that book was inspired by a truer conception of our beginnings than we have grown to believe lately. Certainly the human will is possessed of many extraordinary, creative potentialities which we are just beginning to learn about, and the human will is as the mere will of a cell compared to His.

THE BATTLE

Resistance to consciousness. In the previous chapter, we explained the resistance to consciousness by the false personality. Like an addict who identifies himself and all of his activities with the sensations produced in his nervous system by a drug, and who believes that existence would be worthless without those sensations, the false personality has become completely identified with its emotions, and with the sensations produced in his nervous system by the overproduction of hormones incidental to emotionalism. The battle against this type of addiction can only be won by the will.

Positive assertion. It will be helpful therefore if during the day you should pause for a few moments in whatever you are doing, place yourself in the self-remembering state, then calmy and *objectively* make silently to yourself the following positive assertion:

"I am accepting the challenge of life without reservations. Regardless of my age, my present state of health, and my present responsibilities, I am going to hold aloft the torch of consciousness by my will, and I am going to carry it to the farthest frontiers possible to me."

You will find that the simple assertion in consciousness of this determination, often repeated, will achieve the result of giving direction and power to your entire effort.

CORTICAL FIELDS

One field at a time. We explained briefly before that the human cerebral cortex is divided into a number of different sensory fields: that is to say, one area deals with the signals arriving from the sense of hearing; another field deals with the visual impression; and so on. In subconscious man only one field is ordinarily influenced at a time. To help us understand this fact, we might imagine that when a man is using his eyes, only the area of the visual field "lights up" while the others remain in darkness, or that when he is listening, only the auditory field lights up and the light dies down in the visual field, and so on.

Shifting attention. Thus, according to the above, there is a continual shifting of the attention from one sensory field to another. If we gaze intently at a thing, we hear less clearly what is going on around us, and, if we listen intently, our consciousness of the things to be seen around us is lessened, and so on. If we are interrupted by a noise while examining something visually, it annoys us, and if we are listening to someone with full attention, we are irritated by a sight demanding visual attention.

Single-pointedness. Now in hypnotic technique, the hypnotist usually attempts to have the subject focus his gaze upon a small bright object.

Another method is to have the subject sit back, relax, and close his eyes, then to listen only to the voice of the hypnotist while sleep is suggested. More often, however, these two methods are combined: the subject is instructed to focus his gaze upon a certain object held some distance from his eyes, and, at the same time, the operator suggests to him in a monotonous rhythmic way that he is growing drowsy, that his eyelids are growing heavy, and so forth, and in a short time the subject's attention toward the visual object tires, he closes his eyes voluntarily, his attention is switched into his listening channels, where it gradually contracts its awareness until the only thing it hears is the voice of the hypnotist. The subject then is in a state of hypnotic trance.

HYPNOSIS: A NATURAL PHENOMENON

Hypnotizing agents. Contrary to what is generally believed, hypnosis is a *natural phenomenon,* and it is used (perhaps unconsciously) upon us in many different ways every day. All advertising is based upon the idea of hypnotic suggestion. Music is a powerful hynotizing agent, and in the "singing commercial" we have its rhythm incorporated with the suggestion. When a person falls asleep in church, he is really in a state of hypnotic trance, and in that condition receives much more of the preacher's message than those who sit listening in a state of alert awareness. All propaganda is based upon hypnosis, and leaders who can sway multitudes are not necessarily intellectual giants; they are often people of very mediocre mental attainment, who have—either accidentally or otherwise—mastered the techniques of mass hypnosis; Mussolini and Hitler are examples of this, while Stalin, with a much higher degree of natural intelligence, achieved a great deal of his power through having been built up in the minds of the Russian people as a demigod by way of hypnotic techniques.

The easy way. To be hypnotized is not an unpleasant experience; in fact, to subconscious man it is very pleasant, for it rids him of the necessity of struggling with problems beyond his scope. He accepts the suggestions of the hypnotist as answers to these problems and thus lightens his own mental load. In this way whole nations are sometimes subjugated to the will of a single hypnotist and led down the pathway to disaster.

SUMMARY

OBJECTIVE

We might say then that subconscious man is always under the hypnotic influence of others and subject to the will of others. The objective of Creative Realism is to point the way whereby a man can attain consciousness, and so become subject only to his own will, under the will of his creator, so becoming a *conscious* unit, directly serving and contributing to the consciousness of nature and drawing his inspiration and his guidance directly from the consciousness of nature.

NARROWING DOWN

To state it briefly then: to hypnotize another we must narrow down his field of attention. Once the attention is held—either through the eyes or the ears—it is possible to effect the split that permits us to control the interpretative mechanisms and the motivation of the subconscious. When we have another person in such a hypnotic state, he is incapable of interpreting anything on a basis of reality unless we specifically suggest that he be able to do so.

THE SUBORDINATE

The subconscious mind is always subordinate to consciousness. It has no will of its own other than the laws of its basic design, and so must depend for its promptings upon other sources. When the consciousness is immersed in the subconscious, these promptings come from dreams and fantasies, which in turn are the products of desires for emotional stimulation. The consciousness is very weak and hazy in this state, and, if forced to give its attention to something outside of the body—something to be seen or something to be listened to—it does so under protest, as it were. It wishes to return to its emotional world within and to its dreams. It is like a sleeper who when shaken awake wants to roll over and go back to sleep.

GRUDGED ATTENTION

That is why the narrowing down of attention is such an easy matter. The consciousness will leave only the smallest fragment of itself awake gladly, if the rest of it can return to its absorbing private theatre within. This small fragment becomes tired and retreats easily as the consciousness of the hypnotist substitutes for it, and we have hypnotic trance.

SENSORY SIGNALS

An ordinary sleeper is aroused easily by sensory stimulation, particularly if the stimulation be intense, but not so a person in a hypnotic sleep. In ordinary sleep painful signals activate the arousal center by way of side branches from the main sensory pathways, but in hypnosis the arousal center is temporarily isolated and disassociated from all normal sensory impulses.

THE PERISCOPE

It should be clear from what has been said that true consciousness can never be a partial thing. When the arousal center of the brain is fully activated by the will, it activates the cortex as a whole instead of only a limited area. Ordinary man's consciousness, submerged in his subconsciousness, has only, as it were, a single flimsy tentacle connecting it with the outer world. This tentacle wavers between the various sense centers, and, even when his attention is momentarily fixed on an outer object, he is dimly aware of what is going on within his subconscious.

OBJECTIVE CONSCIOUSNESS

Conscious man may narrow down his field of attention also—and at will—but instead of being dimly aware of what is going on within his subconscious, he is dimly aware of the other happenings in his outer surroundings, apart from the object of his attention. In short, subconscious man relates such realities as he receives through his "tentacle of consciousness" to his fantastical inner world, while conscious man interprets his inner experiences realistically in terms of outer realities.

SUBTRACTING

As was before said, ordinarily if we see a thing very acutely, we hear it less acutely, smell it still less acutely, the acuteness of sensory perception diminishing progressively with each additional sense brought to bear upon it. It is as though each sense brought to bear upon an object subtracts from the acuteness of those senses already bearing upon it. One of the most effective of the exercises for the attainment of consciousness. is to reverse this process.

EXERCISE

TECHNIQUE

First. This exercise can be practiced anywhere at any time, but perhaps the ideal place is out of doors in a park or garden. Stand erect and place yourself in the self-remembering state, then try to make the clearest possible visual impression of your surroundings. Observe the trees, for instance, the smooth or rough bark on their trunks, the angles formed by their limbs, the coloring of the leaves, and the way in which they hang. Do the same with the shrubs, the grass. . . . Observe the way in which the paved walks run, and so on.

Second. While *holding* this strong visual perception, listen intently to the background sounds. The twittering of birds, perhaps children's voices in the distance . . . the hum of bees . . . the sound of a distant automobile horn. Become acutely aware of these background sounds as well as the sights . . . and try to hold both sets of impressions strongly.

Third. Now, while still holding the consciousness of (1) yourself, (2) the sights, and (3) the sounds, add the olfactory impressions. Try to catch the aroma of the grass, the trees, the flowers, and all other impressions made upon your sense of smell. Sniff gently high up into your nose, for this is where the olfactory nerves are situated.

Fourth. While holding all of the foregoing impressions strongly in consciousness, become aware of the *feel* of the air upon your face and eyes; perhaps there is a breeze . . . note its direction, and turn your face so that you can feel it on both sides . . . then turn squarely toward it.

Finally. By a supreme effort of will, try to combine all of the impressions of (1) yourself, (2) sights, (3) sounds, (4) smells, and (5) the feel of the air, into *one single vividly conscious superimpression*. At first you may be able to hold this superimpression for only a few seconds, but you will find that it brings with it a feeling of well-being and a sense of élan and of identification with nature that is its own reward.

THE EFFECT

Arousal center development. This exercise is in the nature of an aid to the development of the arousal center of the diencephalon. It tends to bring gradually this all-important mechanism under the control of the will, to the end that it becomes capable of intensely activating the entire cerebral cortex whenever we wish to enjoy a period of tranquil illumination or to reorient ourselves to great nature and her harmonies.

Natural patterns. It was explained previously that within the human nervous system their exists a mechanism (the reticular formation) for *interpreting* the impressions gathered by the sensory nerves, and that this system is built of the memories of millions of years of trial-and-error experiences and intuitive perceptions, congealed into a *natural pattern* capable of interpreting every physical stimulus and of triggering the exact physical response needed to cope with the situation indicated by the stimulus.

Interference. It was explained that the aforementioned mechanisms are interefered with by the introverted consciousness triggering unnecessary responses, by its weaving fantasies and creating artificial situations for the subconscious to work upon. By this the perfect interpretative mechanisms are thrown out of focus, and the results are the psychoses, the neuroses, and all the host of psychosomatic diseases with which our civilization is plagued. We are prevented from fulfilling our normal function in nature and contributing our end-product—*consciousness*.

Separation of consciousness. The foregoing exercise is an important aid to removing the consciousness from its subconscious entanglement, and in placing it where it belongs rightfully—in the dominant role of the mental economy. When this objective is even partially attained, much of the interference is automatically removed from the interpretive mechanisms, and these fall back quickly into following their ancient and natural patterns, to the immense benefit of our health, to our greater happiness, and our response to life as a whole.

CHAPTER 12

Balanced Development

Empty-handed I go and yet the spade is in my hands; I walk on foot, and yet on the back of an ox I am riding: When I pass over the bridge, lo, the water floweth not, but the bridge doth flow.

Fu-ta-shih

WORLD CONSCIOUSNESS

Data storage. We have likened the human subconscious mind to an analogue computing machine. To work effectively it must have in storage a large supply of good data, and so an attempt has been made in this book to supply such data as might enable it to build up the concept of nature as a vast organism, working and growing, even as the body of a child works and grows, toward a preconceived objective—the objective of world consciousness. Without consciousness, living nature would be as completely meaningless as seems the beautiful body of the occasional child born without a cerebral cortex.

The mystic. It is possible for a person to attain to a high degree of consciousness even though he may remain undeveloped intellectually; those who have lived in India and have come into contact with "Bhakta Yoga," where the devotee plunges his whole being into an identification with whatever aspect of God he has chosen, have witnessed this phenomenon. From the Western point of view, however, the attainment of consciousness, without having the intellectual equipment with which to translate the realities perceived into the relative concepts useful to our daily lives, is not a desirable objective. An impractical saint is just as great a misfit as a spiritual moron with a highly developed intellect.

103

The higher way. The great stumbling block in the way of man's orderly development is that when he is preoccupied with things spiritual, he tends to neglect his "analogue computer"—his subconscious—by means of which he must bring the spiritual down to earth, and when he is able to develop a highly efficient. computing machine, he tends to rely upon it completely and to ignore all problems which cannot be solved by means of it. The higher way calls for a harmonious development of both consciousness and subconsciousness.

MIND AND SCIENCE

Intellectual limitations. Newly developed intellectual techniques have enabled us to modify our physical environment to a considerable degree, but these have not added a "cubit" to our spiritual stature. The energy concept has enabled us to tear apart the very building-blocks of matter— the atoms—but natural science has had no success whatsoever in its efforts to discover the nature of mind, the bearer of unconsciousness, subconsciousness, and consciousness. Invisible and intangible, science has only been able to approach it negatively.

Mind not measurable. Science has found that mind is not a thing— for it is not measurable. If it were a form of energy, it would be measurable. But search the energy scheme as it will, no scale of equivalence between energy and mental experience has been discovered. Experience in consciousness is not open to observation through any sense organ and is not provable by anyone beyond ourselves.

Stimulus and response. Yet we know that mind *acts to direct energy* and that in turn energy acts upon mind. In the exercise given in the preceding chapter, for instance, we visually observe the objects in our surroundings, listen to them, smell them, and feel them, and we know that streams of electrical impulses are traveling backward to our brains, and that these cause further electrical disturbances there, but the process of *becoming aware* of these impulses or stimuli—the process of consciousness—the energy scheme does not cover. As we said before, were all the main sensory pathways cut so that the stimuli could not arrive in our brains, we could still be conscious, though not conscious of sensory impressions. On the other hand, were we unconscious, as under an anaesthetic, the streams of stimuli would still be arriving in our brains, but we would not be conscious of them.

Mind a stillness. Mind then would appear to be a stillness rather than an activity: a stillness with the ability to *increase itself qualitatively in response to stimulation either received over the sensory system or directly by means of its own will.*

INVOLUTION

Before there could have been an evolution, there must have been an involution. Just as the *possibilities* of a human adult must be concentrated within the microscopic, fertilized, human ovum, so the possibilities of the immense body of nature must have existed in the first microscopic bit of protoplasm formed on earth. Somehow, somewhere, these possibilities must have been envisioned, abstracted, and brought together, then concentrated in that first living form.

Involvement. We can easily realize that for all of the millions of years of evolution which preceded the appearance of man, nature, like an unborn babe, was entirely involved in its own internal processes. It was completely unconscious of events outside of itself, and the slave of the energy systems it directed.

Detachment. With the coming of man came an increasing ability to detach itself a little from its own internal processes and, to some very slight degree, to substitute will for mere response to necessity. Increasingly, man has discovered that his ability to will is dependent upon his ability to detach his consciousness from his own internal processes.

Integration. When the subconscious computing machine, possessed of sufficient data, arrives at the logical conclusion of its rightful part in the mental economy, it tends to free itself from fantasy automatically, and to fall into the natural functional pattern of its true natural design. This makes the release of the consciousness to its normal functional place so much the easier of accomplishment.

The regulator. The subconscious mind then is no longer frustrated by trying to compute answers from fantastic data supplied by the dreaming, introverted, consciousness; and the body is no longer thrown continually out of chemical balance by being regulated according to these unrealistic fedback answers. The subconscious is cleared to compute the data arriving over the sensory system, and to correlate the answers with the realities perceived by the consciousness.

Responding. The natural ability of the human body to respond adequately to all manner of extraordinary situations when subconscious interference is removed is illustrated by the famous experiment in which a hypnotized subject is suspended between two chairs, supported only by the back of his head and his heels, and tremendous weights are placed upon his abdomen without causing his body to bend. Many other phenomena also attest to this fact, such as the ability of East Indians and Polynesians to walk over red-hot rocks without suffering burns, and so on. The following true incident may point the way in which we can all use a greater measure of our natural physical ability in our daily lives.

THE LAMA

Detachment. Years ago a young Western student of psychology had journeyed to Tibet in order to study some of the lamaistic disciplines practiced there. His teacher, an aged English-speaking lama, had tried to explain that by detachment from the internal affairs of our own bodies, we automatically gained control over them. The young man was doubtful, for this philosophy was contrary to all the principles of Western psychology taught at that time. At last the old lama said: "Very well, tomorrow we shall go to Shigatze, and you shall demonstrate the principle to yourself."

The trip. At daybreak the following morning, the young man and his teacher set off on the narrow, slippery, and winding trail to Shigatze, thirty-five kilometers distant. The path at times seemed to climb almost straight upward and, at others, to drop straight downward, and it was not long until the young man's lungs were laboring and his head spinning in the rarified atmosphere of 17,000 feet altitude. The aged lama though was apparently quite unaffected . . . he strode along rapidly, breathing easily, and keeping up a continuous conversation.

Hope deferred. When finally they came in sight of Shigatze, the young man felt as though his chest were constricted by a red-hot band of iron; he was gasping for breath, reeling from fatigue, and was only sustained during the final two or three miles by the visions of a long rest, then a hearty meal, and then more rest.

The return. They had no sooner reached the outskirts of the town, however, than the teacher turned around and said blandly: "Now let us try to make better time on the journey back." And he commenced walking rapidly back over the trail they had just traversed. The young man expostulated that he could not do it, that his heart would give out, and so on, but the lama merely smiled and kept on walking. Finally he said: "It is not important that you die, since all men must die, but it is very important that you should learn to live."

Beyond weariness. After a time the emotional state of desperation in the young man seemed to change to one of mental numbness. . . . He no longer protested even to himself; he was beyond protesting. He felt almost like a disembodied spirit observing in a disinterested way his physical body in action. Then a seeming miracle took place; his fatigue dropped away, the constriction loosened from his chest, and he moved forward almost without a sense of effort.

The last mile. At last they rounded a bend and came within sight of the home lamasery about a mile distant, and, at the sight of it, all the fatigue and utter weariness seemed to rush back and take possession of the young man. He commenced to stagger and the old man looked back at him with concern: "You seem weary, my son; therefore let us hurry so that we may the sooner enjoy food and rest." And he led the way at a rapid jog-trot. Again the sense of fatigue dropped away from the young man, and he finished that last mile fresher than he had begun the first mile of the journey.

Second-wind. In discussing the phenomenon of second-wind afterward, the teacher explained: "The body does not tire—it is a machine— and so long as a machine is in good repair and is plentifully supplied with fuel there is no reason why it should tire. Since it automatically eliminates its own waste products by sweating and breathing, the body can continue to work indefinitely if the mind is not entangled in its operations. The submerged mind is a monkey and cannot sustain its attention; it wants to hop about and look at this, and toy with that, and dally with some imaginary thing. The introverted mind may only find freedom in which to enjoy introspection and daydreams when the body is idling. To bring about this desired situation therefore, it halts a sustained effort by suggesting to the subconscious controller that the 'body is tired,' that its 'lungs are constricted,' that its 'heart will give out,' and so on."

Forced detachment. The old lama continued: "The introverted mind may be forced to detach itself if the demand to sustain the physical effort comes from another, and is stronger than the effect of its autosuggestion. In such a case, we see the phenomenon called 'second-wind,' but all great athletes learn this secret of detaching their minds from their physical mechanisms. They may learn this accidentally, and perhaps do not fully understand the nature of their power themselves, but look upon the face of a great marathon runner, for instance, and you will see the same expression as is observed in a Tibetan 'lung-gompa' runner . . . an expression of serene detachment."

SELF-MASTERY

First step. We take the first step toward self-mastery when *we learn to stop fighting ourselves.* This applies to intellectual efforts as well as to physical effort. An effort to remember a name, for instance, usually results in pushing the name further than ever from the point of recall. If we shrug and detach our consciousness from the problem, very soon the subconscious will pop the name into our minds unaided. When we learn to live in our consciousness, we shall have mastered this great secret of detachment, and the ability to fulfill the ideal code of conduct set forth in Kipling's poem "If."

CHAPTER 13

Energy and the Mind

That space is full of forces which are unknown to us, and that
living beings emit radiations or effluvia of which we are not
aware . . . are facts that I have long since accepted.

PROF. ARSENE D'ARSONVAL

CHILDREN OF THE SUN

Energy. We are children of the sun. The sun, either directly or indirectly, gave birth to our earth, and under the influence of the sun
those physical conditions essential to living organisms as we know them
were organized. The first living organisms appeared and still under
the sun's benign influence, the great body of nature spread out over
the surface of the earth, and rolled forward in evolution from the simple
to the complex, from the comparatively crude to the finer in form and
function, until at last man appeared on the scene.

Sources of strength. Mankind forsook the jungles and the caves to
till fields and build cities, but though he now warms or cools his surroundings at will, and though his nights are as brightly lighted as his
days if he so wills it, although much of the energy of his body is derived
from foods brought to him by other forms of energy from distant places,
although he has supplemented his body's energy by the energy produced
by the locomotive, the aeroplane, wireless, and so on, the sun is still
the source of all these forms of energy.

Energy and life. So upon this earth we live and move, love and
suffer, get married, have children, write books and poetry, enjoy music,
build business, fight wars, become ill and recover our health, become

neurotic and unhappy, and are restored to tranquillity and happiness . . . upon the energy supplied us either directly or indirectly by the sun. It is not strange that sun-worship became the central theme of man's earliest religion.

ENERGY AND MIND

Control of direction. It is obvious though that mere energy in itself cannot write poetry, fall in love, and conceive scientific theories. Something else is needed; something capable of exercising a control over the direction of the energy. Each of the 92 naturally existing atoms is a little package of stored energy; these combine in certain specific ways to form larger packages of stored energy called molecules, and each of the different types of molecules has a different point, at which, under the right conditions, it will release its energy. We take these various packages into our bodies as food, water, and air, but the *unconscious mind* determines the rate of its release in the process called metabolism. We know that this rate of release is profoundly affected by emotion, depression, and other mental states.

Definition of mind. Let us pause now to consider again the definition of mind offered on page 105 of this book: It was said that mind should be considered as a *stillness* rather than as an activity—stillness with the • ability to increase itself *qualitatively* in response either to stimulation from without, received over the nervous system, or to stimulation coming from within itself by means of the will.

Qualitative increase. When we say that the mind has the ability to increase itself *qualitatively,* we mean that it has the power within itself to increase the value of its function. This, however, does not imply an activity like the brightening of a light; it means the reverse. The qualitative value of a mirror, for instance, would be impaired were the hand which held it palsied; any movement would alter its focus and distort its images. We must regard the mind as being in the nature of a mirror having the inherent power to adjust its own focus.

REFLECTING PATTERNS

Stored memories. We mentioned the fact in Chapter Nine that every living thing is the product of its stored memories. It was mentioned also that the memories may be stored in somewhat the same manner as a tape recorder stores memories of the speaking voice, by the magnetic impulses set into motion by the voice vibrations arranging the molecules of the tape in certain patterns, which have the ability to reproduce the original stimuli under the right technical conditions. We might think of a photograph as a rearrangement of the molecules on the surface of a sensitized film, in this same light.

Colored glass. Almost everyone who has visited the desert has seen bottles and bits of glass colored to a beautiful violet by the action of the sun. Here also we have the phenomenon of a rearrangement of the glass molecules, so that certain rays of the sun are allowed to penetrate it while others are reflected back. When we acquire a suntan, the same thing happens in the layers of our skin.

Automatic answers. Now just as the action of the sun upon a piece of glass rearranges its molecules so as to screen out certain rays and reflect them while allowing others to pass through, the voices of our teachers and others, and the photographs of visual experiences taken by our eyes, become the stored data from which our subconscious makes its computations and these are reflected back into the environment also. Those which are needed for our own inner growth are like those which are allowed to pass into the internal structure of the glass to rearrange the molecules. The process of "rearranging the subconscious molecules" is what Pavlov named "conditioning."

The medium. In all the foregoing examples there had to be a medium for the vibrations and radiation of the environment to act upon—the tape of the recording machine, the sensitized film and the glass. The mind or psyche which inhabits the body of each living organism to co-ordinate its diverse activities into a functional unity must be the medium that is acted upon. We know that at physical death the mind or psyche withdraws from the protoplasm of the body, and that when this takes place, the protoplasm in itself immediately loses the power to respond in the former manner to the stimuli.

ENDLESS RECONSTRUCTION

Inherent power. Further evidence of the inherent power of the mind or psyche to *activate itself* by means of an indwelling will is found in the fact that the evolutionary process is one of endless reconstruction—the fin which swims becoming the limb which walks or the wing which flies; in the human brain fresh organization roofs over prior organization, and so on. Were the mind or psyche a physically limited structure like a metal tape, a sensitized film or a piece of glass, this type of reconstruction would be impossible.

Critical moment. In the evolution of each of the species then there must have arrived certain *critical moments in time,* precise instants at which new organizational patterns were set into motion, dividing moments in time at which the organization of the gills which breathed water commenced to reorganize as the lungs which breathed air, moments at which the organization of the fin which swam changed over to the organization of the leg which walked, moments in time at which the clumsy earth-bound reptile spread its rudimentary wings and soared into flight, moments in which, with no memories and no established precedents to guide it, the mind or psyche *activated itself, by its indwelling will,* into a new and original physical organization, which would make necessary a new and original orientation to nature.

Originality. It was only *after* these decisive original moments of willed change that the mind or psyche commenced to build up the memories of the new dimension entered into, which, in turn, would furnish the automatic responses to the new environment. Those species unable to meet the changing environment by arising to a willed change of structure and function perished and disappeared. A specialization that had outlived its usefulness became a fatal encumbrance.

THE HUMAN WILL

Quality of consciousness. Will is a quality of consciousness. The human being as the physical instrument of nature's consciousness is more richly endowed with this natural creative power than any of the other organisms, but it should be remembered that the consciousness we experience is definitely an attribute, a flower, on the *"stalk of the mind" that we never experience as such,* a mind or psyche which broods over the entire surface of our planet and which activates all living things in the same manner that the unconscious mind within a human body encompasses the activities of all of the billions of diverse living cells which make it up.

Unconscious repercussions. As the mind then is not a form of motion, but a stillness which directs motion by absorbing that which is essential to modifying its own inner structure and reflecting the remainder back into the environment as a "filterate" which may be resorbed, filtered, and reflected back again and again by numerous other "individual minds," thus bringing about an internal change in the mind-stuff of great masses of humanity, its reverberations would also seem to extend down to inanimate nature. For instance, in times of great emotional tensions and wars, there are almost always great natural disturbances, such as floods, earthquakes, and other cataclysms. Perhaps widely shared emotions affect the "metabolism" of nature as a whole.

Stillness vs. passivity. If anything said in the foregoing has given the impression that the mind is a state of *passivity,* that impression is wrong. A thing absolutely passive could have no will. In fact, it would have to be a state of absolute nothingness without any kind of content. Consciousness is a positive state of stillness in which lies hidden an inexhaustible reservoir of possibilities which may be tapped by the awakened will.

The ocean. The old Atavamsaka philosophers compared the detached or liberated consciousness to the immense expanse of a calm translucent ocean, which in stillness reflected all the shining bodies of heaven, but which when agitated lost its power to reflect and became the cradle of roaring, all-devouring storms. We would add to this picture that the consciousness can only be held in stillness and detachment by its own awakened will.

Freedom. Consciousness then is an expansive state of extremely alert awareness, in which we are detached from the events that we contemplate, a state in which we are free from doubt and undisturbed by the intellections and emotions of the subconscious, and in which we can see things as they actually are in all their natural relationships, a state in which the will may set original events into motion, a state which is the generator of all truly creative effort.

MOVING UPSTAIRS

Final causes at work. Today, the biologist writes: "We can only understand an organism if we regard it *as though* produced under the guidance of thought for an end, as a final cause at work." Now assuming that in a developing embryo there resides a mind or psyche, containing all the possibilities of the individual to be, the mind or psyche, faced by the step-by-step how's of the situation, would be helpless unless it already was possessed of a memory, a memory of the how's already mastered by repetition. We cannot imagine a mere aggregation of cells doing what they are doing for the first and only time, forming limb-buds and shaping these into arms and legs, in *preparation* for a form of locomotion the cells could know nothing about; we cannot imagine mere cells organizing on their own initiative, two separate eyeballs finished to a single standard, so that their two pictures could be read as one—and all this in complete darkness in preparation for the light of a new environment. At every stage in the development of the embryo, there is evidence that a phase of the mind directing the construction detaches itself from the processes and moves "upstairs," as it were, to initiate new construction on a higher level.

Detachment from memories. In short, long established memory patterns in the mind or psyche are activated by something akin to will; when these memories, acting in a manner somewhat similar to the colored glass of our illustration, are attuned to the energy scheme unfolding, they continue to accept and reject automatically, and the creative phase of mind is able to detach itself and attend to the next stage of operations.

Genetics. It is known that the physical characteristics of an organism are governed by genes. The genes are infinitesimally small units, about the size of giant protein molecules, and are carried in threads in the nucleus of the egg-cell. These multiply themselves many billions of times during the growth of the body. It is thought that these genes manufacture a ferment or enzyme, and then grow in it, once they are activated. We might then regard the genes as preparing the field in which memories are activated. That mind is a matrix of innumerable memory patterns, and the genes prepare the physical media in which only specific memory patterns may become operative; perhaps when there is a hitch in this process and two conflicting memory patterns become operative side by side, we have a deformity.

SUMMARY

TWO CONJOINING PRINCIPLES

What has been said in this chapter, then, may be summarized as follows: According to the theory of Creative Realism, the world as we know it, is the product of two conjoining principles.

First. There is the energy scheme by which our solar system moves and is moved and to which the energy of our sun contributes.

Second. There is motionless mind, which by absorbing certain quanta of energy as "memories" becomes modified, and so reflects back into the environment in increasingly creative patterns the balance of the energy which impinges upon it.

Third. If we can see the end of a thing, we know its cause. Consciousness is apparently the final cause which has activated evolution since life first appeared on earth, and drove it forward with resistless purpose despite all natural opposition from earthquakes, fires, floods, droughts, and other cataclysms.

Fourth. There is evidence that at certain periods of time in evolution, a certain quality or property of mind acted in contravention to all existing natural principles, as when the first organisms left the seas, and when the first organisms left the ground in flight, and so on. A quality not dependent upon the accumulated existent data of memories, but something entirely different in a qualitative sense from the automatically "absorbing and reflecting" phase of mind. We have called this quality of originality *will*.

WILL AND CONSCIOUSNESS

Interrelationship. Will is an inherent property of consciousness; without consciousness there can be no will and without will there can be no consciousness. By virtue of the will, consciousness has the ability to *increase itself qualitatively,* and the qualitative increase in consciousness is apparently the final cause of life.

Functional strata. It would seem that the will and the consciousness are only freed to operate on a higher level when each preceding stratum of memories has been integrated as a functional unity. In the realm of biology, for instance, those memories essential to the internal processes of the cell had to be accumulated and woven into a structural coherence before the next *original* step—the co-operative activities of a group of cells, working as a single organism—could be taken.

The human organism. We may follow this process in the development of the human embryo upward from the single cell, as more and more structures are organized and welded into functional coherence, until finally, after birth, still higher control centers are organized, and connected up with each other and with the developing supercontrol center—the subconscious mind. With this the infant gains the ability to accumulate memories as an *individual,* memories which may be in some measure different from those accumulated by any other individual. As he becomes more conscious, he may decide upon which types of memories he shall accumulate in order to modify his mind—those pertaining to engineering, medicine, or any of the other arts, sciences, or trades. He will then attend a school or college where such memories are supplied, and expose himself to them. In due course his mind becomes modified by the absorption of these memories and is able to reflect back creatively into his environment, along the lines of his chosen work, the balance of the energy which comes to him.

SUBCONSCIOUS

Data storage. His subconscious mind, his analogue computer, is the specialized segment of mind in which these memories are stored as data, and the answers furnished to outer problems by his subconscious represent the "reflected back energy." The memories within his subconscious, however, must have a structural coherence, first, in order to operate efficiently, and, secondly, in order to release the consciousness with its will into a still higher field of creation.

Assimilation. Unless the data stored in his subconscious mind is integrated into a functional coherence, there is conflict, with consequent distortion of the product. The genius of Freud first recognized this fact, and psychoanalysis is the art by which he hoped such conflicts might be removed. When the conflict is resolved, Freud thought that the "unconscious mind" would be released to do creative work. Creative Realism holds that the *consciousness* may be so released from its subconscious involvement, but that it can only increase itself qualitatively and functionally, even when release by analysis has been made possible, through the effort of its own will.

CENTRAL PHILOSOPHY

Basic framework necessary. No complete subconscious integration is possible unless all elements are drawn within a basic framework of a satisfactory philosophy of life as a whole. In times past religion fulfilled this basic need, as it still does for many, but with the growth of materialism due to the rapid development and the spectacular achievements of physical science, the "conditioning memories" supplied in the classroom and those supplied in the churches are somewhat mutually exclusive, and the influence of religion as a basic integrating philosophy has declined.

FREUD AND CREATIVE REALISM

Sex. Freud held that sex was the prime motivating force in life, that repressing and distorting the impulses arising from the sexual instinct was the cause of most of our mental aberrations. Creative Realism holds that a "wish"—suppressed or otherwise—is the expression of a need, and that needs are based upon the requirements of the organism. The physical organism of a narcotics addict may *need,* due to a semipermanent perversion of function caused by repeated dosages of the narcotic, a continuing supply of the narcotic in order to maintain the perverted functional equilibrium so acquired. In this same sense, an overproduction of a hormone in response to daydreaming builds up a specific addiction, which creates the "wish." The hormone may be testosteron, in the case of sex, or it may be adrenalin in the case of the individual who seizes every opportunity to fly into a rage, or it may be some other hormone to which an addiction has been established. But in every case, Creative Realism holds that the addiction is sensation producing, or sensation eliminating, and that this craving for sensation is the real villain in the piece. With the preceding facts in mind then, we shall in the chapter which follows consider some means of correction.

CHAPTER 14

Psyche and Soma

In the pigeon suffering from beri-beri runs dramatic improvement of the impaired respiratory process of the brain, along with dramatic relief of its other symptoms by vitamin B_1.

R. A. PETERS

LIBERATING THE CONSCIOUSNESS

The aim. If we consider the aim of the present study to be the liberation of the consciousness and its will, we must take into consideration all of the factors which have a bearing upon mental action, factors which may distort our mental reflections, though they exist apart from the mind.

Energy. The sun's energy comes to us transformed into foods, water, air, drugs, and so on, which are again transformed—by the memory patterns—within our bodies in a long series of delicately balanced steps into the types of caloric and bioelectrical energy used by the human organism. These steps are carried out by means of complex chemical particles called "enzymes," of which more than two hundred have been identified. These act as catalysts which produce chemical reactions, without becoming altered by the reaction themselves.

Hormones. A hormone is a secretion of an internal gland, which has the property of stimulating specific areas of vital and functional activity. Thus when the production of a given hormone is overstimulated by being repeatedly triggered through emotional daydreams, those enzymes involved in the production of the hormone are under an added stress. If the capacity to produce them is exceeded, often the gland goes "into reverse" and stops functioning, as in Addison's disease, when the adrenals go on strike; diabetes, when the pancreas take a permanent holiday; and sexual impotence, when the reproductive glands grow weary.

Perhaps not mental. In many of these cases, however, the cause of the trouble is not mental, but mental pathology may be the result of a deficiency state. For instance, some of the vitamins act as enzymes in the body, while still others act as co-enzymes—that is to say, they are partners of the enzymes, as it were, and must be present in the body for the enzymes to be able to do their work effectively. Anyone who has observed the mentally deranged victim of pellagra, or the profound depressive condition of the beri-beri sufferer, and realizes that a dramatic cure can be obtained by the administration of a few of the right vitamins, can realize fully the relationship between nutritional deficiency states and the neuroses and psychoses.

Vitamins. Reports of the spectacular results obtained by researchers together with the commercial exploitation of these wonderful substances, the making of exaggerated claims, the packaging of them in chemically unsuitable vehicles, and combining them in "shotgun dosages" in single capsules, which probably renders some or all of these inert through the exchange of ions, encourages many people to try them. In many instances, the results have been disappointing; nevertheless, their vital importance to the living process is unquestionable.

Deficiency states. Farming on the same ground year after year without crop rotation depletes the soil of certain of the more subtle elements not replacable by commercial fertilizers. Then due to our modern methods of milling, canning and processing and cooking, even the vitamin-poor cereals and vegetables grown on the depleted ground are deprived of a large proportion of these chemically unstable particles. Consequently, it is probable that the average human intake of these vitally important substances today falls far short of that of our grandfathers, and still farther short of that of primitive man living off wild berries, roots, and wild meat.

INSTINCTIVE APPETITE

Hunger. Hunger is an instinctive demand, and the lower animals are led by their instinctive centers to seek the particular foods their bodies need from hour to hour. We have all noticed cats and dogs upon occasion searching patiently through the grass or along the hedges for a particular herb, which they will eat. Through seasoning and the complexities of good cooking, modern man has lost the guidance of his instinctive center in this respect, but its needs are expressed through the nervous system nevertheless. They are expressed as vague and uncrystallized yearnings or wishing.

Hunger dream. The "hunger dream" in which starving people dream that they are seated before tables loaded with luscious foods, or the smoker's dream (when deprived of tobacco) of smoking, is a phenomenon often discussed by psychologists and others.

Satisfaction. Freud points out that the function of the dream is often to still a wish arising from the organism by pretending that it has been met and thus preserving sleep. We would go further than this and say that the dream indicates a *need* of the organism, and that this need is not removed by the dream, but merely prevented from disturbing the arousal center for the time being. Thus, the need expressed by the dream will continue to be a disturbing factor in the subconscious until it is satisfied.

Vitamin hunger. Hunger for food or for sexual satisfaction can produce typical and unmistakable dreams, but what about vitamin hunger? The amounts of vitamins contained in the various foods per pound weight are so infinitesimal that specific dreams based upon the hunger for specific vitamins would hardly be possible. Again the physiological effects of a vitamin deficiency are so subtle and diffused that they are almost impossible to find by means of our present techniques. It is thought that vitamin deficiency causes what is known as "biochemical lesions" within the cells themselves, and that these lesions interfere with the cell's normal biochemical activities. Thus we might expect the dreams arising from vitamin deficiencies to be vague and troubled, and we might expect that they would express themselves by means of any visual symbols stored in the brain cells *in terms of frustrations.*

Waking repercussions. We might expect that the needs expressed by such confused and troubled dreams would be expressed in the waking state in terms of irritability, depression, nervousness, fear, and forgetfulness; and in known vitamin deficiency cases, this is exactly what we find.

Transference. We have mentioned the wrong work of the control centers before, but here it is pointed out that this wrong work is often a result of deficiencies. The instinctive center, let us say, cannot satisfy an existing need within its domain, and so the subconscious calls upon the emotional center for a "hormonic stimulation" to speed up the fading work of the cells affected by the deficiency; the emotion releases hormones from the pituitary, which trigger the release of hormones from the adrenals, pancreas, thyroid, and gonads, and the fading cells are temporarily stimulated into faster action. The stimulation of the sex glands, however, triggers a corresponding psychological "desire-state"; or the moving center may be stimulated, with resulting restless pacing and gesticulations accompanied by a psychological state of irritation and impatience; the intellectual center may be set in motion, and it may rationalize the trouble as being due to coffee or to something else; and so it goes.

TWO PRINCIPLES

Mind and energy. It is emphasized again that life is the result of two conjoining principles—mind and energy, or matter—and that each principle has a modifying effect upon the other. While it is obviously true that daydreams are usually based upon the fact that they produce sensations, and that the sensations are the result of the daydream's triggering an overproduction of hormones, the reverse of this is also true. A state of vitamin deficiency can exert a demand upon the organism for continual hormonic stimulation far in excess of the normal order of things, and this in turn can create an abnormal psychology. It might be added that emotional states can create a vitamin deficiency, even as a vitamin deficiency can create emotional states.

Nutritionists. Nutrition is a new science. While it has made astonishing progress during its short life span, the extra training it requires in biochemistry, cytopathology, and kindred subjects, at the same time offering less financial returns than might be expected from the other specialities, has apparently discouraged most medical students from entering this field.

The check-up. Consequently, as few practicing physicians have either the time available, the specialized knowledge necessary, and the special equipment at hand to enable them to offer a diagnosis of preclinical avitaminoses, the reader may have difficulty in getting a proper check-up on his nutritional status. As it is always desirable to commence a course of these vitamins with a series of massive injections of the leading ones while taking others of the same series orally, your physician, should he agree with the facts set forth in this chapter, may help you should you have any of the symptoms referred to. The day will undoubtedly come when the psychiatrist and the nutritionist will join forces in the assault on psychosomatic disease, and the results are likely to be really spectacular.

Interaction. From the subconscious mind organized mental states, such as plans, daydreams, and sleeping dreams, extend an influence downward through the fine network of nerves which make up the "reticular" system to every cell group, gland, organ, and structure in the body. On the other hand, every cell group, gland, organ, and structure gives off impulses which are conducted back to the subconscious mind through the comparatively large "A" fibers.

Computations. The impulses coming from within are organized into stimulus images at certain centers, and these stimulus images become the *internal data* which the subconscious must use, together with the external data stored in the brain cells after arriving from the outside over the sensory nerves, in making its computations. Thus, so far as the subconscious is concerned, the intellectual possibility must also be possible in terms of the physical machine. Otherwise, we become disinterested in the possibility. We say: "Yes, maybe it *is* possible, but not for us." Yet we find it difficult to explain just why it should not be possible for us.

Interpretations. The possibilities of the physical machine are governed by the impulses gathered from the various glands, organs, joints, muscle fibers, and so on, and sent to the subconscious mind where these—as stimuli images—are interpreted. These interpretations are then sent to the proper centers and become the criteria by which the activities pertaining to the centers are regulated automatically. If similar impulses continue to arise over a period of time, and specific interpretations are repeatedly sent to a certain center, it becomes a "fixed" interpretive system, through which all orders received from the subconscious are translated for execution.

Example. An example of this is the individual with a knee injury which causes a limp. Owing to the injury, it is difficult to step down or to go up stairs except sideways. Long after the injury is healed and the knee restored to full function, the injured man will catch himself favoring the leg by going sideways up stairs and stepping slowly and cautiously off a sidewalk. The interpretative pattern laid down in the moving center at the time of the injury is still to some degree operative. The moving center tells the leg: "Be careful. You cannot do that safely."

False interpretations. While living in his natural state, a high degree of objectivity was forced upon man. Like any other animal his survival depended upon his alertness, and so interpretive patterns such as the above were quickly erased and the normal pattern restored when the need of them no longer existed; but with introspective, civilized man, the recipient of special consideration and sympathy because of an injury, the story is quite different. Most of us function largely on false and outworn interpretations. These are the self-limiting factors which not only determine our intellectual interests, but which prematurely age us by rendering our physical functions less and less able to cope with the give and take of civilized living. Thus, when considering the effects of vitamin deficiency states, we must be careful also to consider the symptoms—both mental and physical—produced by these outworn interpretive patterns.

THREE HORSEMEN

In this writer's experience, the three factors outlined in this chapter —(1) vitamin deficiency states, (2) hormone addiction and daydreaming, and (3) limiting and false interpretations—are present in every functional disease and state of unwellness. Perhaps, by destroying the natural resistance of the organism, they are also a predisposing factor in infectious disease.

But we might go much further and say that these "three horsemen" ride some part of the way at least in each of our lives, and all of the way in the lives of the hungry hordes of the East, where illiteracy and hunger make their rule absolute.

SELF-REMEMBERING

Changing your perspective. By the persistent practice of "self-remembering," and by working hard at the other exercises given previously in this book, you will be withdrawing the consciousness which is the "cement" of these useless false interpretative patterns; you will be withdrawing your consciousness also from its "land of dreams" in the subconscious and thus be able to effect greater efficiency of that harassed computing machine. Your doctor will help you correct any prevailing deficiency condition, and the changed perspective incidental to all this will speak for itself as to the correctness of the theory. In the chapter which follows a method for helping yourself still more will be discussed.

CHAPTER 15

Black Magic

From "I am He" I mounted to where is no "to" and I perfumed
existence by my returning.

Ibnu 'I-Farid

THE MACHINE

Mind and energy. In the preceding chapter a concept was offered
of the human organism as a machine, formed of two conjoining principles—mind and energy—and it was pointed out that the two principles
act upon each other; in short, they are mutually conditioning principles.
Therefore, to achieve the greatest possible degree of functional harmony
or health within the organism we must give equal consideration to both
of the principles.

Not mechanical. With the achievement of a degree of functional harmony in the *mechanical* co-relationships of the two principles, it becomes
easier to release or liberate the third principle of consciousness-will,
which is nonmechanical, original and creative. When integrated as an
independent mental principle, the possibilities of consciousness seem
almost limitless. It is apparently able to superimpose at will, for at least
short periods, new behavior patterns over the ancient, functional, "memory patterns" which regulate the structure and functions of the living
body.

Separation. When the conscious-will is separated from the subconscious, either as the result of the personal attainment of consciousness or
as a result of complete unconsciousness induced by hypnosis, the human
organism may be directed to perform many feats impossible to it while

in the usual state—feats similar in nature to those recorded in the Bible as "miracles," feats not explainable by the laws of physics nor the laws known to any branch of the physical sciences.

THE WATERSPOUT

Common phenomenon. Waterspouts are a common phenomenon. A funnel-shaped column of cloud-filled wind dips downward to the ocean from an ordinary cumulus or cumulo-nimbus cloud and whirls a column of water from the ocean upward; then the column, remaining in suspension, moves across the ocean at the pace of the cloud.

Two principles. In the waterspout we have an illustration of a temporary union of two different elements producing a phenomenon which neither of the elements—air current or water—could possibly produce alone. Now let us consider the human organism as being similar in principle—a temporary union of mind and physical energy. Even as the air and the water forming the waterspout obey different laws of nature ordinarily, and one supports birds while the other nurtures fishes, so mind and matter (the matter incorporated in the human body temporarily) obey different sets of laws. We have learned something of the physical laws, because physical phenomena are subject to physical measurement. We have learned little or nothing about the laws of mind.

Difficulties. We have learned practically nothing about mind because we ourselves are part of that which we would explore. Even as our bodies and brains are in their material aspect but differently organized aggregations of the same elemental particles which form the distant stars and the dust clouds of interstellar space, our minds also perhaps are but localized organizations of that awesome mind which set the stars in the infinite and ordained their courses.

THE RELATIVE AND THE ABSOLUTE

Phenomena. Laws belong to the relative, material universe, but the absolute could not be bound by laws other than its own will. Thus, mind, when acting in conjunction with the energy-concept of the material world, modifies its possibilities to conform more or less to the laws of physics. Upon occasion, however, we encounter phenomena in which apparently the laws of physics have been either circumvented or superseded.

Removal of limitations. This type of phenomenon is not confined to nature but occurs during the course of human events. For instance, take the case of man who as a result of brain injuries accidentally comes into possession of unusual powers ordinarily acquired only by long and persistent disciplines. Such an instance is the recently reported case of the Hollander, Peter Hurkos, a house painter, who, after a fall from a ladder with consequent severe concussion of the brain, found himself in possession of powers which enable him to diagnose obscure illnesses in others; to solve crimes which have baffled the police; to conceive instantly complex chemical formulas, although untrained in chemistry; to detect hidden flaws deep down in complicated machinery, although untrained in engineering or mechanics; and so on.

"Super-sleuth." It was reported in a magazine article that Peter Hurkos receives a huge retaining fee as a consultant to Phillips and Company, one of the world's largest radio, television, and electronics manufacturers. It is said also that Hurkos is retained by the police departments of various European countries as a consultant, and that he is the man who led Scotland Yard to the recovery of the famous "stone of Scone" when it was stolen recently from Westminster Abbey.

"Hadad." In his outstanding book, *My Six Convicts* (Rinehart and Company, 1951), Donald Powell Wilson tells of his experiences during three years as a research psychologist at Leavenworth Penitentiary. One chapter tells of a convict named "Hadad" who apparently committed suicide by hanging himself in his cell. After being cut down, the body was examined by the prison physician and the man pronounced dead. It was thought that death must have occurred several hours earlier. The physician ordered the body put on ice.

Resurrection. Some days later three doctors gathered in the prison morgue to perform an autopsy on the body, but when the first incision was about to be made, the "body" sat up and said that "he would rather they didn't." As a demonstration after this, the "ex-corpse" delayed the seizures of all the patients in a ward filled with deteriorated epileptics, for three days, and he claimed to have accomplished that tremendous feat telepathically. Ordinarily, no known drug can cause a three-day remission of seizures in such cases.

POSSIBILITIES

Evidence. In citing the foregoing two cases at this time, the purpose is to submit facts which have already been widely publicized as evidence that the mind contains possibilities far beyond those accepted at present by our Western science. Obviously, Peter Hurkos seemed to possess a certain degree of "mental omniscience" to be able to describe the exact details of a crime and to give an exact description of each of the participants, though the crime had been committed a week or more earlier.

Superimposed patterns. In the case of "Hadad," apparently he had achieved by training a separation of his will and consciousness from their subconscious entanglement, and had thereby gained an enormous degree of control over his physical body. Not only that but his freed consciousness apparently possessed the power to temporarily re-establish a pattern of normal functional behavior on the deteriorated brains of the epileptics—a pattern which lasted for three full days.

STIGMA OF "MAGIC"

Removing the barriers. Science has no explanation at present for these types of phenomena; but a number of independent investigators in different countries—men such as W. Grey Walter of the Burden Neurological Institute of England, Penfield of the Montreal Neurological Clinic, and Rhine of Duke University, North Carolina, and others, are gradually removing the barriers imposed by the stigma of the word "magic" which has long stood in the way of an explanation. After a lapse of half a century or more, hypnosis has become an essential tool of psychiatry, for under its influence we are able to see how wide and how deep is the influence of the mind over all organs and all functions of the body.

The emotions and cancer. Recently it was reported in "Science News Letter" that Drs. West, Blumberg, and Ellis, in charge of the Tumor Clinic of the Veterans Hospital in Southern California, had established a definite correlation between the personality patterns of cancer patients with the relative rapidity or slowness of cancer progression in individual patients. Drs. Thomas F. Dougherty and Jules A. Frank of the University of Utah have identified a mysterious substance "X" which seems to be produced when mental or physical stress takes hold of a human being or an animal and that this has an influence on the course of many diseases. It seems to have a bearing on the fatal disease leukemia, as well as on arthritis, tuberculosis, and cancer.

The key? As pointed out by Grey Walter, in hypnosis, the hypnotist gains access to the inner workings of the "learning mechanism" without diverting or distorting the basic properties of brain function. Personality patterns are *learned* patterns, and therefore may be modified by learning.

PSYCHOLOGY

Definition. Psychology then might be defined as the study of the mind's action while it is associated with the "physical waterspout" or body—in short, the study of the manner in which the mind acts in conjunction with physical energy produced by the body within the body.

Limitations. It should be clear by now though that the action of the "air currents" trapped within a "waterspout" would by no means cover the field of its possibilities. The air current would be associated with the cloud brought into contact with the ocean by the waterspout.

Wider horizons. Floating above the ocean at an altitude of several hundred feet, were this cloud conscious, let us say, it would have a much wider perspective than would that portion of itself trapped within the waterspout and whirling in a cycle of furious activity. But again, the moisture-laden cloud in itself is not pure air, but a mixture of water-vapor and air, much less concentrated than the mixture within the waterspout—a sort of "astral-body" of the waterspout as it were.

Perspectives unlimited. Now that portion of the air making up the cloud in itself is a part of the atmosphere which embraces the entire earth, and so its perspective would be practically unlimited. Were it conscious, it would in its lower aspect know everything taking place on the surface of the earth, while with its upper surface it would be conscious of all taking place in the vast reaches of the heavens.

Analogy. We might conclude the above analogy by imagining that that portion of the waterspout meeting the surface of the water would contain more water and so would be more subject to the limitations of water than would be that portion uniting with the cloud. We might imagine then a zone extending downward a short distance from the cloud as comprising a "subconscious mind," and below this, we might imagine the air, tightly concerned with the tumultuous activity of the waterspout only, as being the "unconscious mind." We can imagine the cloud itself as the free human consciousness, a creation of the world atmosphere (consciousness) of which it remains a specialized part and with which it is in consonance.

SCIENCE OF MIND

Origins. A "miracle" is defined as "a happening outside of the *known* processes of natural law," and such miracles produced by mental means have been recorded in the earliest annals of human history, even as they occasionally continue to make the headlines today. Before the birth of physical science, a rudimentary science of mind existed. The priesthood of ancient Egypt called this science "magic," and it included techniques of healing, the casting of spells, and predicting or prophesying.

Moses. Moses, we know, learned his magic from the Egyptians, and every great leader whose life significantly contributed to the enlightenment and development of the human race possessed some knowledge of this science. For scores of centuries the holy men of India and Tibet have been performing "miracles" by their techniques, and healings by the "word of a Yogi" (one who has achieved union) are common even today. Hippocrates used "magnetic passes" of his hands to cure disease. And he said: "It is thus known to the learned that health may be impressed on the sick by certain movements and by contacts, just as some diseases may be communicated from one another."

Aesculapius. Aesculapius was capable of allaying pain by breathing on the site affected, and by passes of his hands would throw patients into a long and refreshing sleep. This evidence from the past has never been invalidated by modern science. The "miracles" performed by Jesus are as unexplainable by the present conceptual schemes of physical science as are the lesser "miracles" performed by Peter Hurkos or Hadad. Reason is not "reasonable" when it rebels at an idea and rejects evidence because that idea and evidence lie outside the realm of intellectual and sensory perceptions to prove according to current dogmas.

NARCISSISM

Psychoanalytical terminology. According to Greek mythology, Narcissus was a beautiful youth who fell in love with his own reflection in a fountain. He pined away in desire for it and so lost his humanity and was changed into a lower order of thing—the narcissus—which had beauty but no soul capable of beholding it. Narcissism in psychoanalytical terminology means self-love or selfishness in the deepest meaning of the word.

Introspection. Everyone who lives by introspection among his self-created subconscious fantasies, and thus his own reflection in the "inner fountain," is to a greater or lesser degree narcissistic. This state of being prevails until a greater love beyond himself leads his attention away from his own reflection. Narcissism or self-love has often perverted the use of mental power in the past. Even Jesus had to fight a forty-day-long battle against His lower nature which tried to persuade Him to use the powers He had gained control over for His own personal glorification. But the greater love prevailed.

Power used by all. Now we all unconsciously use this extrasensory mind power to some extent every day. The rooting on the football field or at the arena, the chanting in unison at the political convention by the supporters of a candidate, the corn-dance ritual of Mexican Indians, and the rain-dance of the Hopi Indians of the American Southwest, and all such demonstrations, are crude and instinctive ways of attempting to influence the higher phase of mind into channeling a course of events in accord with the desires of those participating. A solemn church service is essentially the same type of phenomenon.

"Black magic." The Narcissistic individual who sends impulses of hatred unconsciously in the direction of another who stands barring the way to the fulfillment of a selfish desire is instinctively practicing "black magic," as it is called. Black magic is the name given, in ancient days, to the destructive and selfish application of extrasensory mind power. Even as today physical science is devoting much of its effort to producing a "science of slaughter" by which millions of lives may be snuffed out in the twinkling of an eye, so in olden times a mental science of black magic was developed by means of which single individuals could be influenced to act contrary to their own wills.

"Wages of sin." Fortunately, though, the practice of black magic brought its own penalty upon the practitioner. A fission was created between the top of the figurative "waterspout" and the "cloud," and the "cloud" sealed itself off from the nefarious activities, the "water" with its entrapped portion of air fell back to the "sea" from whence it had emerged, and the "soul" was dissipated.

"LOVE YE ONE ANOTHER"

Basic law. In nature, ignorance of the law does not excuse a violation of it. The man who unconsciously sends impulses of hatred, envy, and other emotions born of self-love in the direction of others is penalized for the practice of black magic just as is the trained and deliberate practitioner of it. That is why Jesus laid such very great stress upon the necessity of overcoming all the narcissistic or selfishly inspired emotions. His Sermon on the Mount is a classic, considered as a text to be followed preceding and during the study of mental science.

The one sure way. It was said: "What profiteth a man though he gain the whole world but lose his soul?" and that still holds good. The longest life of a waterspout is very brief, measured against the endless span of the atmosphere. In common sense it should be the aim of the atmosphere trapped within the waterspout to rejoin its cloud, to enrich it with its experience to the greater enjoyment of the wider horizons, and no amount of temporary extra power within the waterspout would compensate for the loss of this. The one sure way in which to preserve this heritage of freedom is by the attainment of consciousness, and through consciousness, the infinitely greater love for our resplendent creative source than for our little physical selves whirling in their respective "waterspouts." Remember this constantly when practicing the techniques given in the chapters that follow.

CHAPTER 16

Images as Building Blocks

Neither shall they say, Lo here! or, lo there! for, behold, the Kingdom of God is within you.

ST. LUKE, 17:21

THE IMAGE

Mystery. One of the most profound mysteries of life is the ability of the fertilized egg-cell to reproduce itself and to build hereditary images of its parents. The explanations offered of how this is achieved mechanically rather enhances the mystery. The mystery of the objectified image in the building called the Taj Mahal is not explained away, for instance, by pointing out that the building is just an assembly of marble blocks, laid according to the principles of mathematics. The *image* conceived by the mind of the architect is the reality, and the blocks of marble were simply used to give this image concrete form and substance.

"Accident." We cannot imagine any kind of creation taking place without an image of the thing to be directing its organization. A heap of marble blocks could never on their own become a Taj Mahal. Thus, a creation by "accident" would be well-nigh incredible.

Memory-images. It was explained in Chapter Ten how memory-images are formed and stored in the cells of our brains and nervous systems. From the swarms of electrical impulses streaming over our sensory nerves continuously certain of them are abstracted and organized into images to be stored, while the remainder are unheeded.

Meanings. As each of these memory-images is formed, it is given a meaning in terms of the particular personality storing it. It then becomes a part of the mental "working-capital" of that individual; thus, each

133

stored memory-image is a *meaningful image* and is related meaningfully to the larger image we have called the "false personality."

FALSE PERSONALITY

Origins. The false personality is the creature of lies and fantasies. Its formation commences with one-year-old Johnny's being told solemnly by his parents that he is a *big* boy because he drank all of his milk, that he is a *bad* boy because he pulled the cat's tail, and so on. These assessments of *what he is* are accepted by a child's subconscious according to the law of suggestion, and are added to from hour to hour, and from day to day, by his own dreams and fantasies, triggered by stories of animals which talk, "wolves which dress in grandma's clothes after gorging on the body of the old lady," by wild and bloody movies, in which the child identifies himself with a swashbuckling moron whose trusty six-gun never seems to run out of ammunition, by radio stories of precocious adventurers who do incredible things, and so on.

Modification. This twisted and fantastic personality image, to which all the memory-images become related, is modified somewhat as the child grows older by bitter experience. The fantastic false-personality image does not hold up in the acid test of coping with the real environment; its lies become modified and more rational. For the sake of "politeness," it learns to gush over those whom it secretly despises, to become perhaps a smug hypocrite with a carefully camouflaged exterior, behind which it still dreams of "desperate deeds of derring-do," finding in these fantasies the fulfillment denied it in reality.

The environment. The organization of such false personalities, of course, is unavoidable under present circumstances. The false personality is the product of our whole environment, and we cannot change that overnight. Consequently, the foregoing should not be regarded as a criticism of humanity for doing something it might have avoided— the false personality is an unavoidable phenomenon—but it is a *fact to be coped with* in the liberation of the consciousness.

STABILIZED MEMORY-SYSTEMS

Functional systems. Stored memory-images become functional units. When they are organized into networks or complexes, they become functional systems. In essence the fertilized egg-cell is a compressed complex of memory-images, all related to the image of the person to be. As the embryo commences to grow, these compressed images become objectified as each builds its little "Taj Mahal," as it were. Within the egg-cell, however, this complex of memory-images has been stabilized through hundreds of thousands of years of facing the acid test of coping with the realities of the environment. All of those images which were distorted and unrelated to reality have been eliminated from the associated complex of images which forms the unconscious mind of the embryo.

Semistability. The ultrastability of the unconscious mind, after it has reached a certain point in its expansion within the embryo, permits the organization of six "subsystems"—the six control centers, which are only semistable and flexible. To acquire stability these semistable systems must incorporate new memory-images from the environment with those inherited from the unconscious mind. In short, they must be "educated."

The subconscious. When the six control centers have become more stabilized by the child's learning to walk, to talk, to eat, to assimilate unfamiliar foods, and so on, there is a co-incidental development of the "super" semistabilized system which co-ordinates the functions of the six control centers with situations arising in the outer environment. To be able to assess these situations, it is organized after the fashion of a natural analogue computer whose "feedback" or summations trigger the indicated responses in the six control centers.

Stages. In each stage of the embryo's development, a degree of functional stability must be secured before a new pattern-image awakens to take over the organization of the next phase. These ancient steps in stability are evidenced by the evolutionary "recapitulation" of the embryo referred to in an early chapter.

Warped growth. The law of life is evolution—growth. Due to the impelling power of mind within every living organism, it must either push onward, or, like the great reptiles of ancient time, drop out. Only reality has a survival value, and a false personality, warped by fantasies and lies at its beginnings, can only grow by adding more fantasies and lies. Gradually, the selections made from the arriving stream of stimuli and the organization of these into memory-images become governed by the inflating false personality, and then the individual has great difficulty in accepting, or even considering, many realities, because these are unassimilable into the false structure.

Release. Not only is the survival value of the false personality zero, but it is quite impossible for it to achieve the degree of stability within the subconscious that is necessary to the release of the next higher image —the image of consciousness. So most of us pass through our whole life cycle, trapped in our false personalities, presenting a thin shell of pretense to the outer world and tortured by the fantastic stewpot of our subconscious within.

REFLECTION

Inexhaustible reservoir of possibilities. In Chapter Thirteen it was said that mind is not a form of motion but a stillness that modifies its own structure by absorbing part of the energy which comes to it while reflecting the remainder back creatively into the environment. That energy which is absorbed, then, is energy organized by mind into images, and that which is reflected back is reflected back from an image, even as an image is reflected by an architect's mind to become a building.

Reinterpretation. The problem of the psychiatrist is to purge his patient's subconscious of the unrealistic interpretations attached to images formed during unhappy emotional experiences in the past. He does this by regressing his patient in time, step by step, until he can recall the earliest images; then the psychiatrist assists the patient to reinterpret these on a basis of reality. Thus, the ego (false personality) is strengthened to the point where it is better able to cope with the realities of the environment.

The Rorschach Test. In the Rorschach ink-blot test, a spot of ink is dropped upon a sheet of paper, and the paper is then folded and the other half pressed down so that a large irregular blot is formed. The patient is then asked to give a meaningful interpretation of this blot; in short, his mind takes this meaningless image and adds a meaning to it in the way it does with all images. By studying the patient's interpretations of a series of these ink-blots, the psychiatrist is helped to an understanding of the basic orientation of the patient's interpretive mechanism. If it is oriented to reality and to creation, the interpretations indicate this, and, if oriented to fantasy and unreality, the interpretations indicate this fact also.

The T.A.T. In the Thematic Apperception Test the patient is given a set of twenty cards, nineteen of which bear pictures indicating ambiguous situations and the remaining single card blank. The patient is asked to write a story about each of the cards, and these stories are studied by the psychiatrist. All people tend to interpret an ambiguous human situation in the light of their own past interpretations of similar situations, and so his invented characters in the stories often reveal facets of his own false personality which would be difficult to bring to light under direct examination.

IMAGES AS BUILDING BLOCKS

Emphasis. The foregoing techniques of psychiatry are briefly discussed because they emphasize the fundamental importance of the image as the building block of the human personality. If we examine a picture printed in a newspaper, we can see that the print contains a screen, the lightness and darkness of various parts of the picture being produced by the density of dots in the respective areas. If we view the picture at a distance we cannot see these individual dots, for they all coalesce into the single impression of the picture. We can imagine the human personality as being a multidimensional picture also made up of "dots," but that if we examine these dots closely, we shall see that each is a separate meaningful image, though at a distance they all coalesce into a single impression. If too many of the wrong kind of dots appear in a single area, they distort the whole picture.

The "ego." Now the "ego," as meant by the psychologist, is the individuality or personality of the self-conscious subject, the entity which resists, on the one hand, the threats of the "superego" and, on the other hand, the impulses of the "id" (combined control centers). Creative Realism holds that unless an individual is functioning in the conscious, self-remembering state, he cannot be truly "self-conscious." Obviously, if he is not aware of himself, he *cannot* be self-conscious. Therefore Creative Realism holds that what the psychologists call "self-consciousness" is the introverted and fractionated consciousness entangled in the subconsciousness and forming a false personality. This false personality has acquired a code of morals and a standard of behavior by rote or conditioning, standards not necessarily based upon reality but upon the whims and fantasies of others.

The "superego." The "superego," as defined by psychology, is the "unconscious inhibitory morality of the mind, which criticizes the ego

and condemns the unworthy impulses of the id (emotional centers)."
Creative Realism holds that this so-called superego is the overshadowed
and shackled true personality—the bearer of conscious-will—and that the
salvation of the individual is dependent upon unshackling it and placing
it in supreme command of all the lower and mechanical attributes of
the mental organization.

"Salvation." In almost everyone's mind there is a single image which
has been interpreted by the individual as a symbol of the highest qualities attainable by man in his present form. To Christians, this symbol,
of course, is Jesus. To most Jews, perhaps, it is Moses, the law-giver.
Mohammedans have their prophet Mohammed as a symbol, while in
the Far East, many hold as a symbol one of the aspects of Brahma, the
creator, or Gotama Buddha. By deep concentration and meditation, and
by identifying themselves with the qualities of their interpretations (of
one or the other of these symbolic-images), "salvation" has been attained
by countless thousands of people.

Liberation. What happens in such cases is this: The real personality
—the superego, if you wish—the only element of the entire human psyche
that is capable of developing the higher qualities yearned for, bursts its
shackles by the power of its own awakened will and takes over a measure of *conscious* control, with the result that there is an immediate
transformation of the entire personality, and life for that individual
begins anew. Such is the power of the image.

COMPLICATIONS

Mechanical conditioning. Due to the long period of mechanical conditioning made necessary by our modern technological society, and
to the increasing number of fractional adjustments incidental to our
crowded and hustling living conditions, our false personalities have lost
their swaggering "let's pretend" simplicity, and have become tightly
organized complexes of images, related to larger images which have no
survival value—images for the most part based upon material achievement alone, often not even based upon *constant* images of material
achievement, but upon images born of fantasy, of sensation-producing
delights. Thus, religion finds it much more difficult to assist the individual toward his own liberation than was formerly the case. The false

personality has created its own antidote to religion in an attitude of smug and benign tolerance, to be donned once a week.

Image-forming center. From the foregoing, it should be clear that control of the image-forming center (the imagination), together with the interpretive faculty which endows our images with meanings, is a vital first step in achieving the liberation of our consciousness.

The interpreter. Not only is the imagination the image-forming faculty, but it is also the interpreter of the images. In pain, for instance, an impulse traveling over the "A" nerve fibers from the site of an injury arrives in the brain; instantly, under ordinary circumstances, it is interpreted as a "broken toenail," a "twisted ankle," or something else, by the imagination, which then triggers the appropriate control center into whatever action is necessary to prevent further injury to the affected part. Thus, the weight of the body is instantly balanced in a different way to remove stress from the injured part, and we "limp" in the case of a foot or leg injury.

Detachment. When the imagination is temporarily detached from its function of interpretation, through being intensely concentrated elsewhere, as in the case of a soldier in battle, or a man in an automobile accident, a considerable injury may be sustained without a person's becoming immediately aware of it. There is no immediate interpretation of the stimulus, and, when some time later the imagination is freed to make an interpretation, the response triggered in the control centers may be so violent that the patient goes into a condition of "shock." When the imagination is detached from its function as interpreter of stimuli, by means of an anaesthetic, extensive surgery can be performed without any awareness of what is going on on the part of the patient.

THE SENSORIUM

Interpretative images. The sensorium is the seat of the sensations within the brain, and it is here that the imagination erects its interpretative images which govern the co-ordinated responses of the control centers to the stimuli of the outer world. The sensory information brought to the brain of an infant does not differ materially from the data received by the brain of an adult. The infant, however, has not yet erected a structure of interpretative imagery in the sensorium. The infant first sees a thing; then it knows that it sees a thing; and, finally, it interprets what that thing may be. In the adult, the seeing and interpreting happen simultaneously, if an image exists in the sensorium similar to the thing seen.

Re-education. When we experience a sensation for the first time, *what we perceive of it* represents the best interpretation we are able to make of it at that particular time. This depends upon the interpretive images stored, as the result of childhood training, experience, and . . . daydreaming. For instance, people born blind, who later recover their sight through surgery, are unable to recognize objects until they have gone through a laborious process of learning the art of creating visual images, and interpreting these, to replace the sound, smell, and tactile images formerly used. An adult may know the feel of a triangle and a square, for instance, if he has been blind from childhood, but he will be unable to distinguish visually, one from the other, until he has created and interpreted visual images of each. With the foregoing in mind, then, we are ready to consider in our next chapter techniques for bringing this all-important faculty under the control of the consciousness.

CHAPTER 17

Hypnotism

And a thing is not seen because it is visible, but conversely, visible because it is seen.

PLATO, *Euthyphro*

HYPNOSIS

Power of suggestion. Hypnosis is the art of directing the imagination —either one's own or that of another—into forming images of things not present to the senses. When such images are formed at the suggestion of the operator, the subconscious of the subject adjusts itself to them as though the images were of things actually present to the senses. This is the basis of all the ancient systems of magic, of modern stage hypnotism, and modern hypnology as employed in the psychiatrist's office.

Potent tool. Due to the spectacular demonstrations of stage hypnotists, the overdramatization of this natural phenomenon by sensational writers, and the wholesale employment of its techniques in "brain washing"—present-day Communist methods of political persuasion—and conditioning the minds of masses of people into accepting spurious images as realities, many people fear hypnosis as an evil influence; yet any influence can be evil in the hands of evil people even as any influence can be good when directed by good people. The influence in itself is neither good nor bad; like atomic energy it can be used to bring light into darkness, to fight disease, mental tensions, and poverty, or it can be used destructively. It is merely the most potent mental tool available to man for modifying his own subconscious attitudes.

141

Practical applications. When we observe a mass of people yielding their reason and identifying themselves with a ranting demagogue, we are witnessing a phenomenon of hypnosis; likewise, when we go to church and yield ourselves to the influence of the solemn music, the intoned sermon, the chanted psalms, and so on, we are partaking in another hypnotic demonstration. When we listen to the singing commercials over our radios, and the positively stated suggestions of the advertisers, again we are being subjected to hypnotic influence. In fact, we can extend this right down to the rhythmic crooning and rocking of a babe by its mother, and say that from the cradle to the grave we are continuously, and often deviously, directed by the hypnotic influences of our environment.

Acceptance and rejection. Some of these hypnotic influences are bad and some are good. Obviously to yield ourselves up to the influence of a ranting moron might prove disastrous, yet we know that when we yield ourselves up to the influence of a good church service, the general effect upon our minds is salutary. We leave church with a new sense or orientation to the real values of life. We may afterwards feel humiliated if we yield to the influence of a stage hypnotist, yet after a session under a skilled psychiatrist, using this same influence, we may feel strengthened and refreshed. To be able to either accept or reject a thing, we must understand it. Otherwise we may fall victim to the thing we fear through our very ignorance.

SELF-HYPNOSIS

Freeing the subconscious. Self-hypnosis or autohypnosis, as it is called, is a tremendously effective technique for helping free the consciousness from its subconscious involvement, but here a warning is given: Unless the student has acquired the ability to practice "self-remembering" at will, he should only practice what is called "slight hypnosis" upon himself, except under the guidance of a psychiatrist trained in hypnology.

Escape. If there is any tendency on the part of the student normally to escape from reality into his own daydreams, the practice of the deeper stages of autohypnosis, by giving his fantasies and daydreams a more vivid reality than ever, may lead him into hysteria and neurosis and a deeper involvement with his subconscious than ever.

Domination. Properly speaking, hypnosis is the art of the "more conscious" dominating the "less conscious." In heterohypnosis, we have the conscious operator dominating the less conscious subject. In autohypnosis we should have the detached consciousness of the student, acting in the same manner and in the same relationship to *his own* subconscious as the consciousness of a hypnotist acts in relationship to the subconscious of his subject.

Slight hypnosis. Slight hypnosis may be practiced with perfect safety to help free the consciousness, for if instructions are carefully followed, there is no danger of going into the deeper trance states spontaneously. We all practice slight hypnosis upon ourselves continually though unknowingly. For instance, when we "count sheep" in order to woo sleep, we are practicing a form of autohypnosis. When we completely identify ourselves with a character in a play or a movie we may be watching, or when we "lose ourselves" in a book, we are also in a self-induced state of light hypnotic trance.

ANTIDOTE TO FEAR

Understanding. The antidote to fear is understanding. We only fear the unknown, and so as a first step toward removing the element of fear from this tremendous instrument, we shall give a brief summation of the generally accepted principles of hypnosis, as they are accepted in the Western world, that is.

Eastern techniques. In the East, various techniques of what we now call "hypnotism" have been practiced for at least forty centuries by the priests, prophets, magicians, and healers. At ancient Thebes a bas-relief has been uncovered showing the passes of Mesmerism, and Tibetan gomchens (learned lamas), Hindu yogis, Buddhist monks, and others, have been performing seemingly impossible feats by name of them since as far back at least as their recorded history goes.

Jealously guarded. There is a difference, however, between the methods of hypnosis practiced in the East and those practiced in the West. In Asia the chela (pupil) is given a long preparatory training by his guru, or teacher, and only after this has been satisfactorily completed is he permitted to practice the techniques of autohypnosis. These techniques are jealously guarded, and no student is permitted to hypnotize another until he has mastered the art of autohypnosis.

New science. Western hypnotism, on the other hand, is a comparatively new science. It dates back to Anton Mesmer, who was born in 1734. After receiving his degree in medicine from the University of Vienna, he developed the method called "Mesmerism" and practiced it in Vienna for about ten years, rolling up an impressive score of spectacular cures. So successful did he become that he was made also the target of persecution and criticism by the court physicians of Maria Theresa, and so he left Vienna and went to Paris which was then the center of science, and he again became tremendously successful.

Decline of Mesmerism. The number of Mesmer's patients became so great in Paris that he attempted to treat them by passing his curative influence to various inanimate objects such as water, wood, and glass. Thus, popularity destroyed "Mesmerism." For a while Mesmer was undoubtedly the most popular physician in Paris, but wholesale methods cannot be used in any form of healing. A commission investigated his methods and concluded that there was no evidence of the existence of the "animal magnetic fluid" to which Mesmer had attributed his healings, and so he retired quietly to Switzerland, where he died in 1815. To the day of his death at the age of 81 Mesmer never changed his theory regarding the existence of animal magnetism.

De Puysegur. A pupil of Mesmer, the Marquis de Puysegur, continued to develop Mesmer's methods, and he noticed that often a patient in the trance state would be able to prescribe his own cure and even predict the date of his recovery. He found also that some people while in this trance state possessed clairvoyant and supernormal powers.

The French school. Possibly the three outstanding men of this nineteenth-century French school were Deleuze, whose book *Animal Magnetism* stimulated great interest throughout Europe, and La Fontaine and Baron du Potet, who introduced the subject to England.

The English school. The subject was taken up by the brilliant English physician, Dr. John Elliotson, as a result of a demonstration by Du Potet. His success was phenomenal, but, as was to be expected, his colleagues first refused to either investigate his results or to listen to his theories; then they launched a campaign of persecution against him, and he was forced to resign his position as senior physician at the University College Hospital.

Dr. Esdaile. Stimulated by reports of the work of Elliotson, Dr. Esdaile commenced to experiment in Calcutta in 1845 and discovered that hypnosis was the perfect anaesthetic. He then proceeded to perform over three hundred major operations and several thousand minor ones painlessly, using only hypnosis as an anaesthetic. Sir Herbert Maddox appointed a commission to investigate Esdaile's claims and the report was completely favorable. A hospital was placed at Esdaile's disposal and he continued his work. Its further development was stopped, however, by Morton's discovery of physical anaesthesia.

Dr. Braid. With the passing of Elliotson and Esdaile, the end came to Mesmerism, which took for granted the existence of animal magnetism as a therapeutic agent. Dr. James Braid of Manchester, after observing the work of Fontaine, demonstrated that the trance state could be produced by simple fixation of attention plus suggestion, and that therefore it was unnecessary to consider the theory of a transmission of "magnetic fluid" to explain the phenomenon.

The Nancy School. Dr. A. A. Liebault of Nancy, France, began the study of Mesmerism and hypnotism in 1860, and, as a practicing physician, used it extensively in his practice. He was extremely successful and Dr. Bernheim, an eminent professor of the medical school at Nancy, joined him to establish the famous Nancy School of Hypnotism, or as it is now named, the Académe de Psychologique. Here Braid's original ideas were developed scientifically; the "magnetic fluid" theory of Mesmer was dropped and replaced by the science of suggestive therapeutics. Incidentally, it was here that Sigmund Freud developed the theory which pointed out the tremendous influence exerted on human behavior by the unconscious mind and that the value of a suggestion does not depend upon its acceptance by the conscious mind, but upon its acceptance by the unconscious (subconscious).

SUGGESTION THEORY OF HYPNOSIS

Stubborn facts. There were many advantages to the suggestion theory of hypnosis, for it could be kept within exact scientific limits. Although many aspects of it remained as profound mysteries, the mechanics of its induction could be established, and anyone could be taught these. On the other hand, certain stubborn facts kept cropping up, such as the spontaneous exhibition of extrasensory phenomena in hypnotized subjects, which seemed to validate the older theory of an exchange of magnetic fluid. Yet if one accepts magnetism, one must also accept the possibility of occult phenomena, and this would so extend the range of the subject that it would be hampered at its very beginnings. It would be like an astronomer studying the whole range of the heavens instead of limiting his observations to a single constellation or perhaps even to a single star.

Results. Today, modern science knows that everything—even cabbages—both receives and gives off waves of energy, and so it would be far more fantastic to disregard this observable phenomenon in our study of mental influences than to accept the "magnetic fluid" theory of Mesmer. It is a fact also that notwithstanding the brilliant record of therapeutic suggestion, this school has never been able to produce the spectacular results obtained by the old Mesmerists: Anton Mesmer, De Puysegur, Deleuze, Du Potet, La Fontaine, Elliotson, and others.

CREATIVE REALISM

Reinterpreting Eastern symbolism. Creative Realism holds that during the past four to six thousand years of continuous study, research, and experimentation by successive generations of adepts in Asia (who are in no sense our mental inferiors), much more of value has been learned about this science than has been learned by Western psychology in the two centuries since the advent of Anton Mesmer. If we reinterpret the Eastern symbolism into familiar Western terms, certain principles emerge which seem borne out by experience.

First. All living organisms are at once separated and connected by a nonmaterial "ocean of mind" which envelops this planet at least.

Second. This mind is not an energy; it is a "stillness" which has the capacity to form images and to reflect images. The images so formed, and in the manner previously hypothecated, have the capacity to organize and to direct energy.

Third. It is possible for an image formed by one human mind to be transmitted to another human mind, either visually, orally, or by telepathy.

Fourth. Such a transferred image has the power to do work, and to assist in the direction of the energy produced within the body of the "host."

Fifth. When an image is transferred orally or by visual means, it must draw to itself the primary energy from that produced by the host. When it is transferred by telepathy, it arrives in the mind of the host charged with this primary energy, but may be opposed by the energy of conflicting images already stored in the subconscious of the host.

Sixth. Therefore the best effects are achieved by conditioning the host's mind ahead of time into an understanding and an acceptance of the idea, then by using all three methods. Thus (1) a visual image of the symbol should be presented; (2) it should be suggested verbally; and (3) it should also be conveyed by a strong telepathic impulse.

HYPNOLOGY AND HUMAN RELATIONS

Solving the riddle. According to the foregoing then, the science of hypnology can be extended to cover the whole explanation of human behavior. Moreover, it can perhaps become the instrument by which the riddle of our personal arrival and departure as physical creatures might be explained. Be that as it may, there is no question about the fact that this new science in the West is bringing with it new and wider horizons and an almost infinite range of possibilities.

CHAPTER 18

Autohypnosis

It was six men of Indostan
   To learning much inclined,
Who went to see the elephant
   (Though all of them were blind)
That each by observation
   Might satisfy his mind.

JOHN G. SAXE
"The Blind Men and the Elephant"

AUTOHYPNOTIC TECHNIQUE

Polls. As reported by L. M. LeCron in *Personality, Symposia on Topical Issues* (November, 1951), a poll was taken of psychologists, psychiatrists, other physicians, and a few dentists, who work extensively with hypnosis to discover whether they themselves were good subjects. Included in this poll were most of the leading authorities on the subject in the United States. Of 59 replies, 9 stated they had made no attempt to be hypnotized, and of the remainder, 68 per cent classified themselves as poor subjects, 24 per cent as fair, 4 per cent as good, and only 4 per cent as very good subjects.

Experience. It was said in an earlier chapter of this present work that to really *know* a thing we must experience it. If I raise my hand, I experience an act. If I state that I have raised my hand, that is something entirely different—something which is independent of the actual experience and a thing which may be completely misleading, since by saying that I have raised my hand I may be telling a falsehood.

149

The objective. So far as Creative Realism is concerned, the objective of the autohypnotic technique is to enable the student to experience objectively what he is doing—to learn to know, accept, and realize himself as a unique individual, governing his own motivations and his own behavior by a new relationship established between his liberated consciousness and his subconsciousness. Therefore, the following brief explanation of the generally accepted theory of Western hypnotism is not given with the idea that the reader should attempt to hypnotize others. On the contrary, this writer holds to the Eastern view that no person should be permitted to hypnotize another until he has first mastered the art of self-hypnosis and the liberation of his own consciousness.

Contagion. Those who have witnessed a group of sober decent citizens turned into a mob of blood-lusting savages under the hypnotic influence of the leader of a lynching party, or who have listened to the thunderous chanting of a crowd of educated, intelligent Germans under the hypnotic influence of Hitler, have witnessed mental contagion flare into an epidemic; this writer believes that it is possible for a neurotic, poorly oriented operator to transfer quite unintentionally some of his own mental pathology to his subject, and that until an operator has been fully prepared by the mastery of his own subconscious problems, through autohypnosis, he should no more think of hypnotizing another than would a surgeon think of operating with a dirty knife.

WESTERN THEORY

Understanding autohypnosis. To understand autohypnosis, however, it is necessary to understand something of the theory behind the entire phenomenon of hypnotism. It should be realized though that Western psychology has just opened the door to this new dimension a tiny crack so far; that its definitions are purely arbitrary and its hypotheses restricted by self-imposed limitations for the purpose of scientific organization of data. Here then is the generally accepted Western theory.

Three phases. Western psychology divides the hypnotic state into three main phases: (1) light hypnosis (heightened suggestibility), (2) deep hypnosis (lethargy and catalepsy), and (3) somnambulism (complete abnegation of will).

First phase. In light hypnosis the subject usually closes his eyes but feels that he can open them at any time; his body feels relaxed and heavy, but he can hear all that is going on around him. Afterward (in heterohypnosis) the subject will often deny that he has been hypnotized, but the fact that he responds as strongly to posthypnotic suggesion given in this stage as he does to that given in the deeper stages proves very definitely otherwise.

Example. An example of this is a person who was told that at a certain time on the day following, she would walk to a certain spot and practice deep breathing for five minutes. She decided to resist the suggestion and the following day went to town to do some shopping; as the time approached for the posthypnotic suggestion to take effect, she became possessed of a vague feeling of nervous anxiety which developed into a sense of urgency about "something forgotten," although as a matter of fact because of her preoccupation with her shopping she had no conscious recollection of the suggestion given the previous evening. This nervous anxiety continued to bother her all during the day and was only relieved after she returned home by carrying out the suggestion.

Second phase. In the second phase of hypnosis, the body may become quite rigid with complete anaesthesia, or insensibility to pain. In Asia this trance is used by clairvoyants and in the production of various other higher phenomena but its possibilities have been little explored by Western psychologists. While rigidity of a limb can be produced in almost all subjects who pass beyond the first phase of hypnosis, true and complete catalepsy is relatively rare and is only attained after a considerable period of conditioning.

Third phase. The third phase of hypnosis or somnambulism is somewhat similar in nature to the state of the natural somnambulist or sleepwalker, but in the case of the hypnotized somnambulist, he is able to carry on a conversation, to recall in response to suggestion events of his earliest childhood with astonishing clarity of detail. In this state the subject can be directed to perform both physical and intellectual tasks which would be quite impossible to him in the normal state, and will readily perform any absurd antic suggested. There is usually complete amnesia or forgetfulness of what has taken place after he is awakened.

STAGES OF PROGRESSION

Light hypnosis to somnambulism. Hypnosis, according to Western psychology, always commences with the first phase of light hypnosis, but it may progress beyond that into either the stage of catalepsy or of somnambulism. If we can imagine a scale graduated from 1 to 10, with 1 representing light hypnosis and 10 representing catatonic trance or suspended animation, we can consider that it is possible for a subject to recede to any part of this scale once he has passed beyond 1. Each subject, in fact, is different in this respect.

Creative Realism scale. Creative Realism holds that all people live in two alternating mental states—the negative or receiving state and the positive or sending state; that the fluctuations between these states vary with individuals, but that like two-way radios, we automatically switch into sending for a while, and then when our message is "over," we switch into a "listening" or receiving state. It holds therefore that a much larger scale is called for, ranging from .9, representing the passive, negatively oriented individual who spends his life on the "receiving end" and seldom puts forward ideas of his own, who lives in a perpetual state of light somnambulism, to .1, representing the conscious individual, whose "receiving" periods are adjusted to the inflow of realities, his sending periods adjusted to the product synthesized from these realities.

Listening. According to the foregoing, all of us, by relaxing and listening uncritically enter a pre-phase-one condition of autohypnosis, and that hypnosis therefore, as practiced in the laboratory or in the psychiatric clinic, is merely a logical progression of this natural phenomenon, in which the subject is induced to deliberately prolong and deepen a "listening period" by transferring the responsibility of censorship (over the material listened to) to the hypnotist. Thus whatever is suggested by the hypnotist is acted upon by the subconscious of the subject as if it represented reality.

MORE ABOUT HYPNOSIS

Self-censorship. In self-hypnosis there is no transference of responsibility to another. The consciousness must act in the role of hypnotist and the subconscious in the role of subject. The objective to be attained must be soberly considered, intellectually understood, and consciously accepted, before the actual hypnosis is undertaken.

Displacement. During the actual hypnosis, the consciousness is temporarily displaced, and instead of being aware of the outer surroundings, it is introverted, and becomes aware of the inner subconscious world of symbols and fantasies. Only in this case it is not fractionated among the fantasies, and it is not an actor and participant in them. It plays the part of an observer at first, and later as a director.

Danger. Herein is the danger before referred to. The subconscious world of fantasy is such an alluring place, wherein the wildest dreams can become "true" in a flash, and the most ridiculous theories can find apparent complete confirmation. Even as the man dying of thirst in the desert may see lakes of palm-fringed cool, clear water just beyond, or the polar explorer dying of hunger may see a sumptuous banquet table loaded with all his favorite foods, just beyond his reach, so the self-hypnotist is faced in this subconscious dream world by the vivid dramatizations of his most intense desires, and there is a strong temptation to remain in this world of make-believe, or to return to it as a means of escape from the work-a-day world of hard realities. This, of course, is schizophrenia.

The lotus-eaters. This subconscious world is the "rocky isle" of Greek mythology on which the Sirens sing their seductive songs to lure the voyagers to shipwreck; here also is the "land of the lotus-eaters," where the weak of purpose are urged to tarry in seductive idleness. On the voyage to conscious realization, there is no by-passing this treacherous zone, unfortunately, and so our only choice in the matter is either to brave its seductive lures or to accept ourselves as we now are and refuse to make the voyage.

CONTROL OF IMAGINATION

Orientation, dreams or reality. In the ordinary man, the control of the imagination is lodged in the subconscious. He does not imagine a thing consciously but subconsciously, and these subconscious imaginings give his perceptions of reality fantastic twists and modifications which render them creatively useless. The imagination, remember, is the chief executive of the entire interpretive system described in Chapter Ten. All things imagined are imagined in *relation* to something else. All phenomena are interpreted in terms of their relative significance to something else. It could not be otherwise. At present, then, the imagination is oriented to the false personality, and all of its interpretations are made in relationship to this. In Creative Realism, the imagination is oriented to consciousness and reality.

The first step. The first step in our technique of autohypnosis is merely to observe the operation of the captive imagination in the subconscious, playing the part of an observer and realizing constantly that in this zone the imagination is a liar and a cheat; that the fantasies we are observing have no more reality than our usual sleeping dreams have or that the fantasies produced in a sick man's delirium have.

The second step. The second step is to win a measure of conscious control over the imagination by directing its control over the control centers. We commence with the moving center which still operates on a semivoluntary basis, and we teach it to relax every muscle in the body on a certain signal . . . the calling up of a single visual image. This is repeated with each of the other control centers in turn until all are under the control of the consciousness when we so wish, and the rest of the time they are, like six powerful motors, idling along without undue stress under the natural automatic governing mechanism of the subconscious, thus conserving the energy produced by the organism by eliminating the psychosomatic stresses and strains and making the power available for higher purposes.

Not easy. If the idea of using the technique of autohypnosis has given the impression that the conquest of the imagination is an easy matter, be assured that this impression is wrong. The steps mentioned above are only the first few toddling moves of a journey which has no foreseeable end. As Sir Edwin Arnold poetically puts it in "Light of Asia":

Veil after veil will lift, but there will be,
Veil after veil behind.

Yet even these first few steps represent weeks of steady, unswerving, purposeful effort. Compensation though is by no means delayed until complete attainment. Each small advance toward mastery brings with it a greater measure of self-confidence, a greater measure of energy, a freer flow of creative ideas, and an increasing feeling of general well-being and happiness. We know even from the first that *this is what we have been waiting for.* We have the sense of progressing.

SUMMARY

AUTOSUGGESTION

Autohypnosis and autosuggestion are two different things. Autosuggestion is given more or less in the waking state, but autohypnosis *always involves a trance state, however light.* In considering this state, it is interesting to note that practically all animals and insects make use of it upon occasion. Today in the laboratory we experimentally induce trance in chickens, geese, snakes, pigs, lions, horses, monkeys, and even in cockroaches. It might be said that trance is as natural a phenomenon as sleep, although, of course, it is less frequent.

AUTOHYPNOSIS

We shall conclude this chapter by again pointing out that the power to induce a trance in order to obtain extrasensory data goes back to antiquity. All systems of Yoga are based upon it, as are the systems practiced by the Zen Buddhists, Tibetan gomchens, Mohammedan sufis and dervishes, Christian mystics, and others. Each of these systems represents a workable though tortuous approach to autohypnosis. In our next chapter we shall offer a modern approach and a simple technique by means of which any person intelligent enough to understand the preceding chapters of this book should be able to get almost immediate results.

CHAPTER 19

Nonmeasurable Mind

And so these men of Indostan
Disputed loud and long,
Each in his own opinion
Exceeding stiff and strong,
Tho each was partly in the right,
And all were in the wrong.

JOHN G. SAXE
"The Blind Men and the Elephant"

MIND, THE UNKNOWN

Nonmeasurable. The difficulty encountered by science in attempting
to apply the techniques of physical measurement to psychology is that
although mind under certain conditions acts in conjunction with the laws
of physics, it is not in itself a physical phenomenon. Mind can only be
viewed in a proper perspective by using the whole of animate nature
as a frame of reference. Viewed in isolation by its action in a single
individual, the data can be as misleading as would be the data gathered
from the study of a toenail, without reference to the human body of
which it is part.

Experiencing consciousness. No one knows *what* mind is, nor where it
may or may not be found in a physical sense. No one knows what consciousness is . . . save through *experiencing* it. Thus in the realm of
psychology the thing itself and the experience of it are one. If we try
to separate mind from the study of it, we cannot study it, for study is a
mental act.

"Explanations." The subconscious can never *experience* consciousness any more than the tap-root of a tree can experience sunlight like the leaves. The intellect is a subconscious attribute, as is proved by the fact that it is capable of functioning much more efficiently under the suggestion of a hypnotist, when consciousness is completely submerged in a deep hypnotic trance, than it is capable of functioning normally. Therefore all intellectual explanations of consciousness must be as naive as the explanations given of the elephant by the six blind men of Saxe's poem.

THE EXERCISE

METRONOME METHOD OF AUTOHYPNOSIS

Getting the feel. With the foregoing in mind then, try to get the "feel" of what is meant by the following explanation of the technique of auto-hypnosis, as well as the intellectual understanding of it. The metronome method will be first described, because a degree of hypnosis can always be attained by it, and we shall use this degree, whatever it may be, to condition ourselves to the point where we can immediately enter into a light trance at will.

PRIVACY

A warm room should be chosen for the experiment, and complete privacy should be assured for at least an hour. A comfortable arm chair in which to sit should be placed with a single small light behind it. The curtains should be drawn.

THE METRONOME

The weight of the metronome should be moved to the top of the bar and a cardboard disc about the size of a quarter should be covered with tinfoil and placed at the top of the bar where the weight is. This should be placed well above the eye level, though not high enough to cause excessive strain in gazing at it. It should be so arranged that the light from behind the chair falls upon it.

THE SUGGESTION

Take a sheet of paper and write upon it the following suggestion:

"From this time onward, whenever I so will, I shall immediately enter a state of hypnotic trance by simply visualizing the metronome before me, but on no other occasion. This trance will end exactly 25 minutes after entering it and I shall awake feeling refreshed and vigorous."

SILENT SUGGESTION

After reading over the suggestion a number of times, roll up the sheet of paper on which it is written and attach it to the back of your hand by a rubber band. The sensation of the paper on the back of the hand acts as a constant reminder of the suggestion to the subconscious and this method is extraordinarily effective. The subconscious is hypersensitive in autohypnosis.

SIMPLICITY

It is of great importance that only one posthypnotic suggestion be given to the subconscious at a time in this way, and that it should be phrased as tersely and simply as possible. Where there is a multiplicity of suggestions given, one serves to confuse and weaken the other. With the suggestion that we wish the subconscious to work on during the trance committed to paper, and attached to your hand, the next step is to banish the suggestion from the consciousness and to concentrate upon the actual trance suggestion.

RELAXING

There are two movements to be observed in changing positions. First there is the muscular tensions essential to the movement, then there is a subsidence of the excess tensions and a relaxation of the body as it adjusts itself to the new position. Seat yourself in the chair you have prepared, and focus your attention on your body. Are your jaw-muscles relaxed? . . . Neck? . . . Shoulders? . . . Arms? . . . Back? . . . Abdomen? . . . Thighs? . . . Lower-legs? . . . Feet? . . . Relax your body as much as possible, but at this stage do not try too hard or the effort will have the opposite effect.

MONOIDISM

Now fix your gaze upon the silver disc and listen to the ticking of the metronome for a minute or two until you catch its rhythm. Above all, *do not become too anxious to succeed,* for this will cause tenseness and make success more difficult. Now go into the *self-remembering state* and fix your attention upon *one single idea and hold it there*—upon the idea of sleep. At first perhaps you may have some difficulty in establishing this complete monoidism, for your subconscious will try to inject stray ideas, and you may find your attention wandering; resolutely bring it back again to the one idea of *sleep.*

SILENT VOICE

Now in suggesting, you should develop the feeling that the true personality—the "I"—is giving the suggestion to the mechanical body and its subconscious "analogue computer." This true personality is *not* the body, and it is *not* the subconscious mind. Therefore, you should, when addressing these temporary and mechanical attributes, address them as *you* and not as *I*. If you repeat the suggestions silently, they will be just as effective as though you speak them aloud.

ENTERING HYPNOTIC STATE

Now still keeping your consciousness focused upon the single idea of *sleep,* silently repeat the suggestion:

You desire sleep, more than anything in the world. . . .
Your whole body is relaxed and completely free from tension. . . .
Your eyes are getting heavy . . . bit by bit they are closing. . . .
You want to close them, and they are relaxing more and more. . . .
Your eyes are closed . . . you completely desire sleep. . . .

Your body is growing heavy . . . it is completely relaxed. . . .
You are now drifting into a deep hypnotic sleep. . . .
Into a deep, deep, hypnotic sleep . . . etc., etc. . . .
I have complete autohypnotic control over you, and you will carry
    out the suggestion attached to my hand.

PATIENCE

You must persist with great patience in these suggestions, and you
will find that your consciousness at first will dwindle to a tiny point and
you will apparently become immersed in the usual dreaming state of the
subconscious; this is only seeming, however, for even though you bring
no recollections back to the waking state for a while, your consciousness
will remain as a unity while you are in the trance state, and your "rap-
port" with your subconscious and unconscious eventually will approach
100 per cent.

MISLEADING IDEAS ABOUT AUTOHYPNOTISM

Amnesia. There are some things which may be somewhat misleading
to the student at first in the practice of autohypnotism. One of these is
that unless there is amnesia (forgetfulness) as only occurs in the deeper
states of heterohypnosis, he is likely to feel that he has not succeeded in
hypnotizing himself at all. Make no mistake about this: if you follow
the directions just given, *you shall without question* succeed in inducing
a degree of autohypnosis; whether you have felt this to be so or not, you
will have entered at least a light state of hypnotic trance during the
experiment.

Supernatural expectations. The second misleading thing is that the
new student is prone to expect weird, unusual, or even supernatural
experiences when entering hypnotic trance for the first time. This is
based upon a complete misconception of the phenomenon. As explained
in the previous chapter, we have all placed ourselves in the state of light
hypnotic trance spontaneously upon thousands of occasions during our
lives. Every time we concentrate our full attention and listen uncritically
to another, every time we lose ourselves in a play, a movie, or a book,
we enter a light state of hypnotic trance. The only difference is that now
we are doing this deliberately, instead of spontaneously; and we are
doing it for a clear-cut purpose, instead of aimlessly and accidentally.

THE HIGHER PHENOMENA

Discipline. The ability to produce the higher mental phenomena, such as clairvoyance, psychokinesis, telepathy, and the like, is not lightly come by. They are the product of long self-training and discipline, of deliberate conditioning carried out through hundreds of successive periods. The only other way in which a person sometimes (as in the case of Peter Hurkos, "The Man with the Radar Brain," spoken of in an earlier chapter) may develop this ability is the result of accident or disease which damages the inhibitory mechanisms which normally prevent the premature unfolding of these powers, as the hard outer shell of a seed prevents the premature budding of a plant.

Natural development. Premature development is never a good thing, for it leaves an inadequate supporting structure and a lack of normal controls. The natural way of development is to "soften the hard outer shell" of the precious seed by acquiring self-mastery through deliberate self-conditioning, then to cause it to germinate by flooding it with the sunlight of consciousness.

OTHER AUTOHYPNOTIC METHODS

Rhythm of sound, movement. Should a metronome not be available to the student, autohypnosis may be practiced by fixing the attention on the small bright disc alone. Rhythm of sound, however, as well as of movement are extremely effective aids to the production of trance. In primitive ceremonies the rhythm of drums is extensively used, and in our modern practice of religion we customarily use slow rhythmic hymns and music.

The posthypnotic suggestion. The effectiveness of posthypnotic suggestion in autohypnotism is always relative to the amount of countersuggestion already at work in the subconscious. The effect we are striving for at the beginning is to cause our subconscious to immediately act upon a suggestion given by our consciousness—without qualifications and reservations. Overcoming the countersuggestions calls for persistence and continual repetition over a considerable period of time.

Testing trance state. After practicing the trance state before your metronome for five or six days, practice going into the trance state without the use of the metronome. Seat yourself in a chair, relax, strongly visualize the metronome and the silver disc, and, at the same time, recall the auditory image of the ticking. Repeat the sleep suggestions as formerly outlined. If the posthypnotic suggestion written down and attached to your hand on former occasions is successful, you will within a few minutes go into the trance state. If this does not occur, then try again on the day following. Perhaps a certain amount of unusual tension incidental to the new experiment is preventing its success. Unless full and immediate success is attained without the metronome, you should continue a daily session with it, regardless of how often you practice without it by merely visualizing it.

First things first. Remember, the success of all our future work along these lines is dependent upon our ability to deliberately enter the trance state at will. Remember also that by confining our posthypnotic suggestion to this one single thing we shall in the long run make much more rapid progress. With this basic ability once acquired, the mastering of all further techniques is relatively easy. Here, in this exercise, you are taking the first step in breaking away from automatism. You are putting yourself in a position to make your own plans, to supply your own motivation, to regulate your own responses to outer stimuli, and to be master of your own destiny. That is worth any amount of effort.

Easier autohypnotic methods. There are easier methods of teaching autohypnosis than those given in this book. A person can make arrangements to be hypnotized and to have the posthypnotic suggestion given him while in the trance state so that he will be able to hypnotize himself at will. But in this writer's opinion, to teach autohypnosis in that way is about as safe as teaching a child to drive an auto with a jammed throttle and no brakes. The ability to trigger tremendous responses in oneself without the means to adequately control such responses is a situation closely akin to insanity and certainly not to be desired.

COMPENSATION

Self-remembering After each period of exercise in autohypnosis, the student should spend at least fifteen minutes in practicing self-remembering as outlined in Chapter Eleven. This is *important,* for it counteracts any tendencies toward negativism and subjectivity which may have been aroused by the autohypnosis. It will be found that the periods of self-remembering following the autohypnosis are much easier to maintain, and the state of objective awareness is much more vivid than previously.

The intellect. It is very important that control over the subconscious be started with the control over the intellect. As we have said before, the intellect is a subconscious mechanism, with one tiny part of it above the threshold of awareness and the rest of it below the threshold of awareness. This is the mechanism which makes its computations by comparing one image with another, according to the principles of mathematics. It works according to the principle of logic or comparison, and these in turn are dependent upon the interpretations previously given the images.

Intellect and will. The ability to bring the intellect under the control of the conscious-will is dependent upon learning to think in clear-cut images, in well-defined pictures, and in relating these to each other in clear sequences. Concentration of the intellect might be defined as an *uninterrupted flow of related images toward a single purpose.* Concentration can be mastered like any other mental attribute—by practice.

Practicing imagery. A good exercise in the practice of concentration is to take a book on an unfamiliar subject to a busy place where there are many different noises and changing sights, and convert one chapter into a chain of visual images. Close the book then, and an hour afterwards sit back for a moment, relax, and try to recall the chain of images. This should be consistently practiced once every day.

Total conquest. Conquest of the subconscious and the liberation of the consciousness calls for a total effort in every aspect of the mind. Creative Realism is not interested in mere exhibitions and mental "stunts" but in a rounded development of every aspect of the true personality.

CHAPTER 20

Technique of Relaxation

The whole presents itself as one great graduated scale of seething organization. . . . at one time the planet had none of our particular species. Now it has. That is, it has evolved recognizable mind. . . . The planet has thus latterly became a place of thinking.

Sir Charles Sherrington

THOUGHT SYMBOLS

Subconscious and stored images. The subconscious is completely dependent upon its stored images in carrying on the process we call thought. Without these sensory images it could no more operate than could a computing machine operate without data. Each of the images used by the subconscious, however, is more than a mere photograph with soundtrack, and the like, attached; it is a *symbol* charged with a particular and specific meaning relative to the false personality of the individual.

Meanings. If we can imagine a sensitized film representing a particular personality, and capable of endowing the images impressed upon it by a camera with meanings, relative to itself, we should have something of an approximation of the situation. But we might go further and imagine that each particular false personality film, although sharing the basic characteristics of all other films, differs in many respects. Thus the same Image might be seen by two persons, and to each it might have a different meaning; it would therefore call up a different response.

Experiments. A series of experiments conducted by this writer some years ago seemed to demonstrate that a telepathic message may be transmitted by a person speaking one language and received intact by a trained telepathist who speaks a different language, the inference, of course, being that the actual message is conveyed in *meanings* rather than in word symbols, and that the meanings can be translated into any language.

Further experiments. L. F. Cooper, writing in the *Journal of Psychology*, 1952 (Vol. 34, pp. 257-284), on time distortion in hypnosis, states in his findings that a great part of dreams consists of *meaning tone;* that the dreamer knows what a conversation in a foreign language conveyed to him means, but that he is unable to repeat the words exchanged. The conclusion is that this explains why long dreams occupy only a very short time. In short, a *meaning* may be both subtle and complex and difficult to unravel and fit into word symbols. A *meaning* is not in itself a space-time phenomenon, even though it pertains to the world of space-time.

DISTORTION OF MEANINGS

False personality in action. In explaining the distortion of meanings by the false personality, we might consider the following: The more objective and general a meaning is, the higher is its truth value, but the lower is its usefulness in terms of the individual. The concept of a creative spiritual essence permeating and activating all living nature, in the same manner that a creative spiritual essence permeates and activates all the billions of living cells which compose in their totality a human body, has been held by mankind since the beginning of time.

Utility value. The utility value of the *basic meaning* of life in terms of the individual was low. How could he *apply* such a meaning in the solution of his individual problems? If the creative essence operated within him, did it not also operate within his enemies? He observed the rule of tooth and claw prevailing among all living things; from insects to humans, all lived by eating the protoplasm of others; that life is bought and paid for by death is the most obvious fact with which he was faced.

Analogy. Within a human body this same "rule of tooth and claw" prevails; each of the billions of unit-lives which make it up is forced to battle its environment and the countless swarms of conflicting unit-lives during its brief period of survival. Every movement of an eyelid brings death to some unit-lives and birth to others. Cells die and are replaced by new cells; wars are fought against swarming armies of invading bacteria; and sometimes a colony turns renegade and becomes cancerous. Yet in terms of the life-span of these microscopic unit-lives, the life of the organism persists. The *consciousness* of the organism continues to function with scant regard usually to the eternal conflict within.

Consciousness. In the case of a human body, we *know* that consciousness is the only value, in human terms, to life. We know that the value of all the billions of cells of the body consists of the fact that they subserve consciousness. We know that without consciousness neither life nor death could hold any significance.

MIRROR-IMAGES

Working-pattern. To help our subconscious minds establish a rational working-pattern of this theory, we might consider the mind of nature as an invisible mirror, in which the *meanings,* born of a creative will, become crystallized into images. We might think of the original organisms on this planet in terms of such images functioning in the physical environment and passing on reflections of themselves to their descendants.

Image-meanings. As we have seen, the most profound *meaning* occupies no space, although it may take thousands of volumes of word-images to explain in terms which the subconscious mind can use in making relative computations. In this way then, we can think of evolution as a process by which a single tremendous *meaning* is being unfolded by millions and billions of living images.

Conscious meanings. We might think of consciousness as being the dimension of *meanings,* of meanings inexpressible in relative subconscious images. The ecstacy of the Christian mystic, and the Mohammedan sufi, the Brahman samhadic trance, and the Zen Buddhist satori, all describe a state of supreme consciousness in which a human mind is united with the supreme mind of nature and becomes cognizant of a tremendous *meaning* which beggars all description given in terms of sensory images.

Meaning and usefulness. A thing which has lost its meaning has lost its usefulness, and thus, each morning when we bathe, shave, manicure our fingernails, and when we have our hair trimmed, we ruthlessly slaughter tens of millions of unit-lives (cells) which have lost their meanings, relative to the image of the body as a whole. We only attempt to preserve those cells which help preserve the integrity of the body-image.

"Cruel" nature. Nature preserves the integrity of her supreme image in the same way. That which has lost its usefulness and its meaning relative to this supreme image is purged by nature's system of checks and balances. The individual whose personal image does not reflect the image of his creative source, and whose personal *meaning* is not integrated with the great meaning, is like a cell on a fingernail grown too long. He no longer contributes to the integrity of the body-image of nature; he distorts it. When whole nations lose their meanings in terms of the creative integrity of nature, history shows that they, too, become ruthlessly purged.

Restoration. The restoration of our inner images, replete with their individual *meanings,* is the most important project of our lives. The unfolding of our individual meanings supplies the *zest to live* and the power to do. By the attainment of objective, self-remembering consciousness, we can bring about such a restoration.

THE DEVIL

False personality. The real devil which tempts us is the false personality—that creature born of lies and distortions which seeks to subvert all powers and potentialities within us to the gratification of its swollen ego. It is said that even Jesus had to wrestle with this devil and to overcome it before His power was fully established.

Distorter of images. This false personality "devil" is the distorter of images—the twister of meanings—and the trained telepathist can only receive messages by passing beyond this "devil" into a state of completely impersonal unconsciousness. The same is true with a hypnotized subject able to receive a message given in an unfamiliar language. He must be placed in an extremely deep state of hypnosis wherein the artificial false personality is temporarily completely obliterated.

Sensations. As we have said before, the false personality is a "hormone addict," and it draws its lifeblood from sensations. When these sensations are not forthcoming normally, the false personality fabricates fantasies and "horror movies" in order to stimulate sensations artificially. As all of the lower animals are moved by sensations instead of thoughts, and as this rudimentary physical control mechanism is born within each human and its development in a malignant form, using fantasies instead of realities as stimuli follows, it becomes obvious that its conquest is a necessity before we can restore our natural images—our true personalities—to their birthrights.

CONQUER MOVING CENTER

The first step in this conquest of our "lower selves" is to conquer the moving center. Following the technique given for autohypnosis in the previous chapter, we shall now apply the technique to the problem next in line. It should be understood though that the art of placing oneself in an autohypnotic trance at will must first be mastered according to the technique already given. Any attempt to unduly rush the conditioning process will result in either a partial or a complete failure. A slow but steady step-by-step process of psychosomatic control must be built up, and each step must be firmly established and consolidated before the next is undertaken.

METHOD

For your written posthypnotic suggestion this time, write and memorize the following:

The moving center is now integrated as a functional unity, and it responds to orders with a perfect co-ordination of all movements needed to execute them. It will come to immediate and full attention of my consciousness *whenever I visualize the symbol of a "Black Cat,"* and it will accept the orders then given by my consciousness fully and unquestioningly.

THE CAT

In using the cat as our symbol of control of the moving center, there is a reason which will be obvious if you spend an hour or two in studying the movements of this animal. When the cat raises a paw preparatory to striking a dangling string, he uses just the groups of muscles necessary to the movement, and economizes on the rest. When he springs upon a ball, he passes from complete relaxation to lightning motion. When preparing to spring, he wastes no energy in superfluous movements, but sends his energy coursing into those muscles he will presently launch into action.

THE SLEEP SUGGESTION

The sleep suggestion should be given as before, except that this time the trance should be deepened somewhat by adding:

. . . I have complete autohypnotic control over you, and you will carry out the suggestions attached to my hand. . . .

Now you are fast asleep . . . in a deep, deep, hypnotic sleep. . . . I am now visualizing a black cat, and when I visualize this symbol in the waking state, the moving center will be alert to receive a conscious order, which it shall obey fully and immediately.

AFTER AWAKENING

After awakening, visualize the black cat (in the self-remembering state), then, addressing the moving center *as objectively as though it belonged to another person,* give it the order: "You will now remove every undue tension from every part of the body's musculature." Now still remembering yourself, briefly run your mind over your body to check the work of the moving center: eyes, jaws, neck, shoulders and arms, back and abdomen, thighs and lower legs, feet and toes. . . . Be sure all are perfectly relaxed.

EMOTIONAL TIE-UP

In the lower animals not possessing language symbols there is an almost complete tie-up of function between the emotional and the moving centers. The emotions of fear, anger, or love, immediately activate the moving center into making the appropriate response. Conversely, should the moving center of an animal assume the posture indicated by such a response, the emotion itself becomes triggered by the posture. This mechanism is to some extent still operative in most human beings.

Tensions. So it might be said that physical tensions induce emotional states and emotional states cause physical tensions. In a series of experiments reported in the *Journal of General Psychology,* 1951 (45, p. 265), A. S. Edwards reports that as measured by a tromometer, there was an increase in finger tremor by recall of an emotional situation (in a hypnotized subject) of 350 per cent for fear and 438 per cent for anger.

PERPETUATION

The foregoing illustrates the self-perpetuating mechanism of tension. Every one of the six control centers is equipped with a memory of its own. In the case of the moving center, let us say, in an altercation it is triggered into producing a "fighting stance" by the emotional center. Like the cat it throws all of its energy behind the muscular system needed to do battle. This withdraws the energy normally at the disposal of the instinctive center for digestion, assimilation, elimination, and repair, and these processes are abruptly halted. The altercation passes, but not in the subconscious. The person elaborates a fantasy perhaps to compensate the false personality for a "loss of face," and in this fantasy a terrible battle ensues with all the emotional repercussions of an actual battle. From then on, an accidental physical tension may result in a sense of belligerency and irritation, even as a recall of the actual incident may result in a state of physical and nervous tension.

Multiplication. If we multiply the above imaginary incident by all the thousands of tension-creating incidents of a lifetime which have been magnified and dramatized by the subconscious, we cease to wonder why civilized man appears to live in a perpetual state of tension.

Meanings again. When too many meanings of different and conflicting kinds become impressed upon the same image, it becomes impotent and unable to do effective work of any kind. This adds up to exhaustion, the prelude to disintegration. In intellectual terms it adds up to cynicism and intellectual sterility. In spiritual terms it adds up to regression to the subhuman level.

NEW LIFE FOR OLD

To restore the highest natural image of the self to its pristine brightness, and to unfold its meanings in creative work, we must learn to rid ourselves of tensions by getting down to the causes of them, to learn to "yield unto Caesar the things which are Caesar's" by withdrawing our consciousness from them, and *then* we shall be in a position to "yield unto God the things which belong to Him."

Repeat exercise. Continue with the exercise outlined in this chapter until you can immediately relax every muscle, instantly, by simply visualizing the symbol of relaxation—the black cat. Practice this relaxation often during the day. It will only take a moment or two, and do it especially in every situation wherein you find your emotions becoming involved. Make a practice of doing the exercise as soon as you sit down to a meal, and repeat the exercise the last thing at night when you are ready to sleep.

CHAPTER 21

Toward Freedom

Man must lead or go. To lead is all he is fit for.

Sir Charles Sherrington

BASIC LAW OF LIFE

No escape. To live is to work and to work is to live. From this basic law of life there is no escape. Even in our deepest sleep, within the great hushed factory of the body, the swarming scavengers, repairmen, and chemical workers are busy cleaning up the debris left by the day's activities, replenishing the exhausted stores of hormones, repairing the wear and tear on the structures and organs, replenishing the stocks of Nissl granules to power the nerve cells, and building up the supplies of bioelectrical energy within the ganglia and plexuses for the next day's activities. The great central pumping station, the heart, and the lungs which furnish the life-giving oxygen, continue their rhythmic activities without halt or pause. Only the consciousness rests.

Unsleeping subconscious. The subconscious never rests. The stimuli continue to pour in to the six control centers, recording the activities of every cell group in their jurisdictions; this information is analyzed in the control centers, and orders are sent back wherever a change or a modification of activity is indicated. The subconscious mind broods watchfully over the work of all the control centers, and co-ordinates the work of restoration being done, so that the potentiality of the organism as a whole is built up for the next day of waking activity.

Unfinished business. At bedtime there are usually still some problems to be worked out by the subconscious computing machine to "clear its docket," and so assuming that the next day's waking activities will be based upon the answers to these last problems solved, it prepares the physical body accordingly by apportioning the lion's share of the repair and energy producing materials available to those centers which might logically expect to be called upon for the greatest effort.

Energy. In everything we do we are limited by the amount of specific energy available for that particular task. Every thought, every emotion, every organic process, and every physical action, calls for its own specific type of energy. The body is a great and complicated factory in which hundreds of billions of unit-lives are employed in the task of collecting, transforming, and distributing energy. The factory receives raw materials from the outer world in the form of nutrients, and it transforms these into thousands of different types of fuel each with a different "flash-point" applicable to a specific function or process.

ORGAN OF LIAISON

The output. The subconscious mind is the organ of liaison—the link between the mental world and the physical world. It receives stimuli from within and converts these into mentally understandable impulses such as hunger, thirst, pain, and so on; and conversely it receives mental impulses organized from sensory stimuli from without and prepares the body for an appropriate physical response to them.

The controller. Thus, the content of the subconscious mind controls the type and amount of energy produced within the body automatically. If the subconscious content is based upon sex-inspired fantasies, or fantasies inspired by dreams of desperate physical adventures, those systems which would be used in converting the fantasies into physical action receive more than their share of potential energy. In time they become utterly choked with this excess of stored fuel and a violent S.O.S. goes up into the subconscious calling for action to relieve the pressure. Sometimes such an S.O.S. will explode into action as a compulsion too strong to be denied, and we have a "sex crime" or a "murder."

Conflict. More often, however, by desperate efforts, the waking mind is able to keep such compulsions from crossing the threshold of consciousness, but this eternal conflict within exhausts the supplies of the finer forms of energy needed for the higher processes of mentation and results in neuroses and depression.

Fasting. In olden times the practice of fasting as one of the techniques of spiritual discipline was based upon the foregoing. By cutting off the intake of nutrients until the natural loss of stored energy relieved the pressures, the neophyte was in a better position to practice detachment and objectivity. A much more effective method, however, is to deliberately control our subconscious mind through autohypnosis.

STRUCTURE OF GENUINE PHENOMENA

Self-development. It is a basic principle of Creative Realism to teach only that which the student can experience himself. As much harm can result in an ignorant dabbling in the "occult" before all the necessary mechanisms of control are built and the subconscious has been deprived of its addiction to fantasy, we have devoted this present book solely to such preparatory self-development. Nevertheless, it is pointed out now that every type of genuine phenomena *must be supported by some sort of a structure.* Function without structure is simply inconceivable.

Sublimation. The dictionary meaning of the word "sublimate" is to "convert a solid substance by heat to a state of vapor, and to solidify again by cooling. Figuratively, to refine, to purify, to etherealize." It is asserted by the Tibetan adepts in occult science that for an individual consciousness to function after death of the gross physical body, a sublime body (dughpa) must be organized gradually while we are still alive, and that this is done by a natural process of sublimating the finer forms of energy and recrystallizing them into a fine body analogous to the gross physical body. Thus death to the adept means really a rebirth on a higher level. The "Ka" of the ancient Egyptians embraced this general idea, and as a matter of fact some such idea prevails in all religions with the exception of orthodox Buddhism.

The "wages of sin." Denied an adequate supply of these finer substances, it is claimed, nature cannot elaborate this "soul-body," so that death of the physical body in such a case means a complete obliteration of the personality. If this is true, we can easily realize that the teachings of Jesus had a practical significance quite apart from sentiment. "As a man thinketh in his heart" could be interpreted as: "According to his subconscious content, so is he." And again, if we can interpret the meaning of "sin" as the "secret indulgence in lewd, vicious, and murderous fantasies," the meaning of the Sermon on the Mount becomes crystal clear, and we can see why "The Wages of Sin are Death."

PROCESS OF REFINING

Energy. We know that the energy contained in any particle of matter is equal to the mass of that body, in grams, multiplied by the square of the velocity of light, in centimeters per second, and that could we, for instance, convert a single two-pound lump of coal entirely into energy, it would yield about 25 billion kilowatt hours of electricity. Practically though, we would have to burn many millions of tons of coal in a furnace to produce that quantity of energy. Similarly, many hundreds of tons of uranium ore must be processed to provide a few pounds of the plutonium which goes into the A-bombs or which produces the heat for engine-power. We might imagine that a somewhat similar process of refining is necessary to produce the fine substances mentioned, and that an immense quantity of "unassigned" or "unallotted" energy is necessary for the body to be able to produce a little of it.

First call. We might imagine, in short, that the storage depots and batteries of the six centers have first call upon the energy produced by the body, and that when these are normally charged so as to keep the physical body functioning in a normal state of health, the excess is converted into fine energy—providing that *the demand for it exists.*

The demand. From the moment of fertilization, the microscopic egg-cell becomes a human-to-be, an image as a focal point around which a *meaningful structure* will be systematically organized by the collection, transformation, and distribution of energy to form a nervous system, digestive tract, skeleton, and all of the other technological miracles which in their totality add up to a human body. Obviously, there is a *demand* for all this organizational activity, a demand which will not be denied, a demand based upon a meaning—for what is a demand but the pressure of a meaning to unfold?

The meaning. We see this meaning unfolding as the embryo passes through stage after stage of organizational development, and after birth we watch with delight a deeper meaning than mere physical organization commence to emerge from the physical organization as a sparkling, new personality. Our responsibilities toward this new personality now become clear. Even as we provide the nutrients to keep the physical body developing, we must provide the mental and spiritual nutrients which will enable the personality to unfold its inner meaning.

Arrested meaning. The original meaning which activated the entire developmental project from the fertilized cell onward was the unfoldment of consciousness. In a deeper sense, no human being belongs to himself: he was created by nature, for nature's purposes, and to nature he belongs. His purpose in nature is to become a structural and functional unit of her consciousness. But, alas, this meaning has been clouded by the primitive concepts of anthropomorphism, and the fantastic idea that man can do his duty and fulfill his obligations to his creative source by a little "lip-service" and a little extravagant flattery once a week. His *meaning* has been lost in the mists of his subconscious, and has been replaced by the hollow platitudes of an antlike mechanical society. By this, he has unwittingly cheated his creative source, and he has also cheated himself. He has adjusted to subconscious living and to "eating husks among the swine."

Restored meaning. To recover our lost meanings—to reintegrate our fractionated images—we must persist in *willing consciously* to achieve the project. Every day, we should enter the self-remembering state several times, and repeat to ourselves with all the determination that we can muster the affirmation: *"I am accepting the challenge of life . . . regardless of my age, situation, and responsibilities, for as long as I live I am going to push the development of my consciousness to the full limits of its possibilities."*

FREEING INSTINCTIVE CENTER

Autohypnotic technique. In this chapter we are going to use the technique of autohypnosis as a means of freeing the instinctive center from its entanglements with fantasies. The instinctive center controls all of those functions with which we were born, and which we do not have to learn. The repair work within the body, the biochemical processes incidental to the production of energy and its transformation and storage, the production of antibodies and opsonins to fight disease germs, the processes of digestion, assimilation, and elimination, and the like, all come under the control of the instinctive center. Many of the psychosomatic diseases, such as gastric ulcers, indigestion, spastic colitis, diabetes, constipation, gastritis, and a host of other complaints, stem from a dysfunction of the instinctive control center due to subconscious fantasies.

Objectives. Before commencing our work on the instinctive center, let us glance again at the objectives of this system of self-training. It is to free the six control centers from the mechanisms of the subconscious which in their totality we have called the false personality. These mechanisms have been built by the introverted consciousness weaving fantasies in order to enjoy the sensations produced by the artificial stimulation of the various endocrine glands. This false personality, immersed in this "pseudo-life," *competes successfully with reality for the possession of consciousness.*

Ideals. To make its addiction to hormones seem legitimate, the false personality defends itself by tabbing its emotional debauches as "pity," "sympathy," "hatred of injustice," "artistic temperament," and so on. But it is content to merely "emote" about these things. It never takes objective steps to do anything about that which it becomes emotional over. On the contrary, when it runs out of things to "emote" about, it will attend a horror movie, where it can wallow in all of the artificially produced conditions it pretends to "deplore." It is for this reason that it is the mother of gossip, the lover of scandal, and the fosterer of every injustice in the world—from international wars to lynching parties. Before we are in a position to escape from this condition, we must clearly recognize that it *applies to ourselves . . .* and not merely to the "other fellow."

Automatic mechanisms. Each false personality presents a different problem in the breaking up of these old and automatic pathological mental mechanisms. The problem belongs to the individual and he can best solve it if given the techniques and the blueprint of what must be done. Could an individual, say by heterohypnosis, be taught to achieve control of his subconscious mental mechanisms, without first brightening his image of reality and orienting his consciousness to it, and away from the fantastic opium-den in which his false personality lives and moves and has its being, it would be like training a person suffering from pulmonary tuberculosis to be a marathon runner. In short, *unless the orientation be changed from unreality to reality,* we should merely be deepening and intensifying the power of fantasy and the ability to produce greater "shots of hormones."

Protection. Nature built our bodies, built into them protective systems to save us from ourselves. There is complete safety in self-development, because nature does not allow us to proceed too far too fast. She does not want a lot of powerfully developed psychopaths such as Hitler on the loose. Consequently, each man's possibilities are limited by his own desire for reality, by his strength of character and persistence in winning mastery over his own subconscious. The ultimate results are certain in self-development, and they come just as rapidly as is consistent with safety.

AUTOHYPNOSIS

Discipline required. Occasionally students feel disappointed because they cannot immediately achieve the deeper trance states by autohypnosis, and they feel that by the light state of hypnosis they are not achieving results. This is a mistake. We cannot take an automatic reflex pattern, deepened by a lifetime of repetition, and change it into a new type of pattern overnight. The results of posthypnotic suggestion given in the light state of hypnosis are just as effective, and, in fact, often more so than those given in the deeper trance states. Do not expect miracles immediately, but you *may* expect a slow and steadily increasing measure of control over yourself and your reactions to outer events, a sense of greater and greater "release" from strain, tension, and worry, a slow but steady increase in the brightness of your consciousness, and in your general awareness of life-as-it-is-happening, a slow but steady increase in your enjoyment of food, a slow but steadily increasing measure of release from gastric discomforts, a slow but steadily increasing ability to relax into a sound, refreshing sleep, a slow but steadily increasing measure of physical and mental energy, and a slow but steadily increasing awareness *that life for you is really just beginning.*

Monoidism. In the state of light hypnotic trance, in heterohypnosis, it is quite customary for the subject to refuse to believe that he has been hypnotized at all. Often he will say: "Why, I wasn't hypnotized. I heard every word that was said. I knew everything that was going on around me, and I never for a moment lost consciousness." As we have already said, the proof that he *was* hypnotized rests in the fact that his response to posthypnotic suggestion is completely effective. This same thing applies to autohypnosis. Often we feel that we have not entered even a light trance state, but you may rest assured that if you have established a monoidism, if you have kept your mind from wandering, and have held it single-pointed on the suggestions to the exclusion of everything else until the moment that you may have apparently "dozed" when a scattering seemed to take place among fantasies as usual, you have been in a light hypnotic trance. Your response to posthypnotic suggestion will be satisfactory and consistent with the safety-measures mentioned before.

PHYSIOLOGY OF HYPNOSIS

Achieving nutritional balance. In his article, "The Physiology of Hypnosis," published in the *Psychiatric Quarterly,* 1949, B. E. Gordon critically reviews the literature of the past twenty-five years on the physiologic aspects of hypnosis, and points out the demonstrated fact that many gastrointestinal functions are capable of being changed through hypnotic suggestion. Suggestions of eating can inhibit the hunger contractions of the stomach in the fasting patient, and gastric secretions may be produced in response to hypnotic suggestions of eating, and the type of enzyme secreted is specific to the type of food suggested. Similarly, specific secretion of pancreatic enzymes has been noted in response to the hypnotically suggested intake of foods. This demonstrates the effect of the subconscious control mechanisms upon the nutritional balance of our bodies.

Automatic control. The objective of the present posthypnotic suggestion is to return the control to the natural controlling mechanisms of the instinctive center by removing the artificial mechanisms built up and deepened by repetition over the years, based upon food preferences and food phobias. Most of us believe that we "simply cannot eat" certain foods without dire consequences, and so long as we continue to hold those "beliefs," the results will follow; as is pointed out in the preceding paragraph, just as certain chemical processes are induced by suggestion alone, certain pathological processes can be induced by suggestion alone. It is this writer's belief, based upon considerable experimentation and research, that all allergies attributed to foods fall into this classification. Some will object on the grounds that the allergies follow even when one may be ignorant of the content of the food containing the offending substance. The answer is that the "taste mechanism" is never ignorant of such a content. The extreme acuteness possible to the senses under hypnotic suggestion is well known; where suggestion of an "allergy" has been accepted and deepened by repetition and emotion, of course, there is a hyperacuteness of the sense of taste developed that is capable of detecting even minute quantities of the supposedly offending substance.

Adaptability. In reality the instinctive center is the most adaptable of all. Given a balance of protein, minerals, fats, carbohydrates, and vitamins, it can adapt to any diet containing them, whether it be the diet of an Eskimo, a Massai warrior, a Chinese coolie, or a Parisian gourmet. If you follow the suggestions regarding nutrition given in Chapter Fourteen of the present work, and you are still troubled by allergies, you may safely conclude that these are caused by subconscious thought mechanisms and not by physical peculiarities.

Element of time. Recognizing these facts, and accepting the realistic view that it is unreasonable for us to expect to overcome the effects of the lifetime habit-structures built up by our false personalities in a few days or even a few weeks, we can set about systematically freeing our harassed instinctive centers from these a little at a time.

THE EXERCISE

POSTHYPNOTIC SUGGESTION

After seating yourself before the metronome for this exercise, and giving yourself the sleep suggestion in the usual way, you should (after first writing it out and attaching it to your hand) give yourself the following posthypnotic suggestion, addressed to your subconscious:

You have completely dissolved all mental mechanisms based upon fear and the stimulation of fear. The instinctive center is released from all subconscious fear mechanisms to continue its work as thoroughly and systematically as the instinctive center of a fish. Its inherent ability, born of the experience of a hundred million years, is able to cope with any problem belonging to its domain . . . if it is not interfered with by the subconscious. Therefore, you will allow it to work in peace. Whenever I visualize a fish swimming in a tank of water, you will immediately withdraw all mental associations from the instinctive center, and you will allow it to work unimpeded.

EATING

Whenever you sit down to a meal from this time onward, go into the self-remembering state . . . and while in that state, visualize a goldfish swimming in a large tank of water. Visualize the rhythmic pulsations of its gills, the effortless balancing movements of its tail and fins, and realize that this fish is a perfect biochemical factory, unimpeded by emotions and fantasies; that you have an even more perfect biochemical factory within you, if you will only allow it to work under its own management. Try to maintain the self-remembering state during the meal, and resolutely recall the "fish image" afterwards when your subconscious tries to insinuate its old patterns "to prove that it was right."

ALIBIS

Remember, in this work of self-control there are no acceptable alibis. You cannot enjoy your hormones and phobias and your freedom, too. They are mutually exclusive. You must either dominate your subconscious processes or be dominated by them. There is no middle ground.

CHAPTER 22

Nature and Meanings

Many living things are all the time busy becoming other than what they are. And this, our mind, with the rest. It is being made with our planet's making.

Sir Charles Sherrington

TECHNIQUES OF PSYCHOMETRY

Indirection. In dealing with mind, we can at best only use the techniques of physical science in an indirect way and this is more likely to prove misleading than otherwise. All of the modern techniques of psychometry, including intelligence testing, the Rorschach, and Thematic Apperception Test (T.A.T.), give information about such things as the way the subject deals with problems, his manner of approach to them, the efficiency of his use of rational controls, and his response to outer stimuli. In addition to this the T.A.T. is supposed to give information about his attitudes toward family, society, and himself. But all of this is information about the integrated body of fantasies and fictions we have called the false personality. It is, in short, information about the manner in which the subconscious computing machine is functioning and the basic fantasies to which the machine is oriented at the time.

Temporary orientations. The above system of investigation is useful in certain instances, if the psychologist keeps in mind the fact that he is dealing with a momentary constellation of factors brought together by a mood of the moment, a mood which can change with the rapidity of a changing fantasy, bringing about a different grouping of subconscious elements and a whole series of different responses. Furthermore, the responses so measured are determined by the subject's previous conditioning and measure the work of the intellectual center as the criterion of the mentality. Practically, our responses to outer stimuli are never, or at best, very seldom, influenced by our intellects.

Degree of consciousness. Could a test be devised which would measure the *quality of an individual's consciousness* it would be invaluable; but we cannot devise such a test because *experience and consciousness cannot be divided.* We cannot have an experience in consciousness while we are unconscious, and we cannot take an experience out of consciousness to examine it. Consciousness and experience of consciousness are one and the same thing, and so there is no way of discovering whether the quality or wealth of one individual's consciousness is superior to that of another individual.

Differing concepts. Modern analytical psychology is based upon the Freudian concept that: *"Mental processes are essentially unconscious . . . and those that are conscious are merely isolated acts and parts of the whole psychic entity. . . . the psychoanalytical definition of the mind is that it comprises processes of the nature of feeling, thinking and wishing, and it maintains that there are such things as unconscious thinking and unconscious wishing."* *

CREATIVE REALISM VS. OTHER SYSTEMS

Freudian concept. Creative Realism agrees with the basic correctness of the Freudian concept, as it applies to "ordinary man" at this time. Most of us are born unconscious and we pass our entire lives as subconscious individuals, with only a faint glimmer of consciousness occasionally illuminating "isolated acts" briefly. Creative Realism, however, holds that this subconscious state is, in an evolutionary sense, a transitory one. It holds that by self-discipline and the application of the correct techniques, it is possible for all of us to integrate the faint and momentary glimmerings of consciousness into a steady and all-powerful illumination, and that when this is accomplished, the *polarity* of the entire psyche is reversed automatically. In short, then, instead of being hag-ridden by the fantasies and fictions of the subconscious, the subconscious becomes subservient to the consciousness.

* Sigmund Freud, *A General Introduction to Psychoanalysis* (Doubleday and Company: 1953).

Blind leading blind. The foregoing will perhaps serve to explain the basic difference between Creative Realism and other systems. A subconscious individual, never having experienced consciousness, is like a blind man who has never experienced sight. He can only describe experiences pertaining to the subconscious realm; to the energy-scheme of the nervous system, the area of automatic stimulation and automatic response, even as a blind man would be able only to describe experiences pertaining to the senses of hearing, taste, touch, and smell. On the other hand, an individual who has actually experienced consciousness is in the position of a man having vision, trying to describe visual experiences in terms which can be understood by the sightless. If he takes the experience out of the consciousness of it, it simply does not make sense.

Freud's definition. Keeping in mind then Freud's definition, as being applicable to ordinary man at this time, and agreeing that "our mental processes are essentially subconscious (unconscious), that those which are conscious are merely isolated acts and parts of the whole psychic entity," we can see the problem of developing consciousness consists of separating the consciousness—which only "comes to the surface," as it were, occasionally in isolated acts of momentary duration—from its present subconscious entanglement, and then in integrating it as *a new mental faculty.*

WITHDRAWAL OF CONSCIOUSNESS

Consciousness-subconscious entanglement. At the present time, our consciousness is mixed up with the machinery of our subconscious, which it distorts from its normal functions of computing the answers to outer problems and controlling the energy distribution of the body in accordance with these answers to the elaboration of fantasies. When consciousness is withdrawn from the subconscious, the latter is allowed to function in peace, as it was intended to function, and so it automatically becomes more efficient. The energy distribution of the body, no longer regulated by the wild computations based upon fantasies, becomes normalized and adjusted to the realities of the environment, to the immense benefit of our health, and the integrated consciousness allows us to view life from a new dimension.

Heterohypnosis. In heterohypnosis—that is, when another hypnotizes us—it does nothing to extricate our consciousness from its subconscious involvement. Any suggestion given in this way works only upon the subconscious, or/and through the subconscious upon the unconscious. The subconscious cannot produce consciousness since consciousness is not the function of the subconscious. By hypnotic "conditioning" a psychiatrist trained in hypnology is sometimes able to remove some of the most difficult subconscious blocks in the way of the attainment of objectivity and consciousness, but the work of extrication and the development of conscious "illumination" can only be done by each individual himself. Another cannot do it for us any more than another can develop our muscles for us or learn mathematics for us.

Autohypnosis. By autohypnosis we at once separate the consciousness to some extent from the subconscious, and we bring the subconsciousness under the control of our own emerging consciousness. Thus, we are solving our own problems through the exercise of our own faculties. As the attainment of consciousness is cataclysmal and brings about a complete revolution within the entire psyche, the preliminary work is arduous and difficult, and calls for faith and persistence. Mancius was right when he said: "When Heaven wants to perfect a great man, it tries him in every possible way, and forces him to solve his own problems triumphantly."

CONTROLLING THE INTELLECTUAL CENTER

Postautohypnotic suggestion. In this chapter we are going to apply postautohypnotic suggestion to the control of the intellectual center. As we have said before, the intellect is a subconscious faculty; the part of it occasionally illuminated by a flickering of consciousness might be compared to the part of a cash register upon which the computation of the sale is rung up; the act of computation itself is done below the level of consciousness. An attitude of serene detachment is absolutely essential to the correct working of the intellect.

Limitations. Like a cash register or an adding machine, the intellectual center will arrive at the best possible computations if it is furnished correct data. But this data does not arise within itself; it must be fed-in from the outside by means of the five physical senses. It cannot compute that which cannot be seen, touched, tasted, smelled, or heard. To do its work it must be furnished with symbols which can be seen or heard, felt, tasted, or smelled. These symbols may be in the nature of mathematical symbols, or a musical score, or printed letters, or heard words, or a chain of visual images such as were given in the "nonsense" series, or such as are described in Chapter Eleven.

Subconscious meaning. After making a computation, this answer is fed to a subconscious interpretative memory center, where are stored the memories of every experience we have ever had in our lives. These memories are figuratively stored in three categories: pleasant, unpleasant, and neutral. The answer to each computation made by the intellectual center always winds up in one of these compartments, depending upon its nature, before it is sent into the consciousness together with the interpretation for further action. Simultaneously with this interpretation, the appropriate centers are triggered and prepare the body for action.

Subjective interpretations. It is easily seen by the foregoing that the computation itself is neutral. It is clear also that the interpretation is completely subjective and based upon whether a previous similar computation resulted in pleasure, discomfort, or was neutral in its effect. In Pavlov's system of conditioning it is demonstrated that this interpretative mechanism can be easily perverted, and this is so because, as we mentioned before, all interpretations must be made relative to a central *meaning* or theme, a purpose to which all else is related. The lower interpretative mechanism is instinctive and is based entirely upon physical survival. For instance, even an amoeba will move away from the touch of a glass rod or toward food. The central meaning to which all stimuli are related in this case is preservation of the tiny physical cell-body.

HIGHER ORIENTATIONS

Evolutionary ladder. As we move higher up the scale of life, we see the narrow little meaning of the amoeba being expanded to preservation of the species. In the case of some insects—bees and praying mantis, for instance—we find the males sacrificing themselves to bring forth a new generation, and the females going to endless trouble to prepare an environment suitable for the expected new arrivals. When we come to human beings we find these "meanings" parading under high-sounding words such as "personal ambition," "family ambition," "civic pride," and "patriotism," and, unquestionably, all these are virtues necessary to the preservation of the species. But as we climb still higher up the evolutionary ladder, we find a greater degree of detachment from self and a greater degree of identification with life and nature as a whole. We find a new "meaning" dawning which makes its possessor more than man. It makes of him an agent in consciousness of the creative principle which brought him and all other living forms into being.

Evolutionary meaning. This high meaning cannot be brought forth by ritual and pretense; it can only be arrived at through a development of consciousness. But once established it forms a new and higher center of gravity to which the entire psyche and the physical organism as a whole become oriented.

Objective of Creative Realism. Remembering then that the objective of Creative Realism is to help the individual to *experience* consciousness for himself, and to establish a new "center of gravity" in consciousness, in the exercise which follows it will be understood why the aim is the detachment of the intellectual computing machine from its ancient emotional interpretations in terms of pleasure and pain.

THE EXERCISE

PERSISTENCE

In this present book, a comprehensive course is being given for the attainment of self-mastery through the development of consciousness; and since much information must be condensed between its covers to offer a well-rounded program, a month or more of hard work may be represented in one short chapter of explanation and instruction. It is emphasized again at this time that results will come more quickly if work on each control center is continued until a definite measure of improvement in conscious control is attained before undertaking work on the next control center. No harm can result, however, by moving from work on one center to work on another quickly; the ultimate result of liberation of the consciousness will come in spite of this shift in effort, but it will appear to come more slowly because the effort will be distributed over a wider area. The main thing to keep in mind is the fact that in a project of this tremendous scope, persistence and continuous *willing* toward achievement are necessary.

SLEEP SUGGESTION

It is possible to achieve a certain amount of subconscious "conditioning" in these principles by having the material given for the posthypnotic suggestion made into a recording to be played back to us at intervals while we sleep There are machines with a clock attachment on the market, by which we can achieve this, and, unquestionably, it shortens the road to a considerable degree. It must be remembered, however, that the objective is the *liberation of the consciousness* and that all of our work in autohypnosis and upon the subconscious generally is for the purpose of enabling us to develop a higher degree of *conscious detachment and objectivity*. Consequently, following each exercise in autohypnotic control, we should immediately spend a similar period of time in practicing *self-remembering* and the exercises given in the earlier chapters of this book.

THE HYPNOTIC SUGGESTION

Write down the following posthypnotic suggestion, to be attached to your hand in the usual manner:

From this time onward, this intellect will be as completely detached from emotional interpretations as is any mechanical computing machine. It will compute all answers without regard to either pleasure or pain, being solely concerned with providing the correct answers in terms of impersonal, objective realities. I shall at any time achieve complete intellectual detachment by merely visualizing a cash-register.

THE TRANCE

Now seat yourself before your metronome in the usual manner and give yourself the usual suggestion to induce a light trance state. Do not forget that the mere process of putting yourself to sleep with a definite purpose in view will act in itself as a powerful hypnotic suggestion, and the suggestive impact upon the subconscious is intensified by the written suggestion attached to the hand.

DETACHMENT

From now onward you will realize the wisdom of avoiding the use of the intellect in order to bolster "arguments," and you will never attempt to make a decision based upon calculation unless you are able to allow your intellect to make its computation in detachment. The idea of "sleeping upon" important decisions of this kind is a sound one. You will also realize the danger of allowing yourself to be swayed by the "intellectual arguments" of others, when these are based upon that other's self-interest. A cash-register is neither concerned with the good of a computation or the evil indicated by it, since that is not its province; it is solely concerned with making accurate computations based upon the data furnished. Thus, when you discover yourself becoming involved in "good and evil" intellectualizations, strongly visualize a cash-register, and go into the self-remembering state.

REALITY BEYOND INTELLECT

As was said before: we cannot destroy reality; we cannot alter reality; for reality IS. The ultimate human reality lies beyond the intellect in consciousness. The intellect is a useful tool when its computations are based upon this ultimate reality. When its computations are interpreted in terms of pleasure and pain, it can betray us as thoroughly as Pavlov's dogs were betrayed.

CHAPTER 23

Significance of Sex

> Society can conceive of no more powerful menace to its culture than would arise from the liberation of the sexual impulses and a return of them to their original goal. Therefore, society dislikes this sensitive place in its development being touched upon.
>
> SIGMUND FREUD
> *A General Introduction to Psychoanalysis*

LEAVEN

Working ferment. Not so long ago, before the era of widely distributed baker's bread, it was customary for each housewife to bake for her own family. She often made her own leaven for the bread also, keeping a pan of this ferment working for many months by adding additional grated potato, flour, and the like, each time some was removed to make a batch of bread. In this way the descendants of the original yeast organisms which "started" the leaven raised perhaps hundreds of loaves of bread over the months.

Immortal meaning. The functional *meaning* of the countless generations of yeast organisms was preserved intact, so that there was no lessening of the ability of the later generations to raise the bread dough. Obviously, this *meaning* was all-important to the housewife, and she was not in the least concerned about the "private lives" of the individual yeast spores.

Life force. But if the housewife was not concerned about the "private lives" of the individual yeast spores, neither were the yeast spores concerned about the problems of the housewife. They preserved and transmitted a meaning to their descendants, and this meaning was important to the housewife in the baking of bread; but the yeast organisms were completely unconscious of this meaning, and they divided themselves in the endless process of reproducing their kind because of an inner compulsion, a compulsion which in the higher organisms falls under the heading of "sex drive."

Lost meanings. Sometimes, owing to radical temperature changes or other factors, the yeast spores would lose their meaning and the leaven would cease working. When this happened, the housewife would discard the entire pan of leaven and start a new batch, though occasionally she might be able to salvage a small amount which had not entirely lost its meaning with which to start the new batch.

NATURE AND MEANINGS

Preservation of functional meaning. Like the housewife of our illustration, nature is not concerned with the individual and private lives of living organisms as such; she is solely concerned with the preservation of the meanings inherent in each of the species, because in their totality these functional meanings add up to the functional life of the great body of nature, just as the functional meanings of each gland, organ, and muscle of a human body add up to the functional meaning of the body. We, as human beings, are not concerned about the individual cells which form our bodies; we are only concerned that these preserve the functional meaning of their respective structures.

Great meanings. Even as the lesser meanings inherent in all of the billions of individual cells add up to a smoothly functioning organism which will support and sustain a brain, which may become an instrument of consciousness, and even as the development, support, and sustenance of this brain is the ultimate *great meaning* in a physical sense, a meaning which is beyond the understanding of the individual cells, so we might assume that all of the lesser meanings inherent in the swarming organisms of living nature add up to the development, support, and sustenance of humanity, which acts in its totality as the "brain of nature" and which may, at some distant date, form the instrument of nature's consciousness.

Motivation. Pending the slow process of maturation, as measured by human time concept, it was of supreme importance that the meaning of each of the species be preserved and passed down without loss of functional efficiency to succeeding generations, and to insure this nature installed in each organism a "sex center" which transforms the universal force called "the zest for life," "the *élan vital*," by philosophers, into sexual instinct, which motivated a course of action that culminated in reproduction.

HUMANITY AND SEX

Instrument of nature's consciousness. Unless a human being unfolded his "great meaning" as a functional unit of nature's consciousness, he, as an individual, possessed no more meaning to nature than did a yeast organism, which fulfilled only a part of its meaning, to a housewife. The sooner such a yeast organism reproduced others of its kind which might fulfill the meaning of yeast organisms, while removing itself from the scene, the better satisfied would the housewife be.

"Natural eliminators." From the housewife's point of view, it would be an ideal situation were she able in some way to install a mechanism within each of the yeast cells, whereby they would either unfold their meaning or eliminate themselves from the leaven; and nature appears to have equipped every living thing with just such a mechanism. In mankind this self-elimination mechanism is associated with the sex center.

SUBCONSCIOUS CENTER

The sex center is, of course, like the other centers, a part of the control mechanism of the subconscious mind. It is triggered by thoughts and fantasies, and responds by activating the entire sexual mechanism. Steinach and many other investigators have demonstrated the tremendous part played in the body's economy by the hormones of internal secretion manufactured by the sex glands, and of the part played in the aging process by the exhaustion of these glands and the absence of the hormones. The effects caused by an imbalance of the internal hormones, due perhaps to overstimulation, have not yet been accurately determined, but one of these is a certain type of cancer. We know this because the growth can be arrested by a restoration of the balance through injecting a counterbalancing hormone.

Universal meanings. The more universal a meaning is, the greater is its power over the individual. The zest for life, the zest of living things to go on living and renew themselves as new lives, is at once an urge and a motive in everything which lives. No species is without it; innate and inalienable, it impels alike man and bacterium. This tremendous force is expressed as sexual instinct in its "lower octaves of operations" *and as consciousness in its highest aspect.* Both consciousness and sexual instinct are different aspects of the force we have called "the zest for life."

Mutual exclusion. To a certain extent the sexual instinct and the consciousness seem to be mutually exclusive. Perhaps because the individual with an extremely powerful sex drive satisfies his "zest for life" in this expression, and when it becomes exhausted, he no longer possesses enough "zest" for the development of consciousness; the conscious individual on the other hand is no longer dragged willie-nillie behind the wild horses of his sexual passions, and regards it as a supreme expression of love and physical and spiritual unity with his chosen mate. So his "zest for life" to be expressed in consciousness is increased rather than diminished.

"Temptation." The foregoing is probably the reason why many religions advocate a life of celibacy for their priests and nuns, feeling that if during their training they should be removed from associations which might stimulate the sexual instinct, there would be a better chance of elevating the "zest for life" toward consciousness. The investigations of Freud and his successors have shown us the fallacy of this view. That which is not expressed *naturally* is often distorted or perverted and expressed *unnaturally,* figuratively blowing our nervous systems to pieces in the process. The zest for life cannot be eliminated save through death. It may be controlled and directed into the highest possible channels, but it can never be repressed without dire consequences.

SEX SYMBOLS

Role of psychoanalysis. Psychoanalysis has brought to light the tremendously powerful influence wielded by the sex instinct in all the subconscious processes. In fact, Freud goes so far as to infer that *all* dreams are related to sex, and that every symbol used in dreaming is a sexual symbol. Creative Realism holds that this extreme view is an overstatement of the case; that although there is no doubt about the sexual motif of many dreams, there is a different interpretation which can be made of this fact which seems more valid.

Limited symbols. Fundamentally, every thought is the result of a subconscious computation. It is an answer—the best answer which can be furnished—to the data fed into the computing machine. If the data is the product of fantasy—based, for instance, upon daydreaming about sex—the answer will, of course, be related to this subject. As the number of symbols by which these answers can be expressed is limited to those parts of the physical body pertaining to the sexual function, an elaboration of the symbols is usually necessary in order to express the answer fully. As fantastic data must invariably provide fantastic answers, and as the fantastic answers are expressed in elaborated and distorted symbolism, we believe it naive to attempt to read "deep and mysterious meanings" into these fantasy-induced pseudo-phenomena, for the most part, although we concede the value of certain vivid and oft-recurring dreams in indicating the frustration of a deep creative desire seeking to convert itself into action.

THE MIRACULOUS CYCLE

First. To sum up the concept of Creative Realism as applied to dream symbolism and sex: The sex instinct is an expression of the creative power of nature. It is the highest expression, below consciousness, of the "zest for life," the *"élan vital,"* the living principle of nature, which ever presses toward the unfoldment of new and higher meanings through the medium of the organisms which themselves are the physical expressions of her meanings.

Second. Probably the highest act of creation possible to advanced man in his present state of evolution is the creation within his own brain of the center which will directly connect him with the supreme consciousness of nature. The next highest act of creation is to create a child in "his own image and likeness." This act of creation, of course, finds expression through the sexual instinct.

Third. The higher the *meaning* which is unfolded, the greater is its power. A single flash of "cosmic consciousness" transcends all of our previous experiences and leaves us awed, exhilarated, amazed, and transformed by a sense of deep identification with a reality in which physical existence is a mere momentary episode. Next below this transcendental experience is the experience in its fullest expression of real love between a man and a woman. To a lesser degree this also leaves us at once awed and exhilarated, amazed, and transformed, with the sense of a new reality we have found. This explains the power of the sex instinct.

Fourth. By the elaboration of sexual fantasies within the subconscious, a vicious cycle is set up, wherein the sexual glands become overstimulated and produce an excessive quantity of hormones. This adds up to a state of organic "necessity" which triggers a corresponding subconscious mental state, and this intensifies the fantasies to an unbearable degree. The efforts of the waking-consciousness to prevent these subconscious pressures from finding expression in words and acts adds to their power and increases the internal pressures. The results of all this are the premature exhaustion of the sex glands, and as the entire endocrine system is closely related in function, the premature drying up of the sex hormones of internal secretion bring about a slowing down in function of the pituitary, thyroid, adrenals, etc., and perhaps to an alteration of the sex hormones of internal secretion, when the glands near the point of exhaustion, which is carcinogenic or cancer producing.

MORBID CONDITION

Orientation. Creative Realism believes that the foregoing explains the sexual orientation of many of our dreams, but we take the view (at variance with Freud's theory) that most of our "sleeping dreams" are products of our "waking fantasies" or daydreams; that they are the fantastic answers computed from fantastic data furnished by the deliberately induced, hormone-producing-sensation-stimulating fantasies; that those dreams which originate in the unconscious always express an organic need, or a functional distress, and nothing more. A meal of lobster eaten before retiring may produce many fearful dreams. Like-wise overstimulated sex glands may produce more pleasant dreams.

Superconscious dreams. There is another type of dream which belongs to a category different from those mentioned above. They are dreams produced by consciousness rather than by either the subconscious or the unconscious. The books of the English scientist Dunne, *The Serial Universe* and *An Experiment with Time* and the books of Dr. J. B. Rhine of Duke University will provide the reader with some excellent examples of this type of dream, but as this chapter is primarily concerned with the control of the sex center, we shall leave this interesting subject for discussion perhaps in a later book of more advanced instruction.

Detachment. Contrary to what is generally believed, the full beauty of a natural and legitimate sexual experience is utterly destroyed when it is preceded by the elaboration of subconscious fantasies. The fantasy is to all intents and purposes *a substitution for the reality.* The lascivious individual is not in love with women, he is in love with, and the victim of, his subconscious fantasies. Thus, detachment of our sex centers from the tyrannous influence of the subconscious fantasy is an essential step toward the attainment of consciousness.

EXERCISE
THE TECHNIQUE

Whenever we find ourselves becoming sexually stimulated by fantasies, however triggered, the technique is to immediately detach our consciousness by going into the "self-remembering" or objective state. The fantasy should not be forcibly repressed; it should be observed objectively and impersonally, and it—the fantasy—will quickly die a natural death. To assist in this process of impersonal detachment, we are going to insist upon the co-operation of our subconscious by means of the posthypnotic suggestion which follows.

POSTHYPNOTIC SUGGESTION

Write down the following to attach to your hand in the usual way:

From this moment onward, control of the sex instinct is becoming centered in its own natural mechanisms. It no longer initiates fantasies, and neither does it respond to fantasies. It is oriented to *reality* and is a natural component of the zest-for-life expressed as high objective consciousness.

MEANING

The objective of the above suggestion is to clarify the *higher* meaning of sex to the subconscious, and when this is accomplished eventually—

perhaps only after long and patient effort—all interpretations of sexual stimuli will be made by the subconscious in accordance with this higher meaning. We shall then be freed from the curse of automatic, self-induced eroticism, whose fantasies keep our consciousness splintered and diffused among the imaginary ghost actors of the dark unreal world of the false personality, and we shall also be freed from the mechanism of "self-destruction" by which the unfit are removed from the "leaven of living nature."

TRANCE DEEPENING

If you have consistently carried out the exercises in autohypnosis given in the previous chapters, it is now safe for you to deepen the autohypnotic trance as much as possible. Thus, you may add to the usual sleep suggestion the following:

Your eyes are growing heavier and heavier . . . they are completely closed . . . you are going deeper and deeper in autohypnotic trance . . . deeper and deeper . . . I can give you autohypnotic suggestions and awaken you at any time . . . now you are sound asleep . . . sound asleep . . . etc.

CHAPTER 24

Man Against Himself

Emotion as subjective feeling or experience is explained as
arising from a preparatory motor attitude, maintained as wish
or readiness or intention to act, and held in leash pending the
lifting of whatever form of interfering mechanism is holding up
the final action. Preparatory attitude in a motor sense causes
the consciousness of preparation. . . . the emotional feeling
comes from the unexpressed attitude.

N. BULL AND L. GIDRO-FRANK
Journal of Nervous and Mental Diseases
August 1950: 112-97

THE EMOTIONAL CENTER AND ITS POWER RESERVES

Crile's investigations. About forty years ago while conducting his
epoch-making investigation of the cause of shock, Dr. George Crile of
the Cleveland Clinic demonstrated that every cell of a living body is in
effect a microscopic dipolar battery for the production of bioelectrical
current. He showed that the current thus produced is collected by
strategically situated neurons, and conducted to a series of natural storage batteries called plexuses situated within the body from whence it
is fed out as needed to the operational systems, by the control centers
of the brain, acting through their numerous subsidiary control centers.

The sixth center. Five of the centers possess their own "storage batteries" which under normal circumstances provide an abundance of
power with which to operate their respective systems, but the sixth
control center, the emotional center, presides over the massive reserves

of power which can be thrown in behind any or all of the other centers should their own "storage batteries" prove inadequate to furnish enough current during an emergency. The main "storage battery" for this reserve power is the solar plexus.

Impulse to action. Every answer that is clearly formulated by the subconscious computing machine strives to express itself in action. In primitive man the action came usually before the idea explaining the action dawned. In short, the computed answer first triggered the appropriate control center, and *then* appeared in the forefront of the intellect to be touched by consciousness as an idea. There was no clear dividing line between thought and physical action. No hypothetical problems concerned with the future bothered these remote ancestors—they were concerned solely with the practical and the immediate—and so the sensory data to be computed were based upon the immediate physical situation which confronted them.

Flight and combat. Danger lurked everywhere in the early environment, and survival often depended upon the swiftness with which the emotional center threw the reserves of power in behind the instinctive center to charge the organism with the glycogen and hormones for an expected violent effort and the moving center to ready it for flight or combat. The result of this operation being oft-repeated over the tens of thousands of years was the evolution of a "liaison structure" between the emotional, instinctive, and moving centers, a structure of nerve fibres ready to reach out and "clasp hands" so that the instinctive and moving centers would be directly united with the center which controlled the body's power reserves. When this "clasping of hands" takes place, we have a peculiar and generalized sensation known as *fear.*

Evolution. As the centuries went by, the environment became more complicated and civilized and hence less dangerous in a physical sense, so that a corresponding adjustment took place also in the subconscious computing machine in order to deal with the increasing complexities.

THE CENSOR

Shift in emphasis. Gradually the emphasis on life became shifted from the immediately present situation to the hypothetical future situation. It became necessary to plant enough grain and to raise enough meat to feed the entire community through the winter, and so on. No longer was it expedient to "act first and think afterwards"; survival demanded a reversal of this procedure. So the subconscious elaborated a sort of a "filtering mechanism" which would repress those of its computed answers which were inappropriate to the new order of things from erupting into action, while allowing those which seemed appropriate to pass through. This mechanism is called "the censor" by psychologists, and the "false personality" by Creative Realism.

False personality. As civilization became still more complicated, fewer and fewer of the old primitive computed answers which exploded into physical action were appropriate; in fact, such impulsive "thoughts" became almost as great a danger to the individual in this developing reversal of order as would have been an absence of them during the old bloody days of combat and flight. It became necessary to prevent their eruption at all costs, and the false personality called upon the ancient fear mechanism for aid. It pushed down fibrils which connected it with this mechanism, and fear became as strong a deterrent as it was formerly an impulsion.

New connections. Ideally, these fear mechanisms were temporary makeshifts, which should have deteriorated by "an unclasping of hands" of the fibrils, as the light of objective consciousness dawned and became brighter and brighter, to take the individual out of the primitive and automatic reflex type of behavior by furnishing him with the vision and understanding necessary to a self-activating unit of nature's consciousness. Nerve connections are made in response to a demand, and when this demand ceases, the connections are broken and are either reorganized into new systems or degenerate and disappear. Practically, this has not taken place, because we have become sensation addicts and have kept these outmoded connections intact by means of the fantasies of our waking-dream-life.

Reverberations. The situation now is that sometimes an answer, computed from fantastic data, triggers the old fear mechanism and furnishes an impulse to physical action. The emotional center pours its reserves of energy, as of old, into the instinctive and the moving centers, preparing the body for violent action; the highly charged "thought" impulse arrives in the "filtering mechanism," and this calls upon the fear mechanism for help to repress the dangerous impulse. The emotional center is thus called upon to divide the reserve energy of the body, first, into activating the primitive fear mechanism, and, second, into violently opposing and repressing the mental component of the fear mechanism.

The primitive fear impulse to *act* triggers the instinctive center into pouring glycogen and hormones into the blood to suspend all activities other than these and to speed up the heart action and so on. The moving center is triggered into charging the motor system with all available energy, to raise the tension in all of the muscles, and so on.

Pressures. The interference mechanism of the false personality holds up final action, and with the assistance of the power furnished by the emotional center, repudiates the projected action and hurls the idea back into the subconscious. But all ideas, by their very nature, seek to express themselves in action, and all *emotionalized* ideas *must* express themselves in action, either directly or, if this is blocked, indirectly. So the pressure toward action from below, and the pressure to prevent action from above, creates a demoralizing or paralyzing tension throughout the whole subconscious organization, which sometimes figuratively "blows out at the seams" as a psychosis. We often observe this situation manifested as "battle fatigue."

Sexual fantasies. We see a variation of the above, when the sex center is powerfully activated by a fantasy. As you will have gathered from the preceding chapter, the sex center is archetypal and exists in even the most primitive organisms in some form; it has the most ancient and firmly established connecting structure by which it can draw additional power from the energy reserve depots when these are triggered by the emotional center. When a sexual impulse becomes strongly charged by the emotional center, there results an even more powerful battle with the fear mechanism than in the case of fear versus fear. The battling of such an impulse for expression against the power mobilized to prevent its expression creates a state of mental and nervous instability known as neurosis.

One-way street. Once a clear answer has been arrived at—whether or not it be a fantastic answer derived from fantastic data—by the subconscious computing machine, it is on a one-way street toward expression. The only way in which such an answer-idea can be destroyed is to deprive it of its emotional center backing. Deprived of this, it fades away. Since the days of Freud's early discovery of the damage done by these repressed impulses, psychiatry has been mainly concerned with devising ways and means of doing just that.

Wastage. Now disregarding for the moment the pathological out-
me of exhausted endocrine glands, of long-sustained muscular tensions,
long-sustained lethal tensions of the nervous system, and mental insta-
lity (called worry), the wastage of precious energy needed by the
dy for its normal work of repair and replacement, for combatting
thogenic bacteria, and for the orderly operation of the subconscious
alogue computer, is tremendous. A war against an outer enemy is
depressing waste of effort, but the above type of war conducted against
rselves by means of our own energy is simply suicide. Furthermore,
ere can be no surplus from which to produce the "fine material"
eded for the higher type of effort while this wastage is going on.

Ramifications. The fear mechanism, which originally developed as
simple reserve power switch that could be thrown in to enable our .
ysical bodies to better cope with physical emergencies, has become
ormously elaborated as a repressive mechanism by the false personality.
 fact, we might think of the false personality as being woven from the
read of fear. We still use today the fear mechanism which alerted our
dies in ancient days when a stranger was encountered in the jungle,
e wary approach, the holding forth of the weapon-wielding right
and to show that it was empty, the baring of the teeth in an ingratiating
in, which said: "I mean no harm, but behold my fighting equip-
ent lest you should think my inoffensiveness due to weakness."

Fear of weakness. Any display of physical weakness in primitive times,
ny display of reluctance to fight, was fatal, for only the strong sur-
ved in nature's plan to produce their kind. Meat was food and our
mote ancestors were not particular about what kind of meat they ate.
unger might easily furnish the impulse to slay a companion, and doubt-
ss often did; were the impulse not denied physical expression by an
terfering fear mechanism, it is probable that Homo sapiens would
ave become extinct long before this fear mechanism became elaborated
 the point where it could develop a hydrogen bomb.

Fiction of equality. Fear brought forth the fiction of "equality." If
ll men were only equal, it would not be necessary to fear each other, and
 laws were made which would confer equal rights upon the weak and
e strong. But there is no equality in the physical aspects of nature; the
ody of nature has evolved through a ruthless process of competition in

which the weak are eliminated. She could not have built her tremendously resilient globe-covering body by any other process.

Fear mechanisms dominate. The physical body of man was perfected at least a hundred thousand years ago, and so physical competition has long been outmoded. The competition has now shifted to the mental area, where the mentally strong prey upon the mentally weak—though not often consciously. We call this "social injustice" and deplore it even as we perpetuate it. Thus fear mechanisms continue to dominate us. We subconsciously fear our competitor in business, in love, in social eminence, and in politics, and we still approach him stiltedly, baring our teeth and extending our empty right hand as of yore.

The future. All of our science has been organized upon the business of predicting or anticipating the future; and so have our lives as nations and as individuals. Things must be brought together from widely dispersed points at a certain future point in time, and they must be manufactured and redistributed in advance of their need. Our own future must be provided for in advance and provision made in advance to take care of our dependents when we die, and so on. Yet the fear mechanism, elaborated as a false personality, is quite inadequate to this task. It is essentially repressive, not creative. The false personality is not so much motivated by the idea of creating a future condition, as it is by *fear* of losing the prevailing condition. Evolution is a progression and no present condition can be preserved: a condition must undergo change; it must either go forward to a better condition or deteriorate and disappear.

SUMMARY

THE FALSE PERSONALITY

The false personality, then, is a complex, automatic, fear mechanism designed to filter all impulses to action through a meshwork of fear before releasing them. We do not "love our neighbors as we do ourselves" while we live and move and have our being in the false personality; we fear them, except for those few whom long experience has taught us we need not fear. We fear the future, fear the present, and only the past is glamorous—because it need not be feared.

MOTIVE POWER

The false personality draws its motive power from the emotional center. Deprived of this power, it fades away and the miasma of fear we have hitherto lived in is banished by the sunlight of consciousness. Freed from its parasitic fear mechanisms, the great energy reserves of the body presided over by the emotional center become available for a higher type of work, which we shall discuss later.

SELF-REMEMBERING

Henceforth, when you feel an emotionalized idea arising, detach yourself from it by self-remembering. Do not repress the thought, but objectively observe it, and it will quickly die away. Try at such times to recollect the gist of this chapter and this will help in diffusing the power concentrated in the idea.

POSTHYPNOTIC SUGGESTION

In working toward control of the emotional center by autohypnotic suggestion, achieve the deepest trance state possible as suggested in the previous chapter. The posthypnotic suggestion to be copied down, memorized, then attached to the wrist is as follows:

From this moment onward, every emotional impulse which arises will automatically trigger the self-remembering state. I shall immediately attain detachment from the emotion and shall not be moved, either mentally or physically, by it.

PERSISTENCE

It is again stressed that this work of gaining control over the centers calls for great persistence in exerting a deliberately *willed effort*. We cannot expect to attain the tremendous benefits which ensue from this course unless we work at it. As was stressed before, however, the rewards are not delayed until final victory has been achieved; some worthwhile results will be obtained even from the first.

CHAPTER 25

Conscious Evolution

Imagination creates things that could be, or could happen, whereas fantasy invents things that are not in existence, which never have been, or will be.

CONSTANTIN STANISLAVSKI

FORCES OF NATURE

The invisible and immeasurable. However great the part played by blind physical forces in shaping the original microscopic bits of living matter formed upon this planet into their present complex and diversified forms, we are going to have to admit that something else also had a hand in the shaping. That this hand is invisible and immeasurable in terms of energy makes no difference; the evidence of its directive control is unmistakable.

Evolution. Consider this miraculous shaping of bodies: first, the organization of protoplasm from the inert and lifeless minerals, then the forming of it into the elementary engine of life, the cell, with nucleus, containing all of the complex mechanism of gene-containing chromosomes. The original genes must have contained the catalytic capacity for reproducing themselves, and not only that, but for organizing quintillions of bodies of different specific types—and all this *in advance* of their development.

The riddle. In the development of the microscopic human egg-cell into a man or a woman, we see structures taking form in *preparation* and in *advance* of conditions to follow. We see the gristly organization of bones in advance of the elastic muscles to clothe them. We see the lungs shaped as solid glands which will miraculously hollow with the entrance of the first air. We see the machinery of sight, hearing, feeling, taste, and smell being prepared in advance of a condition of existence in which these will be needed, a condition of existence that the foetus, a semi-aquatic parasite, can know nothing of.

Walking back in time. The science of genetics does not elucidate the above riddle. It adequately explains the present fully operational machinery, but this only pushes the riddle further back. If in imagination we walk backward in time, and assume that all of the machinery necessary to produce a man is contained in the human egg-cell, we find this was produced by a man who was produced by an egg-cell, which was produced by a man, and so on. Inevitably, we come back to the first protoplasmic egg-cell formed on the planet. We must then assume that the machinery for the next step forward in evolution was placed within this egg-cell in advance of the experience, in the way that a present-day foetus develops or organizes the machinery of sight, and the like, in advance of the experience of light, and so on.

Imagination. Memory does not explain this riddle. An egg-cell could not recall experiences that it never had. The grouping together of conditions and the bringing of them into a sharp focus in advance of their actual occurrence is not an act of memory. It is a feat of *imagination.* Memory records that which has already happened, but only imagination can inform us of *what is to happen.* Therefore, to prepare itself in structure and function in advance, for each forward step in evolution, we must either credit the humble amoeba with an extraordinary creative imagination, arising from within itself, or we must believe that this microscopic bit of protoplasm acted as a *resonator* to a creative imagination existing beyond itself.

MIND OF NATURE

Analogy. It is not difficult to conceive such a concept. We might think of a great mind surrounding our planet even as our atmosphere surrounds it. In the enveloping atmosphere of air are a number of different levels of density from the fifteen-pound pressure per square inch at sea level to the insignificant density of the top-level of the ionosphere 250 miles up. We can think of the mind of nature symbolically in a similar way: the spiritual ionosphere representing consciousness; a lower stratum representing a cause-and-effect computing machine (like a super-human subconscious); and the lowest level representing a purely automatic stratum which responds to stimuli but does not initiate them. We can think of this stratum in terms of a superhuman unconscious.

Incarnation. We can think of this enveloping mind of nature entering into a relationship with matter with its lower aspects first to prepare the machinery with which to sustain the higher aspects. This would mean both a descending from above and an ascending from below in a continuous process of evolution. It would explain why no absolutely new species have been brought forth during the past million years or so. When a stratum of nature's mind is completely involved or incarnated in matter, the "species" it represents is "fixed."

"Purpose." Of course there arises the question of why such a supreme mind should desire to imprison itself in inert matter. As to this we can only hazard a guess. Every living organism is an energy-system which uses a part of the energy it develops to maintain itself. It draws in nutrients from its surroundings, and throws out of its system by excretion energy no longer suitable in pattern. Finally it generates new systems, independent of itself, as young individuals of its own kind.

ENTROPY AND CREATION

Continuous process. Physics tells us that the universe is progressing toward an ultimate heat death; that when some billions of years hence a state of maximum entropy is reached, all space will be at the same temperature and the processes of nature will cease. *Living nature is anti-entropic.* As the "material" systems of nature are running down, the "living" systems are building up and evolving, at least on our planet, and we might assume that a similar process is going on elsewhere in nature. In fact, it may ultimately be discovered that a simultaneous process of entropy and creation is taking place continuously; that the processes of nature observed by physical science are but a fraction of the picture; that the mind which enables the physicist to understand his observations has not taken time out to observe itself because it is physically immeasurable.

Reconstruction. In short, the energy dissipated by such nonliving systems as, for instance, our own sun is collected and transformed and used to build up finer and more complex types of energy systems called "living systems." The known facts of evolution are evidence that the whole trend of these living systems in their totality is creative.

Reproduction. On our planet all organisms reach a stage of their evolution called maturity, and then they reproduce new organisms of their own kind, so passing on the work of creation. The impulsion to reproduce is the most compelling and the most universal of all instincts. The whole of living nature is certainly more than the sum of its parts, but we might assume that the mind of nature surrounding our planet and clothing itself in a physical "body" woven from inert and lifeless minerals is impelled also by an inner necessity to reproduce itself . . . as perhaps it, itself, is a reproduction. Perhaps the physical cocoons we call bodies are necessary to the achievement of a separation and a crystallization of individual creative minds, from the great mind of nature, and that eventually each human mind which accepts the challenge of evolution is destined to become a great mind of nature to people the earth and the air of another planet with the physical substructure which shall support a race of men as the inheritors of its high creative consciousness.

IMAGINATION

Definition. So much for the hypothetical why of things; let us now return to a discussion of imagination. As is evidenced, imagination is the nonmaterial or mental phenomenon that *must precede* all material construction.

Imagined machines. The dictionary definition of "machine" is: "Any mechanism, simple or compound, for applying or directing force." Before we can attempt to build or create a thing, however simple, we must create a mental picture of it. It is impossible for us to create a thing otherwise. That which cannot be imagined, cannot be created, and, conversely, anything which can be imagined *can* be created. We are not speaking of "fantasy" now, but of the properly visualized and closely integrated imaginary "machines" conceived by the creative mind.

Genius at work. A study of the biographies of creative geniuses reveals many widely divergent personality types and characters, but the stories of their creations all reveal the same process—the sudden, or painfully slow, conceiving of an imaginary integrated machine which explained some hitherto unknown or misrepresented function of nature. Such imaginary machines (as in the case of Planck's quantum theory or Einstein's theory of relativity) directed the energy of millions into new channels and became rungs of the ladder of human evolution.

Final cause. Once an imaginary machine has been created and checked by all available means and evidence as to its workability, it acts as a final cause by directing the energy of those associated with it or sharing it into the channels clearly defined by it. A little thought will demonstrate that our entire lives are regulated and ordered by the imaginary machines others have conceived in the past. The houses we live in, the beds we sleep upon, the clothing we wear, and the packaged foods we eat, the automobile we drive, and the road that we drive it upon . . . all these things, together with our acquired abilities to read, write, and reason, were once imaginary machines without any substance.

Nature's imagination. To return to the proposition offered in the first two paragraphs of this chapter, it would seem evident that creation of living nature on this planet must have been preceded by the creation of a gigantic imaginary machine, and that this acted as the "final cause" or blueprint which channeled the energy of the blind physical forces into shaping the first globules of protoplasm and guided their evolution upward to the race of mankind.

UNDERSTANDING

Organizing data into machines. We only understand that which we are able to reintegrate as imaginary machines in our own subconscious. We can memorize data, but unless we can organize them structurally by our imagination into machines, the data have no meaning . . . we do not understand them. Thus, imagination and understanding (know how) are essentially one and the same thing. Those among us who have experienced occasional flashes of clear consciousness know that it is only describable as a sudden illuminating flash of *understanding*. It is like a brilliant lightning flash suddenly illuminating a dark and hidden landscape that we have been feeling our way toward, showing all objects for an instant in sharp outline and in their proper relationship to each other.

Understanding and meaning. Nature then is a tremendous *meaning,* gradually unfolding in the process of physical, and now mental, evolution. Consciousness is that which *understands meaning.* By understanding a meaning consciousness becomes a part of the meaning . . . is united with it, in other words. And imagination and consciousness are one.

WILL AND CONSCIOUS CREATION

Definition. Will might be defined as the *ability to do* in an individual sense. Ordinary man does not possess this ability to do. He merely possesses the ability to *react* to circumstances initiated elsewhere, or brought together by the laws of chance. When the imagination is freed, it is a self-controlled system illuminated by consciousness and possessing will. Then and only then does man become an initiator of causes and a conscious creator.

Three-storied house. Man then is structured like a three-storied house. He is provided with the first and second stories, but he must build the third himself. The first story is structured by nature in the same manner as are the physical bodies of all other organisms. It is purely a mechanical engine for the collection, transformation, and distribution of energy. The second story is an analogue computer—the subconscious—with control centers which operate automatically in response to the answers furnished by the computing machine; in this second story, the embryonic imagination runs at random and is known as "fancy," the producer of fantasies. Once in a while the front end of the computing machine is touched by a faint glow of consciousness, and we are pleased to call this our "intellects."

The third story. Now our further development depends upon fashioning fancy into imagination; with the aid of the tiny glow of our intellects at first, we strive to coax our fancy into some sort of an integrated effort and to form our subconscious filed data into some sort of a coherent, logical pattern related to the rest of nature. To do this we use the technique of autohypnosis, alternated with periods of practicing the technique of self-remembering. By autohypnosis we are able to direct our fancy into an increasing degree of directive control, and the will we exercise in the process gradually becomes merged with it, so metamorphosing fancy gradually into creative imagination. By *self-remembering* we free for a moment or two the integrating embryo will-fancy, as we might pull upward on a buried post after working it from side to side and loosening a little from its cloying attachment to the earth.

Ascending control. As we gain control over the two lower stories of our house, and set these in order, fancy and will become united as imagination in the process until the time comes when we are able to pull "the imbedded post" up full length at will and to hold it there according to our pleasure. Then we are in a position to turn to the control of the finer forces of nature, as individually conscious units of the great consciousness of nature.

CONSCIOUS EVOLUTION NOT EASY

Like the acorn. It is re-emphasized that there is nothing easy about this process of conscious evolution. Nature creates men wholesale, knowing that like the acorns, for every million brought forth just five or six will root, and of these perhaps only one will develop the fortitude to withstand the hazards of the laws of chance and develop into an oak capable of transcending them. Of all the billions of human beings who have passed through the cycle of material life, probably less than a million have developed a clear consciousness of their individual identities—the "Me" spoken of by Jesus, when He stated that such people would never know death. The vast majority of us come into physical existence unconscious and go back into the great reservoir unconscious. During our period here we pass our time in a world of dreams with only a flitting moment of occasional consciousness. Can we hope to accomplish in death what we could not accomplish in life?

The means. Even as the acorn has within it the *means* of its own evolution into an oak, should the laws of chance cast it into a fortuitous combination of circumstances, such as the right soil, and so on, and its escaping the notice of prowling wild hogs and squirrels, the same is true of human beings. Each of us is born with the *means* of our evolution into conscious and immortal individuals, and should a fortuitous set of circumstances trigger our realization that we can become such, and stimulate us into making the *first self-willed efforts of our lives* toward our own higher development, and should we escape the dangers inherent in mass subconscious thinking long enough so that the shoot of our own consciousness may emerge, we enter into a new field of higher endeavor of unlimited possibilities.

Identification. We are always subconsciously "identified" with many things. For instance, let us suppose that a man is a physician by profession; he is always aware—sleeping and waking—of his calling. He is a man, but he is a particular *kind* of a man. Moreover, he was not born as this particular kind of a man, but only became such a man after he had organized, through long study and effort, a complex subconscious mental machine which enables him to deal effectively with the problems presented to him by his patients.

Other identifications. Our man, however, is not only a doctor; he is many other things as well. So we will "imagine" that this subconscious mental machine is geared to his subconscious computing machine in the same manner, let us say, that a lathe might be geared to a drive-shaft which transmits power to a long line of different machines in a factory. In the "factory" of the subconscious are many machines, each of which has been built by mental effort. Our man, let us suppose, is also married and has a family. He has built up a subconscious machine for dealing with the problems incidental to this phase of his life. So he identifies himself with his profession and with his family. In addition to these factors, he has been born, let us say, in New Zealand, and the conditioning effects of his environment and education in his early formative years have built up another "identification machine" for dealing with his duties and responsibilities of citizenship.

Still more. Our man who identifies himself by reason of his specific machines as a physician, married and a New Zealander, might play chess; another machine is built for handling the problems peculiar to the game. Should our man also enjoy golf and tennis, more machines are created, and so on. The number of such subconscious machines which may be created within the subconscious of a given individual seems well nigh unlimited. Michelangelo is an example of this.

Split power. All of these machines consume power, just as do the machines of a factory; moreover, they are all dependent upon the main computing machine of the subconscious to work out the answers to their problems. Thus, if we have too many "identification" machines in gear at the same time clamoring for answers from the computer, it is unable to adequately serve any; the power available is also divided and all of the machines in gear are slowed down to the point of uselessness. The result is a muddled and confused state and an inability to clearly think through any problem.

Knowing. Now if we ran a factory on the above basis, we would go bankrupt in short order. Without a manager no factory could operate efficiently. If each mechanic at each machine threw his machine into gear when he felt like it, and threw it out of gear again in the middle of an operation when he felt bored; if half a dozen mechanics clamored at once for the services of a computer, and there was no understanding or knowledge of the end product to turn out; we should not have a factory, we should have a madhouse. The knowledge of each mechanic would be a mere fragment of specialized knowledge, and an over-all knowledge would be necessary to the proper direction and co-ordination of all the fragmented "know-hows."

Fancy. The random and erratic running of all our little subconscious machines is what we know as "fancy." Our problem is to co-ordinate their work until they run properly and consecutively toward turning out a worthwhile product at the end of each operation. Each machine must be thrown into gear when it is needed, and promptly thrown out of gear and detached when its operation is finished. Thus power is conserved, the computer is able to work effectively, and all unnecessary worries caused by the simultaneous operation of too many machines are avoided.

Purpose. The first step in accomplishing the above is to create by our imagination a big machine which will give purpose and point to the entire "factory" and automatically regulate each machine to its proper place. This machine must give us a new identification, which will embrace all of our little separate identifications. It must identify us as creative units of the great mind of nature.

THE EXERCISE
VISUALIZATION

Our exercise for this chapter is going to be a little more difficult than usual. It might be well to take a sheet of paper and on one side draw a picture of the world. The artistic merit of the picture is unimportant, the idea is to fix a concrete picture in your subconscious for it to use as a symbol.

THE FIELD

Now take a red pencil and draw a thick red band around your "world" and mark it "unconsciousness." Next, draw a blue band of about half that width, and mark it "subconscious." Lastly, draw a yellow band on the outside, about twice the width of the red and blue bands together, and mark this "consciousness."

PRECIPITATION

Now sit back, relax, and strongly visualize this picture you have created. Endow it with imaginary life. Create in your mind's eye a visual image of our world as a mighty sphere slowly revolving in space. Visualize it as being surrounded by the glowing tricolored envelope of mind. Visualize the dense, lower layer of red settling on the surface of the earth as a raincloud might precipitate . . . and imagine that like a raincloud this layer is composed of individual different-sized droplets.

FERMENT

Visualize each droplet as it meets the earth starting a muddy "ferment" called "protoplasm" and from this imagine different, tiny bodies organizing. Each of these bodies is an engine for the collection, transforming, and distribution of physical energy toward the accomplishment of a new creative purpose, and each little engine is equipped with a resonating system which keeps it attuned to the automatically balancing, cause-and-effect vibrations set up in the "blue layer" as on the one hand the activities of the living bodies send vibrations to it and it sends down responses to the totality of these to co-ordinate the over-all upward evolutionary movement of all.

SYNTHESIS

Many types of these one-celled animals resonate to only fractional notes of a scale, as it were, and when their development as individuals has been completed, they suddenly unite with others of their kind to form "full notes" and from the single-celled algae and protozoa, we see the metzoa type of animals, made up of numbers of cells working co-operatively, forming. When the development of this type has proceeded, we imagine certain of them resonating to chords of simultaneous vibrations of similar pitch, and we imagine that in response the more complex organizations of cells, such as the worms, mollusks, crabs, fish, and so on, emerge; and in response to still more complex chords still higher forms evolve as reptiles, birds, and hooved animals, then the apes, and lastly . . . man.

SUBCONSCIOUS

Imagine that these last creatures to evolve—men—incorporate in miniature two of the three phases of the great mind of nature—the red phase which builds and operates his body in common with those of all other living creatures (and this forms the unconscious) . . . and a "blue phase" organized into a little cause-and-effect structure he calls his subconscious.

CONSCIOUSNESS

On top of this "blue subconscious structure" we might imagine a pale blue bud just touched by white occasionally at the very tip. This man considers as his conscious mind. Imagine that its roots are entangled in the machines of the "blue subconscious layer" and that in order to thrust up its stalk and open its flower it must, by its innate will-imagination, organize the haphazard "factories" of the "blue subconscious layer" into an orderly functional system. Imagine that this chain of clearly formed pictures will help accomplish this.

AUTOHYPNOTIC SUGGESTION

Now write the following suggestion on the reverse side of the paper containing your sketch.

The visual images I have just conceived will *cause* your machines to arrange themselves in a corresponding and coherent pattern. Only the appropriate machines shall gear themselves for each particular operation, and the others will not interfere. Your whole factory will respond appropriately in this way to my visualized commands.

SLEEP SUGGESTION

Now start your metronome. Attach the paper to your hand in the usual manner and go on with the autohypnotic technique.

CHAPTER 26

Stairway to the Stars

And the world passeth away, and the lusts thereof: but he that
doeth the will of God abideth forever.

I JOHN 2:17

MENTAL FORCES

Work. We have presented a concept of nature as a space surrounding our planet, traversed by lines of mental force, to which all organisms
resonate and respond according to their species. This response is known
as "work." To live is to work, for life *is* work. Stating it in another way,
work is the activity of mind acting in conjunction with matter; when
this activity is halted completely by disease or accident, *we cease to live,*
at least in a physical sense.

Obedience. All living things are subject to the physical and mental
laws of nature, and below the level of humanity these organisms are
ruled by chance and bound by the laws of probability. All are equipped
with resonating mechanisms, but nature knows that of all the millions
of seeds put forth, only a chance-favored few will reach maturity and
reproduce their kind. Only the comparative few will develop to the
point where they *achieve obedience* to the higher octaves of law.

Review. Against the tremendous backdrop of the inscrutable universe
we have tried to illuminate our tiny world with meaning . . . and a
purpose. We know that for ages, in the processes of its forming, the
earth would have seemed both meaningless and purposeless to an observer in space—a place of seething torment, of deadly gases, of earthquakes and erupting volcanos; of land masses and mountain ranges

flung aloft, only to be swallowed in a succeeding cataclysm. Yet out of all this horrific tumult were born the oceans, the land masses, and the atmosphere.

Life. Again to an observer, the emergence of living forms from the mists of this lonely little planet would have appeared equally meaningless and purposeless at first—microscopic bits of protoplasm slithering about in the mud, continually changing their shapes; then with these primary building blocks once formed, shape after shape emerging, crude and fantastic bodies of leaping, crawling, and flying things, struggling against each other and the pitiless, unbridled forces of nature for a place on the ladder of evolution, each species bringing forth uncounted millions of its kind to suffer, struggle, and die horribly and be devoured by other living things which coveted their protoplasm. How senseless and purposeless it would have all seemed.

The climb. The observer would see nature ruthlessly putting an end to types which it had brought forth when these had outlived their usefulness. He would see a gradual refinement and specialization taking place in the species which remained. Almost imperceptibly as the aeons rolled forward in time, he would become aware of a change taking place, of an increasing order and harmony emerging from the chaotic confusion, of a growing volume in the obbligato of mating calls and bird songs to counter the discordant clamor of the hunting packs and the terror-wrung cries of the doomed.

Beauty. He would sense the development of the intangible quality of beauty as life grew in importance and the great living body of nature grew in height, width, and depth on the planet's surface. Then perhaps he would realize quite suddenly the unimportance of death; that although individuals, like ripples on an ocean, die and disappear, they are replaced by other similar ripples; that the great ocean of life never dies; that the changing forms on the surface of the ocean of life are due to a change taking place within the ocean; that the visible is an expression of an invisible reality which nothing can halt nor stay; *that nothing ever dies but death.*

THE CONSCIOUS

The irony of nature. Perhaps our observer would muse upon the irony of these countless living things, precipitated into physical life like raindrops drawn from an ocean, and returning thereto at physical death, having no knowledge of identification of their source, the ocean, but believing that death would mean extinction of this precious raindrop of life forever.

Debut of man. Then he would mark the appearance of man—an ugly, hairy, long-bodied, bow-legged creature, with a couple of bony ridges like the ape for a forehead, an underslung lower jaw, and great canine teeth. He would, could he see inside the skull of this creature, note the slow development of a complex brain. Commencing with the bulb at the top of the spinal cord of the primitive vertebrates and fishes, our observer would see fresh organizations of brain tissue roofing over prior organizations, the skull changing in shape to accommodate this enlarged brain, the forehead lifting to make room for the frontal lobes.

Language. As a result of these new organizations, our observer would hear the inarticulate mumblings, screams, and grunts of the creature evolve into a language, a language of sounds by which this man creature would learn to express the *meanings* awakened in his mind by the streams of stimuli pouring in through his eyes, ears, nose, skin, and taste-buds, a language by which he would one day learn to express things far, far beyond the power of his present imagination to conceive.

Sparks. To acquire a new skill, we must build a new brain organization to make it permanent, and we must direct millions of individual brain cells to this task. To acquire a division and development of its creative powers, and perchance to create and reproduce itself in a similar way on other planets, we can assume that our parent, the supreme consciousness of nature, divided its mind, the bearer of its consciousness, among its children and heirs.

Degrees. Each one of these sparks of itself had to be awakened by experience to an understanding of itself by pitting itself against chance-born circumstances to achieve separation from the circumstances, then domination over them. In this way two things would be accomplished: (1) a gradual awakening of awareness within the embryonic creators of the sleeping meaning or final cause within themselves, (2) the gradual reversal of entropy by collecting, transforming, and applying the energy given off by the physical systems to new meaningful creative systems.

CREATIVE REALISM AS A STAIRWAY

Unfolding the theory. It will take at least five books in addition to this present one to fully unfold the theory of Creative Realism. Each book should be regarded as a stairway leading to a landing. It is hoped that the reader, through practice of the suggested exercises, will climb by testing his weight on each individual step until he reaches the landing directly above him. When he reaches that landing, he should pause long enough to orient himself fully to the new perspective this elevation gives him before commencing the climb to the next platform. Before Mount Everest may be scaled, the climber must adjust himself to altitude, and he can only do this by camping briefly at a number of succeeding levels. Life has climbed the slopes of evolution in a similar manner . . . stage after stage.

Diversity. The tree grows as a unity formed of billions of different individual cells, and from this unity it produces seeds, each having the innate capacity to grow into a tree similar to its parent. Under the influence of external radiation received from the sun by the seed's resonators, the innate meaning of the seed—the tree—commences to unfold, and it swiftly begins to organize roots, shoots, trunk, branches, and leaves. *The meaning* automatically imparted to the seed by its parent governs the direction of the energy-scheme unfolding within the seed. We might think of this *meaning* as the "will of God."

The meaning of life. Like the seed, each human child is born into physical existence with an innate meaning locked up in inframicroscopic particles called "genes," which will unfold and direct the energy-scheme within into building a physical structure similar to that of its human parents. But there is another meaning also locked up within the evolving body, which will only begin to unfold after a certain degree of physical maturity has been reached. This meaning is *consciousness.*

Relationships. Unconsciously we are related to all other living things within the great body of nature. The waste gases exhaled by the trees and the plants form the breath of life to the oxygen-breathing animals, including man, and the waste gases exhaled by us form the breath of life for the plants and the trees. The protoplasm of our bodies is dependent upon the nitrogen fixed by bacteria in the soil and plankton of the ocean so that it becomes available to plants, animals, and fish, which we in turn eat as food. Subconsciously we are related by the currency of ideas; by education, literature, and all communicated information and misinformation, our individual subconscious machines are meshed into "national subconscious machines" and all national subconscious machines are loosely related to each other in a world-wide sub-conscious machine. Such is the status of the collective mind of mankind at present. There have been many pauses in the collective climb to this present level, and many climbers are still on the rungs leading to it, but there are so many highly conditioned and thoroughly mechanized intellects crowding it that it is becoming intolerable and a few are starting the climb upward to the next higher level—the level of consciousness.

SCHOOLS

Uniformity, conformity? With the universal spread of education and the building of millions of schools for the standardizing by conditioning of the subconscious minds of the rising generations, there is, of course, a drab sameness and unanimity about civilized life, about the way people think and the things they think about. An individual dares to think independently at his peril, for unless his ideas conform to the standardized conditioned ideas parroted by the orthodox, he becomes an "outlaw" and may expect no mercy. The only conflict allowable is the conflict between dogmas, for a dogma escapes from the "evil" of being an individual thing. In fact, a dogma only exists when a lot of people surrender their rights to think independently and conform to stereotyped patterns of thought concerning religion, politics, finance, business, industry, education, and so on.

"Narrow is the way." Yet the ladder to the next higher landing of consciousness is narrow, and we must mount it one by one. We must grasp the rung above our heads before we may safely reach down to help the person on the rung below us. There is no way in which we may reach the landing of consciousness simultaneously like a marching army or like a class of undergraduates standing in line to receive diplomas. We may only reach it as individuals by transcending, through struggle, the mechanicalness within ourselves, the mechanicalness we have built into false personalities by a lifetime of effort, the mechanicalness by which we are geared like tiny cogs to our mechanical society.

Loneliness. The transition from the subconscious level of mass thinking to conscious individual thinking is difficult, and those on the ladder often suffer from loneliness at first. To fight our own weaknesses single-handed is the supreme test of individuality; to be satisfied with self-approval and a feeling of inner worthiness instead of seeking the approval and the acclaim of others calls for a basic reorientation of the entire personality. Many are unable to make this adjustment at first and retreat down the ladder again to the old level, trying to adapt the new wine of Creative Realism to their old bottles of automatism. This, of course, is like a chicken trying to return to the egg from which it was hatched, and they soon discover the impossibility of the situation and recommence the climb.

The group. It helps when a few individuals organize themselves into a group which by discussions and experiments may keep the interest alive. A group of individuals sharing a common aim, the aim of overcoming their individual weaknesses and by so doing climbing to a higher level of consciousness, sometimes succeeds in raising the status of larger groups to higher levels of creativeness. The group which included Shakespeare and Bacon furnished a nucleus for the generation of a steady and fresh flow of creative ideas.

CREATIVE REALISM AND CREATIVE ENTERPRISE

Gymnastic exercises. The span of human physical life is limited to a few short years and we can by no means carry the physical things we create here beyond the portal of the grave; but the value of creative effort transcends the material things created, for by creating new and better enterprises here, we attune ourselves to creation and develop within ourselves the possibilities of a higher state of consciousness. Creative enterprises are in effect gymnastic exercises through which we may develop ourselves as free individuals.

A system of techniques. Creative Realism is a system of techniques by which the *individual* may escape from the hypnotic condition in which man lives at present into the higher reality of consciousness. We all live in a state of hypnosis, bound by our fantasies and illusions and believing these to be realities. We have become this way through the suggestive influences imposed upon us from the earliest days of our childhood. Hypnosis is exercise of control over the imagination and the subconscious of others by reiterated, monotonous suggestion. All good advertising displays the technique of hypnotic suggestion to a high degree;

all news released is slanted to convey the hypnotic suggestion desired by the publicist; and the intoned sermons and repetitous rituals of our churches are also hypnotic techniques.

Self-hypnosis. Instead of depending upon the hypnotic techniques of others, the Creative Realist uses this potent method deliberately upon his own subconscious mind to condition it to his liking that it may become an efficient computer which finds the correct answers to his ordinary problems from the data supplied by his awakened and co-ordinated senses. In order to employ self-hypnosis in the manner outlined in this book, there must be one part of our minds separated from that part which is hypnotized. With repetition this nonhypnotized part becomes more and more conscious and more and more detached until it assumes a positive relationship to the subconscious on a permanent basis.

Separation. At first, usually, a student will fall sound asleep before his metronome. Later he will become semiconscious of what is going on around him even in the deeper states of trance. Eventually he will become vividly conscious, like the man during the brain-exploration operation mentioned in Chapter Two of this book. From that time onward, auto-hypnosis is no longer necessary, for at a moment's notice he can go into the self-remembering state and give his subconscious an order which will be obeyed with the same fidelity as though he were in the deepest trance state. By the achievement of this separation, he has become a conscious individual, an individual no longer at the mercy of his likes and dislikes, of his emotions and the emotions of others. With the vision of conscious-ness he can clearly see what is to be done, and his subconscious, like a faithful executive, stands ever alert to translate his orders into practical realities.

Reversal of method. In the ordinary course of civilization, leaders in every field of endeavor, exercise, perhaps unconsciously, control over men with the idea of building a political system, an industry, or a commer-cial enterprise. Creative Realism holds that every enterprise should be regarded as a gymnasium for the higher development of every individual associated with it, as a means by which he might overcome his own inherent weaknesses; that under such a reversal of policy everyone con-cerned could not fail to benefit.

Conscious employees. The employer would find his production and his sales records climbing with every slight advance in consciousness among his employees. Labor relations would cease to be dominated by envy and suspicion on the one hand and scorn and impatience on the other. As we have seen, these are purely subconscious traits.

Democracy. Every slight increase in consciousness by the electorate would mean a better choice of representatives and a clearer perspective of the issues involved. Instead of spiraling downward into tight totalitarian systems as at present, there would be a rebirth of true democracy.

Freedom. Creative Realism believes that freedom in consciousness is the meaning and the aim of evolution, that man can never be free except through destroying his inner slavery to his lower self. The techniques offered in this book may prove a sword with which to slay this ancient dragon.

CHAPTER 27

Reality

Misty rain on Mount Lu, and waves surging in Che-chiang; when you have not yet been there, many a regret you surely have; but once there and homeward you wend your way, how matter of fact things look. . . . misty rain on Mount Lu and waves surging in Che-chiang.

SU TUNG-P'O

YOUR REALITY

Your mind. We shall commence this closing chapter by recalling our opening statement that your world is your mind. Heat and cold; light and darkness; sound and silence; form, color, and motion . . . all of these things create sense impressions; without a mind to respond to them, they would not exist as realities, but would be indistinguishable elements of the great isomorphic ocean of space-time. In fact, without a mind to behold it, space-time itself (as such) would cease to exist.

Living. Happiness and grief; joy and sorrow; tranquillity and worry; humor and sadness; faith and frustration; love and hatred . . . all of these are also creations of the human mind, and have no existence without a mind to experience them. Yet these mental experiences are the only coinage in which our wages are paid for our work at the loom of creation. If our creative work is well done, we are paid in terms of happiness, joy, tranquillity, love, and faith; and if it is not rightly done, in conformity with the indwelling evolutionary principles of nature (which the prophets of old described as the will of God), we are paid in the coinage of grief, worry, ill-health, and frustration.

The paymasters. We are our own paymasters. The ten thousand million cells of our brains charge and fire in relation to the patterns we have laid down in our own subconscious minds. These rhythms determine the quality of our subconscious mental activity, sleeping and waking. They determine our intellectual prowess, the soundness of our judgments; they may form a pathway which leads to experiences in consciousness which transcend their ability to either explain or describe, or they may lead away from such experiences and turn us into spiritual idiots who live merely in the false pride of intellects, inferior in efficiency to many of the machines they have created.

SCIENCE AND LIFE

Pattern-seeking pioneers. The development of science is a mental development, the result of pattern-seeking pioneers, selecting from an infinity of phenomena such little bits and pieces as their feeble intellects and dim senses may become cognizant of. The invention of elementary particles to explain the atom, for instance, is a purely mental invention; not so long ago we had a picture of a physical world built of only a couple of elementary particles—and these were sufficient to explain it —but further work with the atom demonstrated that the picture was not complete. Consequently, more elementary particles had to be invented to fill the gaps until today there are around twenty elementary particles, and the list is still growing. Not so very different from the system of the primitives who invented a new kind of god or devil to fill in their explanations of natural behavior!

Structures. The basic principles of our modern science have been laid down by a relatively few *conscious* geniuses, such as J. Clerk Maxwell, Rutherford, Einstein, Max Planck, Heisenberg, and others; upon this structure the ramifications have been elaborated by the *intellects* of thousands of other *less conscious* individuals. Consciousness is the instrument of *direct knowing,* whereas the intellect is the tool of this instrument, a tool for *doing.* The intellect can raise questions and point out ignorance, but it cannot of itself produce enlightenment. Inevitably the intellect must raise questions which it cannot answer. Like any other machine it is limited by the principles of its own construction.

Limitations. With the invention of quantum mechanics, the intellect seems to have reached the limits of its horizons. In the words of Professor Bridgeman,* "We are now approaching a bound beyond which

* P. W. Bridgeman, American Academy of Arts and Sciences, Bulletin 111, No. 5.

we are forever stopped from pushing our enquiries . . . not by the construction of the world, but by the construction of ourselves. . . . The world fades out and eludes us, because it becomes meaningless." The intellect—the second section of the "telescope"—has been fully extended, and to gain new horizons, the third section—*consciousness*—must be pushed forth.

The bridge. It would appear that this last great gift of physical science, quantum mechanics with its field concept, may form the bridge which leads from physics to metaphysics, from psychology to parapsychology, from science to religion. Perhaps it holds the key to the explanation of all these phenomena called "miraculous" from earliest recorded history and lately described as "extrasensory phenomena" by Western investigators. Perhaps it holds the promise of a system of progressive spiritual development and enlightenment emerging to replace the "token worship" of formal religion. Perhaps science has placed within our hands the instrument of our salvation as well as the instrument of our destruction.

THE FIELD CONCEPT

Quantum physics. As pointed out before, the picture of the world offered by quantum physics is one of from ten to twenty interpenetrating but qualitatively different fields filling the whole of space. We might visualize an analogy of this as an ocean made up of twenty intermixed different fluids, each of which retains its own identity and its own properties and produces its own particular kind of bubbles. In the field theory, these "bubbles" would represent the elementary particles, such as photons, gravitons, neutrons, electrons, positrons, mesons, and so on. When a number of the right types of "bubbles" coalesce, they form an atom; a light quantum is a bubble which is carried by waves, forming, breaking and forming again as with bubbles in the ocean, but always moving forward with the waves.

The oversoul. Creative Realism conceives that interpenetrating all of these quantum fields is another much more subtle and important field— *a master field of mind,* perhaps even producing its own elementary particle or "menton" as the significant quantum of protoplasm. This is said at the risk of appearing facetious, but the experiments which are described later in this chapter indicate the existence of a form of energy unknown at present to physical science.

Traveling fields. J. Clerk Maxwell was the first to formulate the theory that electromagnetic fields could exist in free space, distant from magnets and charges. Marconi was the first to demonstrate in a practical way that traveling electromagnetic fields could be deliberately created, that a message could be imprinted upon their structure, to be hurled across space with the speed of light and recovered intact at a distant point.

Imprinting. Today when we hear a friend's voice speaking to us over the radio-telephone from London or Auckland, we know that his voice is being imprinted on the structure of such a traveling electromagnetic field and that it is carried to us faster than it would be were he present in the flesh, and shouting his message to us from across the street. The wealth of detail which may be imprinted upon such fields is demonstrated by television.

Stations. To use these traveling electromagnetic fields for our purposes in the above manner, we must, of course, have transmitting stations and receiving stations. The principle of resonance enables a receiving station to attune its receiving apparatus to a number of different fields selectively. For instance, as you sit reading this book, dozens of electromagnetic fields, each imprinted with a different radio program, are passing through your body and are also impinging upon the antenna of your radio, but neither your radio nor your brain are responding to them. If you sit down before your radio, however, turn on the power and select a program in keeping with your mood of the moment; your radio and your brain will respond to that program and your mood of the moment will be intensified or amplified as a consequence of your tuning in that particular program.

Mental fields. It is the theory of Creative Realism that the "mental field" has properties somewhat similar to the electromagnetic field; that every living organism in nature is a creation of this field; that every living organism is continually and automatically creating traveling mental fields, imprinting its desires, its hopes, and its fears upon these and transmitting them; that every living organism is at once a sending and receiving station, and that it is automatically attuned to "pertinent programs" by its "mood" of the moment. Each of the species would, of course, have its own type of signals, but all would be connected and co-ordinated by the great mental field or oversoul in the same manner that the ten thousand million cells of our brains, comprised of a number of different types or "species" of cells, are co-ordinated by the human mind.

PARAPSYCHOLOGY

Definition. Parapsychology is the young, and at present, somewhat chaotic science which is concerned with the study of such subjects as hypnosis, psychokinesis, precognition, telepathy, and all of those phenomena produced by the human mind which are not explainable in terms of the senses and known physical mechanisms. Dr. J. B. Rhine of Duke University is one of the pioneers of this science in the Western world, and during the past eighteen or twenty years has carried on a systematic program of research designed to determine by the statistical method the authenticity of such phenomena.

"Proofs." The majority of those who have studied Rhine's published reports found the evidence in favor of extrasensory phenomena very convincing. His findings, however, have been questioned by some who hold opposing views on the grounds that his data contain either experimental or statistical errors. Some of these investigators have tried to duplicate Rhine's experiments, and have gotten different results. This seems to be a common experience in investigating extrasensory phenomena. It would seem that the principles governing these become distorted by the very act of observation.

Explanation. The distortion or negation of extrasensory phenomena under laboratory test conditions is easily explainable if we accept the mental field theory. The very mood of scepticism, essential to scientific observation, would be impressed upon the field, and would tend to offset and negate the patterns being impressed by the operator. To use an analogy: the "broadcasts" of the operator would be "jammed" by the "broadcasts" of the observer.

Experience. The foregoing theory was substantiated throughout many years of experimentation by this writer—at least to his own satisfaction. The tremendous potency of extrasensory influence in healing—so long as the patient and his family and friends were kept in ignorance of the fact that it was being employed—was very conclusively established. These effects were either offset or reversed when scepticism on the part of others was introduced. The admonition of Jesus to those He healed—"Go thou and tell no man"—was for a reason. Using himself as a "guinea pig" the writer over a period of years, by creating mental patterns according to the techniques given in this book, was able to successively create calamitous environmental circumstances for himself, in which all the bad luck possible seemed to greet his every effort. By reversing the patterns, the environmental circumstances were reversed. All sorts of fortuitous circumstances unexpectedly developed, and even a small amount of effort seemed to bring extraordinary results. These experiments were repeated twenty times.

SIGNIFICANCE

Organizer of matter. The tremendous significance of the foregoing results are obvious. In dealing with mind we are not dealing with organized matter, but with the *organizer of matter.* We are not dealing with circumstances but with the influence which *creates the circumstances.* Those circumstances which are past are beyond recall. The present circumstances arose out of those that are past, and we can only accept them and adapt ourselves temporarily to them; but we are creating our own *tomorrows* today by our mental pátterns . . . *and we can make these what we will.* To paraphrase Napoleon: every individual carries a marshal's baton, not in his haversack but in his brain.

Organizations. If the above is correct, then the success of every organization—from the family of two or three to the nation of two or three hundred million—would be dependent far more upon the mental patterns of its members than upon its mere technical advancement. It would seem that the enlistment of members of various groups, to train themselves in the foregoing principles and techniques, would hold possibilities for the practical verification of the theory.

Two kinds of knowledge. It must be emphasized again, however, that knowledge is of two kinds. First, there is intellectual knowledge. This type of knowledge is dependent upon the building up through exercises, mostly given at school and college, of an efficient "subconscious computing machine" and the storing of data to be used by it in making its computations. Everything pertaining to intellectual knowledge is imitative and originates outside of the individual acquiring it. This entire imitative intellectual system belongs to what we have called the false personality and it has no way of directly determining the true from the false. It works by balancing one thing against another, so that all of its computations are relative to its stored data. If this data is erroneous in any particular, then its computations will be misleading.

False personality. A good intellectual computing machine is an enormously valuable piece of equipment, for it enables us to deal efficiently with the measurable facts of our daily lives, yet in itself it can give us nothing in terms of *direct living experience.* We have all known men of great intellectual prowess who were petty, mean, cavilling, vain, hypo-chondriacs, who lived wretched ulcer-ridden lives and dropped off long before their time from one of the psychosomatic diseases.

True personality. The second type of knowledge is the result of growth of the true personality or soul. *It is a growth of consciousness,* bringing with it knowledge by direct experience. Unless the knowledge of the intellect is viewed in its proper perspective in the light of this direct knowledge, it has no value in terms of living. In fact, unless all acquired knowledge is checked against the knowledge which grows out of our-selves as the result of direct conscious experience, it may lead us to disaster. Intellectual knowledge alone is but borrowed plumage which never grows; it is knowledge of "how's" and it tends to disregard "why's." Thus a man of great intellectual development, without a cor-responding development of the true personality, may well be a highly dangerous, mechanical, and amoral robot, who applies his twentieth-century technology according to the spiritual standards of the caves and jungles.

THE PAY-OFF

A qualitative state. Our real pay-off in life is a qualitative state of the true personality, a state in which we awaken to greet each new-born day with all the eager expectancy of children. It is marked by a complete absence of fear, and a continual sense of the mystery and miracle of living; a feeling that this world is *our* world; that it belongs to us and we to it forever; a sense of knowing that whatever we do, we are work-ing in our own vineyard and are bettering *our* world. In this state there is no envy and no covetousness. We know that each of us is an essential and individual cell of the great mind of nature; like an individual piece cut from a single great creative unity, and that whatever our job happens to be—whether it be that of washing dishes and making beds, or that of a delegate to the parliament of the world at the U.N.—it is an essen-tial job and contributes to the over-all job of creation.

Work, creation, and evolution. Every job in life is an exercise in creation. The job is not too important in itself. Civilizations rise and fall; cities in time disappear beneath the sands of the desert or the vines of the jungles; great works of art moulder in decay and mighty feats of engineering are forgotten in a new age. The only thing which perishes not is *tomorrow* . . . and tomorrow belongs to evolution. Only your true personality marches with evolution. Your borrowed intellectual plumage with its physical mechanism falls apart at the grave. It is the product of physical energy and without the body to supply that energy it must fall silent. But as was said in an early chapter, the mind of man is not examinable as an energy system and all attempts to find a scale of equivalence between conscious experience and energy have failed. If the mind proper and its consciousness is not an energy system, *then there is nothing about it which can die.* It is immortal.

Awakening. The real creative job, then, is to awaken our true personalities—our immortal selves—to consciousness. This perhaps is the indwelling purpose of evolution. We can use whatever job we may be assigned to as an exercise in calling forth all that is highest and most true within ourselves. We can to some degree exercise the prerogatives of gods in our own tiny spheres, whatever they may be, and in doing so build up permanent values within ourselves which shall remain with us after the curtain has fallen on this act of the play, to be carried forward into a new tomorrow to help us perhaps play a more important part in a new drama of creation.

Knowing. This inner knowledge of "deathlessness" cannot be obtained by intellectual means. It defies intellectual analysis just as every other direct conscious experience defies analysis. Try as we will, we cannot give an intellectual explanation of beauty, for instance, or the strange mutation which takes place in a personality when he or she falls in love. One moment, perhaps, the world is as it has always been, and the next moment, by a subtle mental shift it is transformed into a new world of beauty and wonder and mysterious promise. So it is with the inner certainty of "deathlessness." It marks the assumption of leadership of the true personality in the psychological economy of the individual and the emergence of a higher stage of consciousness.

The prize. This greatest of all prizes is not lightly won. It is not something to be donned on Sundays and laid aside for the rest of the week. Creative Realism strikes straight at the primary fact of existence and its practice always marks a turning point in one's life. Once having practiced it, we cannot return to our former state completely, any more than can a chicken return to the egg from which it emerged. Our yesterdays grow misty and fall away as belonging to another phase of existence, even as the days of our early childhood are now but dimly remembered. We are imbued with a sense of marching, with a "Gung-Ho" élan which leads ever into our tomorrows, which grow larger and brighter as we advance. Neither age nor station makes any difference; we *know* that we have all eternity before us, and the treasure-house of the world is ours for the effort of opening it.

Attainment. The attainment of Creative Realism, however, must be thorough-going and clear-cut to obtain the highest results. It is the product of removing subconscious interference with what is rightfully ours. The wild beast of the imagination must be tamed and taught obedience; the intellect must be trained to do its computing thoroughly and unemotionally so as to "render unto Ceasar the things which are Caesar's," and the true personality must correlate them with "the things which are God's" and the whole personality unified on a new and higher level.

PATTERN-MAKERS

Revolution of the personality. In the previous chapters of this book all of the necessary exercises and techniques for bringing about a complete revolution of the personality have been given, but the completeness of the revolution will be proportional to the amount of effort we put into the practice. There are graduations in the degree of our attainment in Creative Realism as there are in all mental activity. Primarily, Creative Realism depends upon our success in establishing new mental patterns, but these patterns follow *the natural inclination of life* and so are not nearly as difficult to establish as are patterns which run contrary to the normal trend of living nature.

Adventure. By undertaking this program of self-training, you are embarking upon the greatest adventure in life—the opening of a whole new universe to exploration and study. You have nothing to lose but your own ill health, your own frustrations and unhappiness—in short, your limitations. Creative Realism is not a mere intellectual exercise, although the intellect is used as a "pointing finger" to its reality. Creative Realism is a philosophy of character and grows out of the will as the first principle of human life. Even the most brilliant intellect, alone, will fail to unravel all its mysteries, but a strong soul will drink deep of its inexhaustible potentialities. A good intellect and a strong soul together may achieve any height.

Beginning's end. You have read this book, now turn back to Chapter One and commence the serious *study* of its contents. It will be the most rewarding study that you have ever undertaken.

CUMULOUS CLOUD DISINTEGRATED BY PSYCHO-KINESIS. PHOTOGRAPHS TAKEN AT ONE-MINUTE INTERVALS BY W. DALE McLAUGHLIN. ⟶

4

5

6

7

8

9

10

11

12

Appendix

"PROOF"

Determining quality. There is no way in which the *quality* of a state of consciousness may be determined in a laboratory. Many psychological tests have been devised for measuring the intellectual-subconscious processes, and some of these are quite helpful; but no test has been, or ever will be, devised which can determine, for instance, whether an individual is in love, and, if so, in measuring the depth of his love. No one can measure the direct conscious experience which leads to the expression of great poetry, music, or art of any kind. No one can differentiate by any test the qualitative difference in consciousness between the mere "intellectual" and the creative genius.

Knowing. Yet the man in love knows that he is in love by direct experience. The artist feels his inspiration as surely as he feels joy or sorrow or any other emotion. The creative genius has a sense of truth and reality which speaks for itself. All of these states of consciousness emanate from the true personality and have little to do with mere intellection.

Rewards and punishments. The value of life to each of us is determined not so much by the goods we accumulate as by the qualitative state of the consciousness we habitually enjoy. Given a reasonable standard of living which insures cleanliness and decent nutrition, it is possible for every person to increase the quality of his consciousness and with it, of course, his health, his wealth, and his happiness.

MENTAL FIELD HYPOTHESIS

Fear. Fear is the result of a lack of consciousness, not lack of intellectual ability. In fact, the darkening cloud of fear which now envelops the world is the product of pure intellection. Many of our scientists are highly conscious, creative individuals who see clearly the precipice toward which our intellects are inexorably pushing us. Many others, alas, are mere accountants of phenomena, who like the Frankenstein monster have entered the stream of life with unnaturally conditioned computing machines and so have become the terror of their fellows because they have no basic roots in the resplendent reality which brought us to birth as men.

Science and the revitalization of religion. Nevertheless—and rightfully perhaps—science plays a tremendous part in setting the trend of our current beliefs. There seemed no doubt that could the reality of the mental field hypothesis be demonstrated in such a way by the ordinary laboratory techniques of observation and measurement, the revitalization of religion and the resurgence of moral values would follow as a matter of course. If each of us were fully convinced—even intellectually —that what happens to us is the result of what we think in the dark recesses of our subconsciousness, the character of the world would be revolutionized for the better within a few decades. The difficulty was in finding a suitable medium for such a demonstration, one that was unstable enough to be easily influenced and yet that was definitely measurable quantitatively.

Clouds. It was found that the ordinary fair-sized cumulous clouds which float across a background of blue sky were ideal subjects for such a demonstration, for they fulfilled all the requirements. After experimenting with a number of different mental techniques, it was found that a cloud could indeed be *influenced by an act of human will.* Not only could a measurable effect be produced upon a cumulous cloud, but even a cumulo-nimbus or "thunderhead" could be strongly influenced.

CLOUD PHYSICS

Wilson's theory. It is not within the scope of this present book to discuss the physics of this phenomenon, but briefly, in 1920, C. T. R. Wilson, of England, discovered that the earth is negatively charged (electrically) to the atmosphere; that during fair weather, the earth's negative charge was continually and rapidly being neutralized by a steady downward flow of positive ions from the atmosphere. During thunderstorms he noticed that the electrical field was often positive instead of negative, so that large negative currents must be flowing to the earth. He suggested that lightning from thunderstorms happening at scattered points over the world every day supplies enough negative charge to balance its loss of charge to the atmosphere in storm-free areas.

Natural batteries. Wilson's theory visualized a storm-cloud as a natural battery, whose lower pole feeds negative charge downward to the earth as lightning, and point discharges to trees, towers, and other grounded objects, while its upper pole leaked an equivalent positive charge to the upper atmosphere. This theory is now well established.

Problem for physicists. Perhaps by devising a cloud-chamber of the right dimensions, the physicists will be able to discover the exact sequence of physical events which take place when a "traveling mental field," activated and directed by the human will, neutralizes the electrical charge of a cloud and causes it to disintegrate. The cloud-disintegration experiment opens the door to a new world of physical and parapsychological possibilities, a world in which mind and matter blend and interact to produce the miracle of living nature.

THE CLOUD-DISINTEGRATION EXPERIMENT

The experiment. A clear day should be chosen when the wind is moderate and a number of similar-sized cumulous clouds are available at approximately the same altitude. A camera should be set up at a fixed point of observation, and a moment should be chosen to commence the experiment when there are three or more clouds adjacent so that they may be photographed together. One of these is selected by an observer as the "target cloud," and the other adjacent ones serve as "controls." Subsequent photographs should be taken at one-minute intervals of the group of clouds—target and controls. For reasons of health, the experiment should be limited to twelve minutes and should not be attempted again by the same operator for at least two hours after completion of the experiment.

The operator. The operator should place himself in the state of detached consciousness or "self-remembering" previously detailed in this book; he should fix his gaze upon the target cloud, disregarding everything else, and by a detached act of the will—without any subconscious "wonderings" or "doubts"—he should breathe deeply and rhythmically, at the same time *willing* that the cloud disintegrate.

Natural technique. If the technique is rightly conducted, the operator will feel a tightening of his abdominal muscles and a sensation of tenseness behind his eyes. It would seem that the technique is a natural one, for we see it crudely employed by the "rooters" at a football game or at a horse race; an expert at "craps" automatically uses it as he rolls his dice; we see it also in the haka or war dance of the Maoris, in the snake dance, and in the corn dances of the Indians, and in the dances of the Dervishes.

Warning. Nevertheless, a word of warning is necessary here. The cloud-disintegration experiment *should not even be attempted by anyone not in perfect health.* The energy automatically used by the mind in performing it is stored in the large plexuses situated in front of the spine. The body also uses these reservoirs of energy in all of its vital functioning. If they become depleted, the vital functioning will be slowed, with unpleasant consequences. If they become exhausted, a state of "shock" will ensue, with perhaps disastrous consequences. Should the reader have trained himself, however, by following the program and exercises outlined in this book, and should his health be good, he should be able to achieve a significant result with the cloud experiment. By measuring the target cloud in relation to the control clouds at the conclusion of the experiment, and by repeating it one hundred times on different days and under different barometrical readings and wind conditions, he can establish the fact for himself that the mind when directed by the will has power to do work outside of the body.

THE MEXICO CITY DEMONSTRATIONS

Cloud disintegration. During the months of June, July, and August, 1951, in the garden of the Hotel L'Escargot, this writer gave a series of demonstrations of the ability of the human will, when properly trained and employed, to disintegrate completely designated clouds miles away, even when these were heavy with rain and moving across the sky before a considerable wind. Twelve photographs, taken at one-minute intervals of such a demonstration, are reproduced at the beginning of the Appendix (following page 235).

Observers. The Mexico City demonstrations were attended by a number of scientific observers, some of whom had been sent by their governments. There were also a journalist and several hotel guests present during most of the demonstrations. The reactions of the observers to what they were witnessing varied from superstitious terror on the part of some of the casual guests to dumbfounded bewilderment on the part of the scientists, and enthusiastic appreciation on the part of the journalist. All agreed upon one point though: namely, that the demonstrations were a complete success.

Implications. The reaction of the casual observers was that perhaps they were seeing a Western version of the "Hindu rope trick," and they took great pains to avoid getting in the pathway of the "wild hypnotic eyes" which could "blast a cloud" ten miles away. The reaction of the scientists was perhaps typical: "We agree that you have produced 'phenomena of an amazing type,' but the theory upon which it is based does not come within the province of present scientific thinking, and so we are unable to evaluate it at present."

JOURNALIST'S SUMMARY

The journalistic mind, better trained than most to cope with the unusual and to evaluate the incredible, was the only mind present able to sense some of the implications of the demonstrations. Seated in the pleasant garden later he summed it up quietly:

"What I have witnessed here would make the most tremendous scoop in history . . . if anyone would believe it . . . but they won't. All great newspapers are afraid of being hoaxed . . . so they steer clear of the 'miraculous' and the unexplainable as they would poison. What you have done is so incredible in terms of ordinary thinking that few city editors would pass it as a story."

Precedent. The journalist continued: "A long time ago, a man in Palestine also tried to prove a set of basic principles by demonstrating them. He healed the sick, calmed storms, and it is recorded that in a couple of instances at least, He actually raised the dead. . . . Well, you know the rest. The phenomena He produced was of an amazing type, but it did not come within the province of the scientific thinking of that time. . . . Scientific thinking has not yet caught up with the theories He demonstrated. It is my opinion that had science spent even one-half of one per cent of the money in research into the nature of the human mind that they have spent on producing the means—both scientific and political—of destroying it, we should not be cowering in fear among our gadgets today."

RESTATEMENT OF ANCIENT PRINCIPLES

As a thief in the night. "The great and significant movements of human history are seldom ushered in with a fanfare of trumpets and flurry of drums, and I for one believe that we have witnessed the beginnings of just such a movement right here in this garden. I predict that eventually this demonstration will be the means of re-establishing, in a new and modern way, those ancient principles stated and restated by prophets, seers, and sages from the beginnings of our history. . . . This could mean the beginnings of a new age."

Practical demonstration. Since the Mexico City demonstrations a small number of students of both sexes, selected from various walks of life, have trained themselves in the principles set forth in this book. The effects of this training upon their individual lives have been the most satisfying demonstration of all to this writer. In every instance the result has been far beyond expectations and has brought an immeasurable improvement in creative ability, in health, and in happiness.

Basic book. This present book is written as a training manual in the basic principles and techniques of Creative Realism, but other books are planned to carry on from where this one halts. There will always be a "tomorrow" which leads beyond the high-point of today's attainments.

.

Bibliography

To give full credit to all those whose teachings, writings, and researches have contributed to the development of the theory of Creative Realism is impossible, for it would require several books larger than this one merely to list them. The following, however, is a brief list of a few of the later works consulted in the preparation of this book:

LINCOLN BARNETT, *The Universe and Dr. Einstein* (William Sloane Associates: 1948).

LOUIS DE BROGLIE, *The Revolution in Physics* (The Noonday Press: 1953).

V. GORDON CHILDE, *Man Makes Himself* (The New American Library: 1951).

M. A. B. FRAZIER, *The Electrical Activity of the Nervous System* (London, Pitman: 1951).

SIGMUND FREUD, *A General Introduction to Psychoanalysis* (Doubleday and Company: 1953).

B. E. GORDON, "The Physiology of Hypnosis" (*Psychiatric Quarterly:* 1949).

H. GUZE, "Posthypnotic Behavior and Personality" (*Personality, Symposia on Topical Issues:* 1951, 1, 231).

C. L. HULL, *Hypnosis and Suggestibility: An Experimental Approach* (Appleton-Century: 1933).

JOHN MAYNARD KEYNES, *A Treatise on Probability* (Macmillan and Company, Ltd.: 1921).

L. N. LECRON and J. BORDEAUX, *Hypnotism Today* (Grune and Stratton: 1947).

P. D. Ouspensky, *In Search of the Miraculous* (Harcourt Brace and Company: 1949).

W. Penfield and T. Rasmussen, *The Cerebral Cortex of Man* (Macmillan: 1950).

Erwin Schrodinger, *Physics in Our Time* (Cambridge University Press: 1951).

Sir Charles Sherrington, O. M., *Man on His Nature* (Cambridge University Press: 1951).

D. T. Suzuki, *Essays in Zen Buddhism* (London, Rider and Company).

W. Grey Walter, *The Living Brain* (W. W. Norton and Company: 1953).

C. F. von Weisacker, *The History of Nature* (University of Chicago Press: 1949).

Donald Powell Wilson, *My Six Convicts* (Rinehart and Company, Inc.: 1951).

CPSIA information can be obtained at www.ICGtesting.com
Printed in the USA
LVOW12s2205041213

363885LV00039B/2832/P